THE ART AND
OF
INITIAT

THE ART AND SCIENCE OF INITIATION

Edited by Jedediah French and Angel Millar

Lewis Masonic

First published 2019

ISBN 978 0 85318 563 5

Published by Lewis Masonic

an imprint of Ian Allan Publishing Ltd, Shepperton, Surrey TW17 8AS.
Printed in Malta.

Visit the Lewis Masonic website at www.lewismasonic.co.uk

Contents

"The soul [at death] has the same experience as those who are being initiated into great Mysteries.... Wandering astray in the beginning, tiresome walkings in circles, some frightening paths to darkness that lead nowhere; then immediately before the end all the terrible things, panic and shivering and sweat, and amazement. And then some wonderful light comes to meet you, pure regions and meadows are there to greet you, with sounds and dances and solemn, sacred words and holy views; and there, the initiate, perfect by now, set free and loose from all bondage, walks about, crowned with a wreath, celebrating the festival together with the other pure people, and he looks down on the uninitiated, unpurified crowd in this world in mud and fog beneath his feet."

– Plutarch, *c*100 AD

"I approached the very gates of death and set one foot on Persephone's threshold, yet was permitted to return, rapt through all the elements. At midnight I saw the sun shining as if it were noon; I entered the presence of the gods of the underworld and the gods of the upper-world, stood near and worshipped them."

– Apuleius, *The Golden Ass* (*Asinus aureus*), *c*200 AD

"The practices of Highest Yoga Tantra present a spiritual path which enables the individual to attain complete Buddhahood within a single lifetime, prior to the moment of death. Yet, for those who are unable to achieve this, it becomes crucial to use the transformative opportunities offered by the naturally occurring processes of death, the intermediate state and rebirth. Hence, in Highest Yoga Tantra, it is not merely the preparation for a more developed future rebirth which is important, but of more fundamental significance is the personal preparation for using one's own death and subsequent states as a means of achieving liberation."

– The Dalai Lama

"Howbeit we speak wisdom among them that are perfect: yet not the wisdom of this world, nor of the princes of this world, that come to nought: But we speak the wisdom of God in a mystery, even the hidden wisdom, which God ordained before the world unto our glory: Which none of the princes of this world knew: for had they known it, they would not have crucified the Lord of glory."

– 1 Corinthians 2:6-8 (KJV)

"Fundamental Masonry, as you have seen, has for itself a single universal aim, something that morality alone cannot fulfill. The practice of moral decency and social responsibility are, it is true, the apparent object of the degrees – but these virtues cannot be their actual aim. What need would she [the Craft] then have for emblems, mysteries, and initiation? Her purpose is to enlighten man about his nature, his origin, and his destiny."

– Jean-Baptiste Willermoz, *Instruction Secrète aux Grands Profès* (late 18th century)

"We take spiritual initiation when we become conscious of the Divine within us, and thereby contact the Divine without us."

– Dion Fortune, *The Training & Work of an Initiate*

Introduction

Jedediah French

"Do you know, what makes the prison disappear is every deep, serious affection. Being friends, being brothers, to love, that opens the prison by the sovereign power, by the very powerful spell. But the one who does not have this remains in death. But where sympathy is reborn, there life is reborn."

– Vincent van Gogh[1]

This is not an academic book, and it has no pretentions to be considered as such. We want to make that clear from the outset. Some aspects do conform to the rigor and research of mainstream scholarship, but other aspects are deliberately speculative and personal. We have imposed no strict style guide or "house rules" in order to lend the feel of organic difference to the various essays, rather than mechanical uniformity. The goal of this book is exploration, spiritual and religious (whatever you determine those words to mean), and the emphasis is on ritual, Freemasonry, and the esoteric traditions.

In the secluded world of Masonic literature and opinion, a fissure is apparent between those who value experiential, romantic, esoteric-wisdom teachings (e.g. Manly P. Hall), and those who privilege a strictly academic and heavily intellectual form of scholarship drawing on historical research and forensic evidence (e.g. Brent S. Morris). We all know brethren on either side of this divide, all with valid reasons for upholding their respective positions. It is therefore our intention to bring both interpretations of Masonry together in one volume and place them into conversation.[2] There is something gainful in this attempt, not the least of which is a broader and more complete picture of the project's subject matter – ritual initiation.

Another gap we aim to bridge is the political one; a true abyss, which currently ensnares so many of us into, at times, unproductive and confrontational melees of conflicting ideas and beliefs. Not to imply that working out these issues within societies is unimportant. But for this project, and for the sake of spiritual development and inner contemplation in general, we hope to reach above and beyond dichotomous political boundaries to the best of our ability.

That said, some essays in this volume engage seriously with a philosophical and spiritual movement known as Traditionalism, which has occasionally been appropriated by more extremist rightwing and anti-Masonic political orientations. Here, then, our intention is twofold. Firstly, to explore Traditionalist anti-Masonry, especially in regard to Julius Evola. And, secondly, to study and explore the esoteric ideas of Traditionalists to try to understand how they viewed the process of ancient initiation in a modern setting, whether they felt it was still possible or impossible, and why or why not. Since Masonry is a modern initiatic institution laying claim to, according to its own literature, a legitimate initiation ritual extending into the distant past, it is useful to examine what Traditionalists such as René Guénon said about modernity, esoteric practice, and ceremonial transmission.

For me personally, the theme of this book arose as a desire to understand and emphasize the importance and function of *initiation* within Masonic rituals and the broader ceremonial rites grouped together under the rubric of esotericism. For a while I had been following and admiring the work of Masonic author Angel Millar, so I approached him with the idea for this project and asked if he would be interested in writing an essay and assisting with some of the editorial duties. He agreed, and as we discussed and developed the theme, we determined it would be best for me to write the introduction and for Angel, also being an artist, to provide the cover art.

Angel and I have shared as well as individual ideas about the process of initiation, yet we are both deeply invested in the subject as a whole and its importance for Freemasonry. The word itself – *initiation* – has roots in an equally enigmatical word – *mystery*. For a long time, both terms have cohabited with what we today call "religion," particularly when it comes to esoteric or secretive practices and the apprehension of higher knowledge. In the words of one contemporary Classicist:

> Mystery originally appeared in Greek in the plural, *Mystêria*, as the name of the festival that we currently call the Eleusinian Mysteries … for obscure reasons, the Romans used the term *initia*, also plural, to translate *Mysteria*, and this usage became the basis of our term initiation, whereas Latin *mysterium*, eventually, became our 'mystery'. Unfortunately, the etymology of *mystêrion* is not wholly clear. Generations of scholars have connected *mystêrion* with the Greek verb *myô*, which means 'to close the lips or eyes', and they have explained it as referring to Demeter's commandment in her Homeric Hymn to keep the rites secret... More recently, Hittite scholars have explained the Greek term from the Hittite verb *munnae*, meaning 'to conceal, to hide, to shut out of sight', rather than 'keep secret, be silent about'.[3]

Scholars continue to debate the origin of these terms, but for our purpose it is safe to assume that a central element of initiation rests in its being performed outside the normal social spaces of every day life. The idea of creating a "sacred space" has been used to try and conceptualize this process of removal, of willing extraction from the time and space of a group's surrounding society and culture to enact prescribed rituals apparently unintelligible by society *en masse*.

The first scholars of religions (plural), beginning in the first quarter of the 20th century, developed a binary of the sacred and profane to account for the pervasiveness of these customs across cultures and history.[4] These theologians, anthropologists, and sociologists attempted to describe what they thought took place within the sacred realm as being communion – whether individually or as a small group (or a collective *cultus*) – with the divine world beyond the mundane. To account for the various social factors involved in shaping what happens in the sacred realm, this approach has, in recent years, been justly criticized by religious studies scholars.[5] Still, there is something to be said for the "experiences" that people have while undergoing a ritual of initiation, which is one of the main reasons we were interested in producing this book.[6]

A further component of initiation, in addition to experience, is the transmission of private knowledge. This type of esoteric knowledge, reserved for initiates, is contained within a specific community and only revealed within a specific ritual setting.

For example, early copies of the Hebrew Bible canon, such as the Dead Sea Scrolls, look nothing like legible, modern-day books, with helpful punctuation and grammar, but are simply rows and rows of Hebrew consonants strung together in such a way that it resembles something like computer code. How were the rabbis capable of reading such a text? They could read it, in part, because of a process of oral transmission known as the Oral Torah, which conveyed private knowledge and interpretation via an unbroken initiatic chain passed down from generation to generation. There were no vowels in Written Torah (ie, the Five Books of Moses), so they utilized a system of diacritical signs called *niqqud* marks that instructed them how to distinguish between various pronunciations of the letters of the Hebrew alphabet. We could characterize this as part of the specialized, private knowledge of early Judaism. Greek also developed something similar, as did Arabic, so that when a Muslim recites a passage of the Qur'an in melodious verse there are textual marks to assist in the pronunciation of vowels.

In the Vajrayana Buddhism of Tibet, the novitiate is exposed to increasingly more complex and esoteric mantric texts during progressive ceremonies of initiation. During these ceremonies, the moment when the initiating lama *breathes* or recites the revealed mantra into the ear of the receptive candidate is the only permissible situation in which he or she may hear this mantra or teaching. For the candidate to be exposed to these mantric texts in any other way than through this classic method of initiatic instruction would be sacrilege, a betrayal of the mysteries.

Thus, we may identify two important aspects of initiation: experience and instruction. For this book, a basic working definition of initiation might read as follows: *Initiation appears to be a set of practices, and/or processes of realization, through which certain human beings across time have endeavored to achieve deeper knowledge and higher wisdom.*

Building on such a definition, the essays compiled in this volume cover a wide variety of topics, from more practical aspects of Masonic ritual to the angelic invocations of ceremonial magic. Is there a link between these? We believe so, and we hope this link will come into focus as you read through the book. The contents are broken into two parts: The Science of Initiation, and The Art of Initiation.

Part I focuses on the idea of initiation from a more practical historical perspective and attempts to understand the process and function of initiation. This section includes insights from Traditionalism, as well as essays on classical mystery cults, early modern feminine Masonry, and the material culture of the Craft. The essay on material culture may seem out of place, but we include it in this section because of the important role physical objects and relics – as well as the preservation of their history – have played in all initiatory organizations, religions, and rituals. Part I culminates in a lengthy essay on the philosopher René Guénon (the founder of Traditionalism), which, though quite in-depth, is a piece Masons should grapple with, for it is crucial to get a comprehensive picture of what Guénon thought about the possibility of initiation in the modern world – since A) that is the time in which we live, and B) that is the work in which we are engaged.

Part II focuses on the creative and imaginal results of initiation and paints a picture of how realms of spirit might interface with lived experience. This section includes essays on astral magic, esoteric history, Aleister Crowley, Neoplatonism, and, most importantly, personal accounts of initiation. Certain Masons may feel the themes in this section have little to do with the Craft as they understand it. However, we feel it is necessary to include material on magic and esotericism – although such topics can sometimes draw us into polemics, similar to the Traditionalism in Part I – because we want the Freemasons who are reading this to grasp the different ideas being discussed in the literature of esoteric schools. Part II culminates in a longer essay describing spiritual initiation on the astral planes, and a history of the magicians, Masons, and quasi-Masons who have sought such an initiation in the Western Mystery Tradition.

Why create such a book? Because the world is in crisis. We feel it is the duty of Masons to assist as custodians of the societies they helped usher in through the Industrial Revolution. The duty of a Mason and the oaths he takes are no small thing. They are of the utmost importance and seriousness. The initiations the Mason undergoes should not be squandered but rather produce real transformational change down to the roots of the soul. For this reason, it is imperative that we learn to understand, harness, and enhance the Masonic initiatory rituals to their fullest capacity. Only this will bring about the type of change in Being, and in Thinking, that we will need to be successful in moving forward. The greatest possible folly would be for our comprehension of these initiatory practices to decline more than it already has.

It is therefore our contention that Masons should not become better men, but the best. The duty of every true Mason must be to view the entire world – regardless of race, skin tone, sex, class, or creed (or lack of creed, for that matter) – as one human family, as one interconnected lodge. When economists today speak of the Fourth Industrial Revolution (4IR), to our mind this is where Masons should be especially active as the work force and foundational infrastructure of our societies yield to advanced technologies and robotics. Masons must make sure this new industry does not lose sight of the spiritual implications of this massive change and help guide these technologies toward the spiritual wellbeing and betterment of everyone on the planet. As the operative Masons who built the cathedrals strove to fashion base matter into spiritual harmony for the good of the souls of local people, so should modern Masons strive for the same in advanced technology, turning the scientific and engineering laboratories again into sacred spaces and altars dedicated to the spiritual upliftment of all.

Jedediah French, California, USA

1 Translation by Jedediah French: "Sais-tu, ce qui fait disparaître la prison c'est toute affection profonde, sérieuse. Etre amis, être frères, aimer, cela ouvre la prison par la puissance souveraine, par le charme très-puissant. Mais celui qui n'a pas cette demeure dans la mort. Mais là où la sympathie renait, renait la vie." Letter from Vincent van Gogh to Théo van Gogh, Cuesmes, July 1880.

2 A current example of such a synthesis is the Masonic Academy of Reflection, started by Charles (Chuck) R. Dunning Jr. and established in the Valley of Guthrie, in the Orient of Oklahoma: https://academyofreflection.org.

3 Jan N. Bremmer, *Initiation into the Mysteries of the Ancient World* (De Gruyter, 2014), vii.

4 See, for example, the work of Nathan Söderblom (1866-1931), Rudolf Otto (1869-1937), Émile Durkheim (1858-1917), and Mircea Eliade (1907-1986).

5 See, for example, Russell McCutcheon, *Manufacturing Religion: The Discourse on Sui Generis Religion and the Politics of Nostalgia* (New York: Oxford University Press, 1997). As a crucial response to McCutcheon's claims, see, for example, Elaine Fischer, "Fascist Scholars, Fascist Scholarship: The Quest for Ur-Fascism and the Study of Religion," *Hermeneutics, Politics, and the History of Religions: The Contested Legacies of Joachim Wach and Mircea Eliade*, ed. Christian K. Wedemeyer and Wendy Doniger (Oxford University Press, 2010), 261-284.

6 For rethinking the uniqueness of religious and/or spiritual experiences, see, for example, Ann Taves, *Religious Experience Reconsidered: A Building-Block Approach to the Study of Religion and Other Special Things* (Princeton University Press, 2011).

PART I
The Science of Initiation

Paths of Initiation: Freemasonry, Initiation, and Counter-Initiation

Angel Millar

While initiation has played a central role in human society since before recorded history, a fully developed notion of counter-initiation first emerges with the "perennial philosophy" or "Traditionalism" founded during the 20th century by French metaphysician René Guénon (1886-1951).

Though not widely known today, Traditionalism has had considerable impact on contemporary spiritual thought and politics, influencing – in very different and even incompatible ways – Prince Charles of Great Britain,[1] Steve Bannon (controversial advisor to Donald Trump in the run-up to the US elections of 2017), and Alexander Dugin, the Russian neo-Eurasian theorist and thinker often considered to be the architect of Vladimir Putin's worldview.

What concerns us here is not politics but spirituality, especially in relation to Traditionalist notions of initiation and counter-initiation. Since "Traditionalism" is sometimes drawn into political movements that are anti-Masonic (as well as anti-Semitic, etc.), and because contemporary Traditionalists can be openly hostile to Freemasonry, we will look at this doctrine in relation to the Craft and show, moreover, that accusations against Freemasonry emanating from this worldview are false.

First, however, we will look briefly at the life of René Guénon.

René Guénon and the Perennial Tradition

Guénon was born in Blois, France, and died in Cairo, where he had lived for the last twenty years of his life. By the time of his move, the French metaphysician had already "moved into" Islam and had joined the Sufi Order of Shadhilites, taking the name Abdel Wahed Yahya. In Cairo, Guénon lived as a devout Muslim, avoiding the areas of the city frequented by tourists and staying away from the trappings of modern life.

In his early life, however, he developed an interest in mathematics and philosophy. He involved himself with Roman Catholicism and was fascinated with religious and spiritual questions. He seems to have been restless, and at the same time, Guénon also began to explore the world of alternative spirituality, especially Theosophy and fringe Masonry.

In 1908, Guénon was consecrated Bishop in a Gnostic Church. Regarding fringe Masonry, he helped organize a large spiritualist-Masonic conference, with plans to revive the fringe Masonic Order of the Temple. He was initiated into the Masonic *Loge Symbolique Humanidad* (under the jurisdiction of the *Rite National Espagnol*), and the head of the Order, Charles Teder, also initiated Guénon into both a French Swedenborgian Masonic Rite (under the jurisdiction of *La Grande Loge Swedenborgienne de France*) and into the elaborate Rite of Memphis and Mizraim.

While Guénon became disillusioned with the spiritual and religious organizations of France – and while he contributed to both Masonic and anti-Masonic periodicals early on – he retained a respect for Freemasonry and reviewed books on the subject and referenced its symbolism and doctrines in his writings throughout his life. In an editorial note to *Studies in Freemasonry & the Compagnonnage*, we read: "Recognizing that the symbolism and ritual employed by Masonry was for the most part both traditional and esoteric, he labored to discover, define, or create a Freemasonic initiation that would be compatible with Catholic Christianity, as it supposedly was when the Masonic guilds designed and built the great cathedrals of Europe."[2]

For Guénon, the "regularity" of a Masonic jurisdiction or Rite, based on lineage and history, is not what is important. Rather, it is Masonic "orthodoxy" that is the question, and that depends, fundamentally, "in faithfully following tradition," in preserving the Masonic symbols and rituals, and in resisting the encroachment of "modernism."[3] Small details might change, but the "initiatic teaching" must not be distorted.[4]

No doubt it is because of Guénon's early immersion in fringe Masonry, and more broadley because the esoteric and spiritual milieu of France, that some of the doctrines of Traditionalism resemble the ideas found there.

We find, for example, the notion that there is an exoteric and an esoteric (or inner) knowledge, or, rather, levels of knowledge that can appear more and more refined in line with one's own spiritual awakening (and hence the need for initiation).

Man is, in some sense, seeking a connection or reconnection to, or a reintegration with, the deity or the divine. Like regular Freemasonry, which, for much of its history, has recognized the validity of different religions – Christianity, Judaism, Islam, Hinduism, Buddhism, and so on – and as such has enabled men of different faiths to come together in lodge as brothers, Traditionalism has regarded these major world religions as exemplifying eternal truths.

According to Traditionalist philosophy, there existed a "primordial tradition" – a pure religion or *prisca theologia* as revealed by God. This tradition, however, disappeared over time, but its essential truth was retained and filtered into the major world religions, which became different expressions of the "perennial" or "primordial tradition."

Masonic initiation is, for Guénon, concerned with "the attainment of integral Knowledge" or "Gnosis" (ie, direct knowledge of God – Arabic: *'Irfan*).[5] In a Masonic context, this gnosis is descended from the union of Rosicrucianism (which Guénon believes preserved the "gnosis" of the Middle Ages) with that of the stonemasons' guilds (which he implies were already aware of Hermetic knowledge).

Guénon suggests, too, that the three Craft Degrees of Freemasonry follow an archetypal pattern representing "birth, growth, and production," respectively. He claims that because the Craft Degrees are "symbolic," the Blue (or Craft) Lodge can only create "Masons who are only symbols of true Masons." True initiation, and the "true Mason" can, as such, only be found among the higher degrees, to which the three Craft Degrees serve as an introduction.

This claim is more in line with the history of French Freemasonry, which has tended to privilege the "higher degrees," than with

Freemasonry in the English-speaking world, where degrees beyond those of the Craft are generally viewed as "additional," optional, and sometimes of *historical* importance only. The term "symbolic" is, of course, used in Freemasonry to refer to the representation of stonemasonry's tools, as symbols for contemplation, and not, as Guénon imagines, as relegating Craft Masonry to a mere introduction to the York or Scottish Rites.

Julius Evola and Anti-Masonry

Perhaps Guénon's best-known and almost certainly his most controversial disciple was the Italian esotericist, mountaineer, painter, and political theorist Julius Evola (1898-1974). During the 1990s, Evola's writing began to enter the consciousness of the more serious and dedicated spiritual seekers in the English-speaking world through translations of his writings on alchemy, magic, the Holy Grail, Buddhism, Tantra, and spirituality more generally. His political writings were less well-known and, in most cases, went untranslated, though his political magnum opus, *Revolt Against the Modern World*, was published in 1995 by spiritual and New Age publisher Inner Traditions, which had published many of Evola's spiritual works, including his writing on Buddhism, magic, and Hermeticism.

Other English translations of Evola's more obscure works have been published in recent years, including *Fascism Viewed from the Right* (Arktos, 2013), and a collection of essays entitled *A Traditionalist Confronts Fascism* (Arktos, 2015). Both texts are critical of the fascist movement. Nevertheless, as an alleged influence on Steve Bannon (former advisor to the then presidential candidate Donald Trump), Evola has been frequently mentioned by journalists (who apparently have not read any of his work and merely quote blurbs on the back) since 2017.

Often described as "Baron" Julius Evola, the controversial Italian thinker sought to revive a spiritual aristocracy founded on a pre-Christian European ideal (though, as noted, Evola wrote extensively on many spiritual traditions, such as Buddhism, which he respected). Toward this end, he inveighed – like Guénon – against modernity and its reign of quantity over quality.

Although "Tradition" would come to occupy a central place in Evola's thought, his life was colorful and non-conformist. As a young man he was involved in the Dadaist movement in Italy and is sometimes described as one of its foremost painters in that country, though the movement there was small. Evola's paintings do not stand out as examples of great works of art, unfortunately, and his figurative works are particularly clumsy and vulgar, even making concessions for the conscious embrace and elevation of the absurd and irrational by the Dadaists.[6]

Evola later became involved in an occult circle known as the Ur Group and was introduced to Guénon's writing, and to the very notion of Tradition, by Arturo Reghini (1878-1946), a thirty-third degree Scottish Rite Mason active in the group.[7]

Despite his early involvement with Dadaism, Evola's later writing on modernity was often dry and dogmatic and at times petty-minded. Like Sayyid Qutb[8] – the ideologue whose writings shaped the modern Jihadist movement – Evola condemned Jazz music as primitive and degenerate.[9]

Unlike Guénon and Reghini, Evola was never involved with Freemasonry or fringe Masonry. Perhaps surprisingly, considering his life-long interest in initiation, he was almost entirely unconcerned with the symbolism, rituals, and initiation of Masonry, and, instead, his assessment was almost entirely political.

This may have been influenced by his activities during World War II. Though the Nazis were suspicious of Evola and found his notion of "spiritual" races rather than biological ones incompatible with Third Reich doctrine, he worked briefly for the German regime, studying the archives of various "secret societies."

Although his *Ride the Tiger* is often thought to be his final book, Evola's last work, published before his death, was a collection of essays entitled *Ricognizioni* (Recognitions).[10] Included is an essay on Freemasonry called "Orientations on Masonry." What is striking about this essay is that Evola views Freemasonry through a purely political lens. Except for the briefest of remarks, the Italian esotericist demonstrates absolutely no interest in the rituals or symbols of the fraternity, and his historical analysis is questionable at best. (He associates the "operatives" with spirituality and Freemasonry post-1717 with the "secularization" of the fraternity – despite his familiarity with the Scottish Rite.)

While he clearly believes the fraternity is opposed to Tradition, Evola explicitly objects that Freemasonry is hostile to authoritarian regimes (which he associates with Tradition, spirituality, and aristocracy), claiming that it was one of the main agents behind the ushering in of liberalism and democracy (both of which are undesirable in Evola's view).

No less extraordinary, Evola presents Freemasonry as an enemy of the Church. Though he takes the side of the Church here, he was a life-long opponent of Catholicism, and his anti-Catholic stance would have been widely known by the time of the publication of *Recognitions*. Evola would undoubtedly say that he attacked the Church only after its Traditional essence had been expunged. But Catholicism was still the living religion of the Italy of his time (and ours) and its monasteries were, and are, still there for those who want to live a traditional life.

Evola's attack on the Church and his almost willing ignorance of Freemasonry as a spiritual and initiatic tradition suggests that what really affronted him was not their alleged modernism, but the thought of no longer being an outsider intellectual, courting adulation and notoriety, writing about and bringing to public attention traditions such as Buddhism, Tantra, and Mithraism (of which Evola had no authentic experience).

In both *Men Among the Ruins* and *Recognitions* Evola mentions a ritual of the Knight Kadosh in which a crown and a papal tiara are stabbed. This fixation implies that not only did this have an emotional pull on the author but that his knowledge of the fraternity was extremely limited. For the Italian Traditionalist, the crown and tiara are the symbols "of the double traditional authority" of state and religion.[11] Leaving aside Evola's anti-Catholic views and desire to replace the Church with a revived "pagan *imperium*," it is remarkable (a) that he did not know that Freemasonry is not monolithic – or that he chose to ignore the fact – and that rituals have varied throughout time and from one jurisdiction to the next (not all of which might be "recognized"), and, more importantly, (b) that he takes the symbolism literally. (In his own work on Hermeticism, Evola talks of androgyny, "incest," and "killing," which he does not mistake for, or offer as, prescriptions for life, but recognizes as symbolic of specific stages in internal, spiritual awakening – the union of opposites, killing the ego, and so on).[12]

Although Evola may have noticed actual political and anti-religious elements in Freemasonry in Italy (which must be distinguished from Freemasonry in the English-speaking world and those jurisdictions recognized by regular Freemasonry there), his conception of the fraternal movement was largely influenced by *The Protocols of the Elders of Zion*. Generally considered to have been created by the Russian secret police in France at the end of the 19th century, the *Protocols* was published in serial form in the pro-Tsarist newspaper *Znamya* (Banner) in 1903. Notably, the newspaper was edited by P. A. Krushevan, who had instigated a pogrom against Jews at Kishinev, during which more than a thousand Jewish homes and businesses were destroyed, several hundred injured, and forty-five killed.

With German, Polish, French, British, and American editions published in 1920 – though exposed as a forgery in *The Times* of London the following year by the newspaper's Istanbul correspondent Philip Graves – the *Protocols* has proved a highly influential text in radical politics (eg, National Socialism), being described by historian Norman Cohn as a "warrant for genocide." The text has remained influential. It is freely available via the World Wide Web, and various editions have been published in the Middle East in recent decades. There, too, we must note, we find Freemasonry widely regarded as a subversive movement in league with Zionism. Most notably, the text is cited in the Hamas Charter of 1988 – replete with accusations against Freemasonry. The Saudi education system has taught that the *Protocols* is an authentic document.[13]

The *Protocols* purports to be the minutes of a secret meeting of Zionists who are plotting to overthrow the monarchies and aristocracies of Europe and control the world through various means – subverting the press, spreading communism and anarchism, corrupting Christian women, and so on. Once there is chaos, the plotters will appear as saviors who will promise to restore order. People, the text suggests, will flock to them, but rather than finding freedom they will be oppressed.

Besides anarchists and communists, Freemasonry is portrayed as an integral part of the "Zionist" plan. According to the *Protocols*, those plotting world domination are busy subverting Freemasonry and corralling important figures into the lodges (which the plotters are setting up in increasing numbers) so that they can be manipulated and used against the people. (The belief that Masonic lodges are used by powerful politicians to plan wars, terrorist attacks, and more, is popular in contemporary conspiracy theory circles.)

Evola knew that the *Protocols* was a forgery – or at least he conceded that it was likely a forgery – yet he did not believe this detracted from its merit. Instead, he claimed the text was a kind of mythology that expressed the feeling of many people, that the "disorder of recent times is not accidental, since it corresponds to a plan, the phases and fundamental instruments of which are accurately described in the *Protocols*."[14] Hence he conceives of Freemasonry as part of a "Judeo-Masonic" plot which promotes liberalism and internationalism over Tradition, embodied to a certain extent – according to Evola – in Italy and Germany prior to the end of World War II.

Initiation and Counter-Initiation

Even though Evola believed that, politically, anti-Traditional forces could ultimately turn against Freemasonry and Judaism as well, the Italian esotericist saw the Masonic fraternity as a "subversive" organization that adopted the "tactic of replacement and inversion" in its symbolism. Evola strongly implies that Freemasonry is a "counter-initiatic" organization. While not influenced by Evola, nor, probably, by anti-Masonic conspiracy theories, the claim that Freemasonry is counter-initiatic in nature has been made more explicitly in recent years by author Charles Upton, who states in his *Vectors of the Counter-Initiation: The Course and Destiny of Inverted Spirituality* that "Ironically, [Guénon] never seemed to have understood that Freemasonry perfectly fits his own definition of the Counter-Initiation."[15]

What, then, is counter-initiation as defined by Guénon? The French metaphysician claimed that numerous organizations exist to confer a "counterfeit" of initiation. Their processes mimic that of the initiatic yet are not only disconnected from the spiritual realm but, if truly counter-initiatic, oppose it. Counter-initiation is the reverse of, and a conscious attack on, authentic initiation, and, as such, its organizations are "satanic."

We cannot deny that organizations exist today that pose as religious or spiritual but are almost solely for social and political action. We find this in the form of churches and their equivalent among other religions, as well as among smaller spiritual groups, where the preaching is political, where the sacred books are interpreted politically, and where the mission is to change society, or to comment upon the nation's leadership, and not to help the disciple transform himself. Indeed, the crisis of religion in the West seems to stem from the seeping away of the spiritual in its own religious tradition. Here, though, we must note that in contrast to the politicization of religious and spiritual groups, lodges under regular Masonic jurisdictions are prohibited from discussing politics.

Guénon held there was another category: pseudo-initiation. This has none of the positive qualities of authentic initiation into spirituality nor the negative qualities of counter-initiation. While also mimicking the initiatic, such organizations do not consciously oppose the spiritual, but, instead, serve to offer distraction. As such, they would be harmless were it not for the fact that, according to Guénon, each acts as a "cog in the machine" of modernity and anti-Tradition.[16]

To be counter-initiatic an organization must be in competition with at least one other organization which offers authentic initiation. (To put it bluntly, to be subversive, there must be something to subvert.) The purpose of such competition would, presumably, be to steal members or potential members away from the authentic, and spiritual to doctrines and a way of being that oppose authentic spirituality.

The problem for those authors and theorists that have attempted to cast Freemasonry in the role of the subversive is that there were, and are, no initiatic organizations to subvert in the West for the fraternity to compete against. As is strongly suggested by the rapid spread and growth of the fraternity in Western Europe, and the founding of competing and sometimes hostile organizations, such as the Gormogons in Great Britain, Freemasonry emerged in an initiatic vacuum. And, unsurprisingly, never has the accusation been made, even by the most rabid conspiracy theorist, that Freemasonry replaced or sought to replace already existing schools of Christian, Jewish, or Islamic mysticism.

Although nearly every culture had initiations into guilds and tribal initiations into manhood, this was not the case in Britain in the 18th century. In France, there existed various guilds under the umbrella of the *Compagnonnage*, yet this was long in decline and was given a new lease of life with the emergence of the Craft in that region and its borrowing from the fraternity.

The Masonic fraternity, too, emerged at a time when, at least in regard to initiatic culture, the stonemasons' lodges were in a state of decay. As Lawrence Dermott claimed in his *Ahiman Rezon*, 1756, the Grand Lodge was formed "to recollect what had been formerly dictated to them." Although made almost a century after the founding of the Premier Grand Lodge, the sentiment is sound enough. Freemasonry was seeking to *preserve* the initiatic tradition that was in danger of passing out of the consciousness of the stonemasons' guild.

Fantastical theories about Templars are often presented as fact, especially by conspiracy theorists – though such "histories" tend to be dismissed by actual historians – but regarding the pre-history of Freemasonry, one dominant theory is that the fraternity emerged out of the stonemasons' guild of Great Britain during the first quarter of the 18th century. The fraternity consciously drew on the initiation ceremonies of the stonemasons for the development of the ritual and advanced a view of transcendence that aligned to Christianity.

In his *Constitutions of the Free-Masons* (1723), James Anderson includes a synopsis of the mythology of the stonemasons' guild from the Old Charges that were known to him. The texts of this mythology, those that we know of, go back to around 1400 A.D. and include some elements and themes that can be found in Ancient Craft Ritual, eg, pillars and geometry.

Although it was founded in Great Britain and spread quickly across Western Europe, with the majority of Masons there being Christians, for much of the history of the fraternity Jews were initiated into Freemasonry, from the first half of the 18th century onwards. Muslims and Hindus were initiated from around the middle of the following century. Today, lodges admit the faithful of all major world religions, as well as deists and those who profess a belief in God (even if conceived of as a universal "force").

Initiates to the fraternity are, moreover, encouraged to practise their faith, whatever it may be. Masonic encyclopedias and research journals have often highlighted the symbols and teachings of religions East and West, existing and extinct. It seems absurd to suggest that a society whose values, worldview, and symbols are compatible with the views of the world's religions, as understood by less authoritarian and dogmatic members, could be somehow opposed to spirituality.

Freemasonry, it is true, has gone through various phases, with the spiritual and the philosophical sometimes being valued more or less by the membership. Yet, with discussions of politics prohibited in lodge, and with the ritual and ethics of Freemasonry encouraging the individual to change himself for the better, rather than trying to change society, the orientation of the fraternity seems clear. Moreover, recent studies have suggested that it is the esoteric and philosophical heart of the Craft that is of greatest interest to Freemasons.

According to a 2016 study of American Freemasons, 56% joined the fraternity because they "wanted to learn philosophical and esoteric knowledge," while of those who went on to join an appendant Masonic body 67% did so because they wanted a "deeper understanding" of philosophy and esotericism.[17] A 2016 survey by the United Grand Lodge of England found, likewise, that 67% of Freemasons there felt that it was either very important or essential "to understand the symbolism and moral/philosophical issues" of Freemasonry.[18]

Nevertheless, Freemasonry has also addressed current-day issues, recollecting what society has forgotten. This is not a replacement for the spiritual or "moral/philosophical" aspects of Freemasonry, but an embodying of the foundation of traditional initiation.

Hence, after the World Wars, and those of Vietnam and Korea, former servicemen joined lodges because they wanted camaraderie and brotherhood. A sense of brotherhood is not initiation, per se, but either a prerequisite to, or an aspect of, traditional, especially tribal, initiation.

Again, in America, in opposition to slavery and official discrimination, Prince Hall lodges worked to instill a sense of dignity in their members and a historical validity for those of African descent. And, after slavery was abolished, the same lodges promoted entrepreneurship, helping African-American men to reclaim their destinies. We must note that in tribal initiations, the initiates are taught the history of the tribe and its relationship to deity. Indeed, Melville Herskovits has argued in *The Myth of the Negro Past* that "cooperation" among African-Americans was, at the time of writing, "principally found in such institutions as lodges and other benevolent societies, which in themselves are directly in line with the tradition underlying similar African organizations."[19]

More directly related to spirituality, during the 18th century, when "reason" – and the belief that man was the final judge of what was and what was not true – was becoming ever more accepted, it was the rituals, symbols, and mysteries of Freemasonry that attracted men into its ranks. Indeed, it was during the "Age of Reason" that Freemasonry saw an explosion of Masonic and fringe Masonic rites and rituals drawing on Christian chivalry, Hermeticism, Rosicrucianism, alchemy, and so on. While these currents of thought had been largely confined to the literary sphere, or to the pursuit of scattered individuals, Freemasonry enabled those interested in such traditions to come together in a spirit of initiation.

Conclusion

We have seen that Freemasonry was not only maligned by Julius Evola during the 20th century but by radical political activists and conspiracy theorists today. Although colored with slightly different language, with the exception of Great Britain (where the press often portrays the Craft as part of a corrupt "old boys' network" behind the police, judges, and politicians), those attacking Freemasonry believe it to be a subversive force undermining traditional norms. In the language of Traditionalist radicals, it is a counter-initiatic society aimed at undermining and destroying the spiritual truth of the perennial tradition.

However, Freemasonry emerged at a time when no initiatic organizations or guilds (such as can be found in ancient and classical societies) existed, at least to any significant degree. As such, the Craft could not possibly have countered any living initiatic tradition. Moreover, the Freemasons who founded the Premier Grand Lodge did so with the aim of preserving the tradition that had been passed down through the stonemasons' guilds.

Although aligned to biblical Christianity and to the morals of society, Masonic rituals and rites soon drew in other currents of thought, such as Hermeticism and Rosicrucianism, preserving the idea of mystery in an age allegedly characterized by reason and science. It drew men together around the idea of mystery and transcendence.

Later, the fraternity initiated men of all major faiths (Islam, Hinduism, Buddhism, etc.), finding them compatible with the basic premises of Freemasonry, and Freemasonry compatible with the premises of these world religions.

The accusation that Freemasonry is "counter-initiatic," opposed to spirituality, or seeks to undermine the essentials of life by which man must live, is thus not credible. It must be said, too, that had it not been for Freemasonry, it is unlikely that Guénon or Evola would have encountered the esoteric currents of thought that they did.

We might argue about what "counter-initiation" means, but it seems clear that Freemasonry's values are universal and timeless enough to embrace the religions and traditions of the world. In contrast, the Traditionalist, the political radical, and the conspiracy theorist seem small-minded in attacking something that – no doubt like some part of their own spirit, which they would rather not look at – they know little about and do not understand.

1 See my book *Crescent and the Compass: Islam, Freemasonry, Esotericism and Revolution in the Modern Age* (Torazzi Press, 2017). See also the website for The Prince's Foundation School of Traditional Arts at https://www.psta.org.uk/.
2 René Guénon, *Studies in Freemasonry & the Compagnonnage* (Hillsdale, New York: Sophia Perennis, 2004), xii.
3 Ibid., 43.
4 Ibid., 44.
5 Ibid., 49.
6 See http://www.juliusevola.net/paintings.html.
7 Julius Evola, *Men Among the Ruins: Postwar Reflections of a Radical Traditionalist*, translated by Guido Stucco and edited by Michael Moynihan (Rochester, Vermont: Inner Traditions, 2002), 32.
8 *Smithsonian*, David Von Drehle, "A Lesson in Hate: How an Egyptian student came to study 1950s America and left determined to wage holy war," February 2006, https://www.smithsonianmag.com/history/a-lesson-in-hate-109822568/.
9 Julius Evola, *Ride the Tiger: A Survival Manual for the Aristocrats of the Soul*, translated by Joscelyn Godwin and Constance Fontana (Rochester, Vermont: Inner Traditions), 20.
10 Julius Evola, *Recognitions: Studies on Men and Problems from the Perspectives of the Right*, translated by John Bruce Leonard (London: Arktos, 2017), vii.
11 Julius Evola, *Men Among the Ruins: Postwar Reflections of a Radical Traditionalist*, translated by Guido Stucco and edited by Michael Moynihan (Rochester, Vermont: Inner Traditions, 2002), 188.
12 Julius Evola, *The Hermetic Tradition: Symbols and Teachings of the Royal Art* (Rochester, Vermont: Inner Traditions, 1995).
13 See A. Millar, *The Crescent and the Compass: Islam, Freemasonry, Esotericism and Revolution in the Modern Age* (Torazzi Press, 2017).
14 Julius Evola, *Men Among the Ruins: Postwar Reflections of a Radical Traditionalist*, translated by Guido Stucco and edited by Michael Moynihan (Rochester, Vermont: Inner Traditions, 2002), 240.
15 Charles Upton, *Vectors of the Counter-Initiation: The Course and Destiny of Inverted Spirituality* (Hillsdale, New York: Sophia Perennis, 2012).
16 René Guénon, *The Reign of Quantity* (Hillsdale, New York: Sophia Perennis, 2002/2004), 244.
17 See http://www.midnightfreemasons.org/2016/03/how-to-solve-membership-problem.html.
18 See http://freemasonsfordummies.blogspot.com/2016/03/ugles-membership-focus-group-study.html.
19 Melville Herskovits, *The Myth of The Negro Past* (Boston, Massachusetts: Beacon Press, 1958), 161. See also Robert Dannin, *Black Pilgrimage to Islam* (Oxford: Oxford University Press, 2002), 21.

Initiation, Present and Absent

In this context it is no doubt peculiar, even perverse, to start by saying that initiation, in its ultimate sense, may not be available to us in the West today. Yet this seems to be the case – or so one could conclude from Mircea Eliade's classic study *Rites and Symbols of Initiation.*

Examining material from so-called primitive cultures, Eliade says that puberty rites are the prime and most important form of initiation. Though they vary from simple instructions about the Supreme Being to intense and painful rites, "it is through initiation that, in primitive and archaic societies, man becomes what he is and should be – a being open to the life of the spirit, hence one who participates in the culture into which he was born ... It could almost be said that, for the primitive world, it is through initiation that men attain the status of human beings; before initiation, they do not yet share fully in the human condition precisely because they do not yet have access to the religious life."[1]

Note here the indissoluble link between initiation into a culture and initiation into the spiritual life. They are, in these contexts, identical. But for us today this initiation is not possible, because our culture does not have a collective spiritual life. I doubt that it was possible even one or two hundred years ago, when Christianity was the official religion of the West. Though many forms of initiation still take place, they are private in the sense that they are shared only by a portion of society – usually a rather small one. Thus the ultimate initiation, at least according to Eliade, simultaneously spiritual and cultural, is not available to us.

Why are puberty rites of supreme importance? Because all members of the society undergo them. Other forms are intended only for some. One such type is initiation into a secret society or confraternity. These societies are not always secret in the sense that may immediately come to mind: their *existence* is not necessarily a secret; rather it is certain elements of their teaching and practice that are kept hidden from the profane.

The third primary type of initiation involves entering a mystical vocation – in many indigenous societies, that of the medicine man or the shaman. Here the aspirant may decide voluntarily to take on this occupation or may feel that the decision is made for him – he experiences a call, which is often a spirit-induced illness. The aspirant has to cure himself by learning and using the shamanic practices that he will eventually apply to others.[2]

These different forms of initiation share a common theme of death and resurrection: the initiate dies to his former life and is resurrected into a new identity. This would appear to have been the case in early Christianity, when baptism, applied to adults who had made a conscious decision to accept the faith, was seen as a kind of death to the secular self and a rebirth in Christ.[3] Paul perhaps alludes to this idea when he says, "Know ye not, that so many of us as were baptized into Jesus Christ were baptized into his death?" (Romans 6:3). But infant baptism, as practiced today, cannot be considered an initiation: the baby is too small to know or remember what has been done to it. For this reason, no doubt, Catholicism developed a secondary sacrament, confirmation, which more closely resembles a classic initiation; current practice is to administer it in adolescence. (Confirmation evolved out of the early Christian practice of chrismation, or anointing, but originally this was administered immediately after baptism, as it still is in the Orthodox church.) There is even a muted death motif in that the bishop slaps the candidate gently on the cheek as a reminder that he is now committed to the faith even to the point of martyrdom.

Eliade is no doubt right from his point of view, but his portrait of initiation relies heavily on early anthropological reports of "primitive" cultures. He says little about present-day possibilities and would no doubt have agreed with the opening statement of this article. And yet initiation persists. Is there any form in which it is not purely vestigial?

For one answer to this question, we can turn to the 20th century French metaphysician René Guénon, who placed initiation at the center of his philosophical system. Actually Guénon would have been chagrined to hear anyone talk about "his" philosophical system, which, he insisted, had nothing to do with him personally and would have had no value if it did. Rather he was expressing what he called *tradition*.[4]

Tradition is a term that can mean almost anything. Guénon's use of this word is not as obvious as it may seem, even to one familiar with his writings. He gives it a specific, almost technical, meaning, and this meaning is indissolubly connected with initiation.

For Guénon, tradition is virtually equivalent to transmission: "Etymologically, 'tradition' expresses no idea except transmission; when one speaks of 'tradition' in the sense we intend, its meaning really does not extend beyond this perfectly normal usage."[5] (This point is often overlooked by Guénon's admirers, who apply any number of uses to the term.)

Nevertheless, *tradition* refers to transmission in an extremely circumscribed sense, and this is precisely the kind of transmission that is involved in initiation. It is a transmission of a certain spiritual influence, which can only be administered to certain individuals who possess the necessary characteristics. This influence, moreover, can only be transmitted in a regular initiatic line, by someone qualified, under specific rites that are designed for the purpose. (Guénon's frequent use of the term *regular* indicates the influence of Masonic initiation on his thought.) This initiation is permanent, rather like the indelible mark left by the sacraments, according to Catholic dogma.

Guénon's thought has become increasingly influential in the 21st century, although it is only the most superficial aspect of his thought (his polemic against modernity) that gets the most attention. But because of the importance he places on tradition, transmission, and initiation, it is worth sketching these matters out.

Tradition, in Guénon's view, goes back to a primordial spiritual center. In prehistoric times, access to this spiritual center was open and easily attained, but over time it became more and more occluded. He links this increasing occlusion to the Hindu concept of the four *yugas* or ages: the Satya, Treta, Dvapara, and Kali yugas. According to Hindu thought (and to Guénon), we are now in the fourth, the last and darkest of the ages: indeed *Kali Yuga* literally means *dark age*. Hence Guénon's attitude toward modernity, which is the inverse of modernity's view of itself (at least until very recent times). Far from being a time of enlightenment and progress, the present time is an age when connection with this spiritual center (which, at this point, exists in a metaphysical realm only and not in the physical one) is attenuated in the extreme. In fact it can only be gained through initiation.

Initiation, then, is a link to this spiritual center. This link is both "vertical" (to use Guénon's own metaphor) in that it connects the candidate to superhuman realms, and "horizontal" in that it extends back in linear time to the primordial age. (The Hebrew name for the Jewish esoteric tradition, *Kabbalah*, has a similar dual significance.) For these reasons Guénon goes so far as to claim that a valid initiatic line cannot have a historical point of origin: "If the origin of any organization whatsoever is fully documented as the work of individuals whose names can be cited and which possesses no link to tradition, one may rest assured, despite the claims, that there is absolutely nothing initiatic about the organization." He thus contrasts Masonry, whose Landmarks go back "to time immemorial," with the 18th century Society of the Illuminati, which was founded by Adam Weishaupt in 1776 and effectively functioned for only about a decade.[6]

Initiation is an inward connection to the tradition, which, as we have already seen, is effectively the transmission of spiritual influence. It can only be administered to candidates with certain qualifications. To anyone who objects that this smacks of elitism, Guénon replies that initiation *is* elitist. It can be administered to some and not others. The reason is not a desire for privilege or exclusivity, but the simple fact that some people possess certain characteristics while others do not. As Guénon takes pains to emphasize, initiation is not being denied to anyone who could derive any benefit from it.

As for qualifications, "the essential qualification, which takes precedence over all the others, is that of a greater or lesser 'intellectual horizon.'"[7] More specific qualifications often have to do with the conditions of initiation *into a particular line* rather than of initiation in general. In regular Masonry, according to Albert Mackey's interpretation of the Ancient Landmarks, "certain qualifications of a candidate for initiation are derived from a Landmark of the Order. These qualifications are: that he shall be a man – shall be unmutilated – free born and of mature age. That is to say, a woman, a cripple or a slave, or one born in slavery, is disqualified for initiation into the rites of Masonry."[8]

Often these qualifications are understood as deriving from the days of operative Masonry, as an anonymous author in one Masonic periodical believes: "Obviously a maimed man could not do as 'good work, true work, square work' as the able-bodied man."[9] Other disqualifications have less to do with operative holdovers than with impediments to carrying out certain ritual functions: "In most Jurisdictions [the candidate] must be 'perfect' with two arms, two legs, two hands and two feet. In some Jurisdictions, if he can conform to the requirements of the degrees, he may lack one or more fingers not vital to the tokens; in others he may not." Here a physical disability is a source for disqualification because it means that the candidate would not be able to carry out the rites fully or accurately.

For Guénon, "if Masonic initiation excludes … men with certain infirmities, this is not merely because those who are admitted used to have to carry burdens or climb scaffolds, as some assure us with a disconcerting naiveté; rather the Masonic initiation could not be valid for such people and could have no effect because of their lack of qualification. The first thing that can be said here is that even if the link with the craft has been broken with respect to outward practice, it nonetheless continues in a more essential way insofar as it remains necessarily inscribed in the very form of this initiation, for if this connection were eliminated, the initiation would no longer be Masonic but entirely different."

Guénon adds that women are disqualified from Masonic initiation for the same reason. They are disqualified from *Masonic* initiation, but not necessarily from other types: "There exist forms of initiation that are exclusively masculine, while there are others to which women can be admitted in the same way as men." In a footnote to this sentence, Guénon adds, "In antiquity there were also exclusively feminine forms of initiation,"[10] but I have good reason to believe that exclusively feminine initiatic lines continue to exist in the West today.[11]

Other disqualifications for Masonic initiation, according to Guénon, include stuttering, which would indicate more of a mental defect than a physical one as such (mental defects are disqualifications as well); moreover, "the ritual 'technique' almost always includes the pronunciation of certain verbal formulas which must naturally be correct above all in order to be valid, something stuttering does not permit in those afflicted by it."[12] Note the similarity to the instance of missing fingers: again the disability has specifically to do with the ability to carry out the rite.

I should interrupt here to explain that Guénon's discussion of initiation focuses heavily on Freemasonry for at least two reasons. In the first place, Masonic rites and texts, although ostensibly secret, have been publicized well enough so that they are more familiar than those of other initiatic organizations. In the second place, Guénon, as noted earlier, believes that the initiatic lines in the West have been extremely attenuated since at least the Renaissance. In fact "the only two [lines] that can claim an authentically traditional origin and a real initiatic transmission, however degenerate they may be through the ignorance and incomprehension of the vast majority of their members … are the Compagnonnage and Masonry."[13] The Compagnonnage in France consists of the descendants of medieval craft orders much like those of the Masons.[14] Guénon grudgingly concedes that there may also be "possible survivals of certain rare groups of medieval Christian Hermeticists" but adds that they "in any case were very restricted."[15]

Guénon regards the Brothers of the Rose-Cross, known also as the Rosicrucians, as a genuine initiatic line, reconstituted with the help of Islamic initiates after the dissolution of the Knights Templar in 1312. Guénon believes that the Brothers (known especially from the Rosicrucian manifestos, published in 1614-16)[16] functioned in Europe in the late medieval and early modern periods, but he takes literally a legend that after the 17th century, they removed themselves to the East.[17] I have some reasons to doubt him, although I do not see it as my place to discuss what connection this line may or may not have to present-day organizations that call themselves Rosicrucian. In fact I suspect that Guénon was ignorant of various initiatic lines in the West that did and do still operate, largely for a reason he regards as intrinsic to the nature of these lines: they are not organizations in any publicly constituted sense, and they had no reason to make themselves known to him. He does not appear to have thought of this possibility.

In any event, in Guénon's view, initiation imparts a certain spiritual influence to the candidate. He does not use the Arabic word *baraka*, which has something like this meaning, but he could have. This influence is itself the initiatic secret: certain signs, handclasps, words, and the rites themselves are simply their vehicles, and they are ineffective unless they are administered by someone who is qualified to do so. In this connection he notes the use of the mantra in the Hindu tradition. This word has come to be used as slang for anything that is endlessly and mindlessly repeated, but a mantra is not quite that. OM is perhaps the most famous, but for the majority of people, it is not a mantra in the strict sense. It only *becomes* a mantra when it is imparted in instruction by a qualified guru. Anyone else who tried to use it, for meditation or any other purpose, would not get the same result; for this reason initiates are often told to keep their mantras secret. "A *mantra* learned otherwise than from the mouth of an authorized guru is without effect, because it is not 'vivified' by the presence of the spiritual influence whose vehicle it is uniquely destined to be."[18] Note again that the mantra per se is only a *vehicle* of spiritual influence, not the influence itself.[19]

For Guénon, the only lines in the West that are even vestigially initiatic are Freemasonry, the Compagnonnage, and certain esoteric Christian lines about which he says very little. One line that he describes as more or less extinct from an initiatic point of view is that of the Carbonari, the Italian guild of the charcoal burners. The Carbonari started as very much like the French societies of the Compagnonnage, but they are chiefly known to history through their influence on liberal political movements of the 18th and 19th centuries. Guénon believes that by this point they had degenerated into a movement that was solely political, and for that reason no longer initiatic: initiatic lines operate in the realm of the sacred only and have nothing to do with profane matters such as politics. Masonry, he adds, experienced "a certain degeneration in the same directions, though not carried so far, as that of Carbonarism." By this he means the well-known role allegedly played by Masonry in the 18th century revolutions in the United States and France, and well into the 20th century.

I could say a great deal more about Guénon's picture of initiation, which seems to me valid in the sense in which he intends it. But at this point we must go back to the perspective with which this article began: that of Eliade. Guénon's concept of initiation is selective in the extreme; what then are we to make of the initiations in ancient or pristine societies, such as puberty rites, which are administered to everyone in the tribe, and which Eliade considers to be the most important?

Guénon explores this issue chiefly in regard to the *upayana,* the Hindu initiations of the twice-born, the three highest castes in the Hindu system. These are universally administered, at any rate to all members of the caste; one does not fully become a member of the caste without this rite. Citing the scholar of religions A.K. Coomaraswamy, Guénon sees these rites not as initiations in the full sense, but more properly as forms of "admission" or "integration" into the caste. He connects this kind of initiation with those of "primitive societies," the very kind that Eliade was principally discussing.

> One can see the error of ethnologists who unthinkingly apply the term "initiation" (the true meaning and real implication of which they evidently have no grasp) to rites that all the members of a tribe or people have access to at any moment of their existence, and particularly when it is a matter of so-called primitive societies. In reality, these rites have no initiatic character at all… Naturally these societies can have authentically initiatic

> rites, even if these are degenerate to some degree (and perhaps they are so less often than one might be tempted to suppose); but, here as everywhere, these are accessible only to certain individuals to the exclusion of others.[20]

Guénon's view of initiation thus differs greatly from Eliade's. The two cannot be reconciled, and there is no point in trying. We have already seen why: for Eliade, the puberty rite is of supreme importance because it is performed on every member of the tribe, whereas for Guénon, this is precisely what disqualifies it.

Nonetheless, one can gain some insight from comparing the two perspectives. Perhaps the most illuminating is the theme of death and rebirth. Both Eliade and Guénon agree that this is practically universal; they even agree about why. Eliade: "Puberty rites, precisely because they bring about the neophyte's introduction to the realm of the sacred, imply death to the profane condition ... The experience of initiatory death and resurrection not only basically changes the neophyte's mode of being, but at the same time reveals to him the sacredness of the world."[21] Guénon: "The change that gives access to the initiatic order corresponds to a higher degree of reality… Initiation is generally described as a 'second birth,' which indeed it is, but this 'second birth' necessarily implies a death to the profane world."[22]

For both Guénon and Eliade, then, the death and rebirth motif refers to a death to the profane realm and a birth into the sacred. Why should the two thinkers reach such diametrically opposite conclusions, one stressing the universality of initiation in the cultures that practise it, the other insisting that it is necessarily limited to a small elite?

The answer lies in a theme already encountered: Guénon's relentless insistence on the idea that we are living in the Kali Yuga.[23] For him, the primordial center is occluded in our time, and it is occluded for everybody, no matter whether they are French Freemasons or Queensland aborigines. There can be no exceptions. For Eliade, who does not hold to such ideas (or at least not in the same way), it is possible for certain cultures to have retained a collective sense of connection to the "sacredness of the world." Thus he sees no innate difficulty in initiation proper being administered to everyone in a tribe.

Clearly there is a long discussion here, which is not relevant to the present point. I think it best to leave with the observation that Guénon is right in claiming that initiation in the sense he is talking about is a rare and adventitious occurrence in the modern West; whether it is so in cultures that are the diametrical opposites of our own is not a matter about which I would rush to judgment. Eliade too is right in implicitly suggesting that initiation, the simultaneous entrance of the candidate into the realm of the sacred and the realm of culture, cannot be achieved in our present society. Like Guénon, he shows contempt for what he regards as "pseudo-initiatory" groups in the 19th and 20th centuries.[24]

Having said all this, I believe it is time for me to add some personal reflections.

When you think about it, *initiate* is a peculiar word. In some occult literature, like the *Initiate* trilogy written in the 1920s and '30s by an anonymous "pupil" (generally identified as the Theosophist Cyril Scott), it denotes someone extremely advanced.[25] And yet *initiate* means *beginner*, someone who has just started something.

We might find a clue to this apparent contradiction in Buddhism, which speaks of the novice as a *srotapanna*, or "one who enters the stream." The image points to a key aspect of initiation: the fact that it opens one up to a stream of spiritual influence offered by a tradition, as, each in his own way, both Eliade and Guénon suggest.

What does initiation entail? There seem to be three basic levels. They may be conferred in formal rituals – of an organization known or unknown – although I suspect that at least in some cases no ritual, or only the most basic type of ritual, is involved.

The first level could simply be called the initiation of *responsibility*. It marks a point at which the individual stands forward and freely agrees to accept the task of his or her own personal evolution – in Buddhist terms, entering the stream. Most people, however wise, educated, or successful, have not made any such commitment. They will develop and grow as the random circumstances of life permit. But the initiate at the first level makes this commitment to work upon self-development. In return he or she is (metaphorically) implanted with a kind of seed crystal that forms the core of the awakening self. Life starts to shape itself around this crystal and serves as a means of purging the initiate of the dross of his character.

This process of purification continues for a long time, years or more likely decades, and probably there are few initiates alive on earth who are not continuing to undergo it. But after the individual has reached some level of maturity, the time comes for a second initiation – the stage when he now takes on the additional responsibility of a task or line of work that he is uniquely able to pursue, such as healing, art, or social action. This is not necessarily a trade or profession in the ordinary sense, although it may well coincide with one's work in daily life. One could call this the initiation of *vocation*.

Having started on this line of work, the initiate then pursues it both for self-development and in service to a higher purpose. Inevitably the individual will make mistakes, will do some things well and others badly and suffer from lapses of judgment or even ethics. But they are all part of the process of learning. If the initiate is made of good material (and the very fact of initiation suggests he is), he will sort through his mistakes and learn the necessary lessons.

The third is the stage of *mastery*. This is not a matter of acquiring amazing mystical powers or superhuman capacities. But it does show that the individual has acted upon the responsibility he took on in the first initiation and developed the skills required in the second. He is not necessarily finished with these tasks, but he has acquired enough ability to work creatively and from his own initiative. He is now enabled to stake out new ground and expand humanity's range of knowledge.

While I am not a Freemason, these stages seem to correspond to the three levels of Blue Lodge (or Craft) Masonry: Entered Apprentice, Fellow Craft, and Master Mason. Those who have been raised to these levels (as Masons put it) may be able to see the correspondences and even explain some of the mysteries of these stages from details of the Masonic rites.

Notice too that these three stages still exist in present-day crafts, which resemble my description above remarkably closely. Here is a definition of how they apply to electricians: "An apprentice is a beginner or trainee who works under direct supervision of a master electrician. A journeyman is trained and experienced and can work on his own under the general guidance of a master. A master originates projects, gets permits for construction and installations and oversees the work of journeymen and apprentices."[26] These specifications form part of the National Electrical Code in the U.S., which is used by all states in licensing electricians. Evidently these three stages retain a great deal of practical value.

Is self-initiation possible? The answer appears to be no, at least if you are defining it as Eliade and Guénon have. If you are entering a spiritual stream, it is a stream that already exists and there must be someone to introduce you to it. While many people have had spontaneous experiences of illumination, these are probably better described as moments of awakening or enlightenment. Others say that they have received initiation on the inner planes. As usual, no one can say they haven't: no one can make any definitive pronouncements about what inner experience another person has or might have had. Nevertheless, such cases seem highly prone to self-delusion or fraud, so they are at best viewed with caution.

Finally, is initiation necessary for spiritual advancement? Again the answer seems to be no. The range of human experience is too vast, too well endowed with spontaneous awakenings and self-discovered insights, to suggest that formal initiation is always required for progress on the path. For some, it is not only valuable but necessary. Others do perfectly well without it. Why? The answer to this mystery no doubt lies in the uniqueness of the human individuality and the wide scope of circumstances that are needed to help it flourish.

At this point I feel the need to address the compulsively pragmatic contemporary mind, which is likely to ask, "This is all very good, but what practical value does it have for us?"

The answer, or the beginning of an answer, lies in this fact: many adult men today are not men; they are boys. Many adult women are not women; they are girls. In our society it is possible to go through all the stages of life, even successfully, without maturing emotionally, much less spiritually. An individual can build a house by himself from the ground up, practice as a respected neurosurgeon, or turn $10,000 into $10 million while remaining a two-year-old inwardly. One can see this even in certain elderly people, who have brought their infantile capriciousness and petulance with them into the advanced stages of life. They have gone from green to rotten without ever having been ripe.

The reasons for this situation are of course complex. The mentality of consumerism, with its drive toward impulsive and needless purchases, certainly plays a major role. But I think we also have to consider the absence of generally accepted forms of initiation in present-day society. You can be initiated into the culture (that is, you can be culturally literate) without being initiated spiritually. Although you can be initiated in Guénon's highly specific sense, that is rare, and is just as likely to make you feel alienated from the wider culture as to make you feel integrated into it.

This problem is, I believe, greater and more pervasive than one may easily imagine. I believe it lies behind many social problems that are apparently unrelated. The back cover of my copy of Eliade's *Rites and Symbols of Initiation* says:

> The absence of initiation in our culture has left modern men and women often isolated from each other, from the invisible powers beyond, and from the myths that sustain daily life. The primal soul desire for symbolic rituals pushes youth into substitutes for initiatory experience: gangs, suicide, car crashes, teenage pregnancy, street drugs. These "symptoms" show the unquenchable urge for existential transformation and the need for elders, mentors, and rituals.[27]

These words were written in the early 1990s. In the two decades that have passed since then, the situation does not seem to have changed in any visible way. I believe that the need for initiation remains more powerful and pressing than ever, but at this point I can offer no suggestions for answering this need that would not seem improbable or even ludicrous. Thus, regretfully, I must end this article not with a solution, but with a problem.

1 Mircea Eliade, *Rites and Symbols of Initiation: The Mysteries of Birth and Rebirth*, trans. Willard R. Trask (Woodstock, Conn.: Spring Publications, 1995), 3. This book was originally published under the title *Birth and Rebirth* in 1958.

2 On the three types of initiation, see Eliade, 2-3.

3 On the relation of early Christian baptism to initiation, see Edward Yarnold, *The Awe-Inspiring Rites of Initiation: The Origins of the R.C.I.A.* (Collegeville, Minn.: Liturgical Press, 1971).

4 Eliade has sometimes been characterized as a "soft traditionalist," having read and been influenced by Guénon to a certain extent. But, as we shall see, their views about initiation differ.

5 René Guénon, *Perspectives on Initiation*, trans. Henry D. Fohr (Hillsdale, N.Y.: Sophia Perennis, 2001), 56.

6 Guénon, 77, 80. For a short account of the Illuminati, see Monika Neugebauer-Wölk, "Illuminaten," in Wouter J. Hanegraaff et al., eds., *Dictionary of Gnosis and Western Esotericism* (Leiden: Brill, 2005), vol. II, 590-97.

7 Guénon, 93.

8 Mackey's Landmarks first appeared in the October 1858 edition of *American Quarterly Review of Freemasonry*, vol. II, 230. See http://freemasonry.bcy.ca/grandlodge/landmarks.html; accessed July 4, 2018.

9 Anonymous, "The Candidate," *Short Talk Bulletin* 8, no. 5 (May 1930); from the Masonic World website, www.masonicworld.com/education/files/artnov01/The Candidate.htm; accessed Jan. 4, 2018.

10 Guénon, 94.

11 For a discussion of some possible avenues, see Cherry Gilchrist, *The Circle of Nine: Contemporary Female Archetypes from an Ancient Tradition* (Newburyport, Mass.: Weiser, 2018).

12 Guénon, 101.

13 Idid., 34.

14 For a thorough discussion of the Compagnonnage, see Jean-Pierre Bayard, *Le Compagnonnage en France* (Paris: Payot, 1977).

15 Guénon, 34.

16 For a recent edition of these texts, see Joscelyn Godwin, Christopher McIntosh, and Donate Pahnke McIntosh, eds. and trans., *Rosicrucian Trilogy* (Newburyport, Mass.: Weiser, 2016).

17 Guénon, 239.
18 Idid., 54.
19 For a similar view, see Agehananda Bharati, *The Tantric Tradition* (New York: Doubleday Anchor, 1970), chapter 5, esp. 111.
20 Guénon, 155.
21 Eliade, 18-19.
22 Guénon, 172-73.
23 For more on these points, see Richard Smoley, "Waiting for the End of the World: René Guénon and the Kali Yuga," *New Dawn, 19* September 2010, https://www.newdawnmagazine.com/articles/waiting-for-the-end-of-the-world-rene-guenon-and-the-kali-yuga.
24 Eliade, 133-35.
25 See, for example, "His Pupil," *The Initiate* (London: Routledge, 1920). See also "Cyril Meir Scott" in Philip S. Harris et al., eds., *Theosophical Encyclopedia* (Quezon City, Philippines: Theosophical Publishing House, 2006), 558.
26 Bob Haring, "Differences between a Journeyman and a Master Electrician," Chron.com; accessed Jan. 4, 2018, http://work.chron.com/differences-between-journeyman-master-electrician-2158.html.
27 This edition of Eliade's book was published by Spring Publications, which at the time was owned by the archetypal psychologist James Hillman. Thus it is possible that these words were written by Hillman himself.

The Theme of Regeneration in Swedish Freemasonry Seen through the Lens of Two Lodges with Female Members

Susanna Åkerman

By observing two lodges with female members before and around 1800 – namely the lodges *La Veritable et Constante Amitié (Vera amicitia constantia)* from 1776 and *DELU* in 1802 to 1803 – we can get a sense of the Swedish Masonic atmosphere in the circles of Queen Hedwig Elisabeth Charlotta and her husband Duke Charles of Suderomannia (Charles XIII), the founder and main designer of the Swedish Masonic system. In doing so we will also dwell upon Swedenborg's proposed path to initiation and regeneration, a theme much studied by Duke Charles, who was a member of the *Exegetic and Philanthropic Society* from 1786, a Swedish Swedenborgian society that studied and translated Swedenborg's writings from the Latin into Swedish.

Swedish Masonry started in the 1730s and was well established by the time Duke Charles began to design a perfect system of higher-degree Freemasonry, which preoccupied him to the point that he, as King, let his German wife and Queen preside in the Council of State in his absence. Her judgment was simply better, he thought, and history has agreed that he was not 'the sharpest knife in the box.' His desire to complete the Swedish Masonic System was, however, genuine and he single-mindedly perfected it in 1802. About this time, he decided to create a mixed lodge called DELU or the *Det eviga husets utvalda*, "Those Elected by the Eternal Light," sometimes read as *Deus Est Lux Universalis*. Meetings were held at Rosersberg, a castle especially designed for esoteric purposes, with a square room for Masonic receptions and an oblong wing featuring a checkerboard floor and windows to conduct DELU initiations. In the garden, there is a grotto with a Masonic Cross reminding some of the Rosicrucian vault. DELU was also called Gula Rosen, the Yellow Rose, referring to the perfected mental state of the initiated.

Before admitting women into the DELU, Duke Charles had prepared the ground by having Hedwig Elisabeth Charlotta set up a female lodge, *Vera amicitia constantia,* most of the members of which were the Queen's court ladies. They probably met in the Stockholm castle where Charles had arranged a Sanctuarium for receptions and spirit séances. Or perhaps more likely they met in one of the many other halls in the great castle – there is also a painting from that time showing the Queen and her female companion being received by the Duke and a male courtier at an altar-like table.

The spiritual world of Emanuel Swedenborg was important to these people because it introduced them to the realm of spirits that are encountered and enhanced by initiation rituals, giving one the invigorating feeling of being surrounded by smiling faces. A 17th century copy in Latin of Swedenborg's work *The Last Judgement and the Destruction of Babylon* (London, 1758) can now be found in the Masonic library in Stockholm. It says that a final rearrangement of good and bad ideas took place in the spiritual world in 1757, giving more freedom to humans to choose righteously. The Last Judgement thus is a purely spiritual event, not an actual destruction of anything real. Importantly, this work also says that marital relations and conjugial love continue forever in heaven.

In his works, Swedenborg used the image of the chrysalis to explain the regeneration of humans, beginning with a closed-up larva growing into a chrysalis and then metamorphizing into a beautiful butterfly. Similarly, the soul develops from being caught up in self-love and love of the world to opening as a flower out through reformation into a purified state of regeneration, in which Good and True, Love and Wisdom flow in and become the ruling feelings. Man thus is a receptaculum for these energies; to receive them, one must open up to the spiritual world, to the guidance of angels and the Lord's loving wisdom.

This follows from Swedenborg's theory of correspondences, that the inner meaning of the Word represents higher ideas and ultimately the process of regeneration. As Swedenborg himself notes in his diary called *Spiritual Experiences*:

> 2475. THAT ALL THINGS IN UNIVERSAL NATURE ARE REPRESENTATIONS OF THE LORD'S KINGDOM.
>
> I spoke with spirits concerning worms that become butterflies; that they are representations of heavenly life, to wit, that they should be little worms, lowly, creeping on the ground, eating herbs, thus the vilest things; and that meantime they are prepared for a certain representative heaven suitable to them; to wit, that thus through the chrysalis state [per nymphus] they are turned into winged and beautiful insects [animalcula], and then are elevated from the ground into the air, their heaven, [and] fly, and apply themselves to their roses, [and] eat the must [mustum] thereof; celebrate [ludant] their nuptials; lay eggs; and so enjoy their felicity: that these are representations of the reformation and regeneration of humble men was sufficiently manifest; and that these things were continued to their posterity, [and] that they represent the eternal with man. Then the discourse was concerning other things, as well in the animal, as in the vegetable kingdom, in general; that nothing is ever given in those kingdoms that does not represent the Lord's kingdom with indefinite variety. This was confirmed by the angels. – 1748, July 1. – Further, that otherwise not anything can exist and subsist in those kingdoms; hence, each and all that are in nature flow so as to be remote images of the Lord's kingdom.

Thus the "hieroglyphics" or symbols used in Masonic contexts can be understood as representing the divine and heavenly aspects of human activity and by applying the theory of correspondences to such symbols one can reveal their inner spiritual sense. Regenerating is a lifelong process of fleeing evil and seeking good but how this replacement of bad inclinations by good ones takes place is not thoroughly explained in the *Arcana coelestia*. Thus, Swedenborgians turned to the development of the personality offered in the Initiation in Masonic degrees and virtues. They were aware of the goal of the Initiations (regeneration) and could provide a framework for understanding what is going on in them on a spiritual plane under the guidance of the Lord Jesus Christ.

According to Swedenborg's theory of correspondences each thing, person, animal, town, people or historical event in the Bible must be interpreted according to its higher spiritual and celestial sense. This seeking for a higher or inner sense appears to some extent also in the Masonic initiations where illuminations or hieroglyphs from the Bible are presented and then interpreted abstractly in the context of virtue. And when regeneration could be likened to the natural development of the beautiful butterfly, and if the spiritual world that opens is like walking in a rose garden, then the initiation of women into Masonic degrees was not seen as an unsuitable practice. However, the content of these degrees had to be modified to suit their female nature.

Therefore Hedwig Elisabeth Charlotta introduced to her select court ladies an order which she thought would promote the virtue and dignity of women and their true and constant friendship. After a request by the Count d'Usson (or Count de Dusson), the letter of authorisation from the French Constitution allowing the royal adoption lodge was signed by the Duchess Bathilde of Bourbon, or L.M.T.B. d'Orleans, Grand Maitresse of all French lodges of adoption, at the garden of Eden (*le jardin d'Eden*) and confirmed by a sigil of the Duke d'Orleans.

According to the State chancellor Fredrik Sparre's diary, those received as "franche maconnes" in May 1776 were the Queen's friend *Eva Sophie von Fersen* (1757-1816), married to Adolf Ludwig Piper, *Hedwig Eleonora (Hedda) von Fersen* (1753-1792) married to Ture Leonard Klinkowström, state lady by Princess Sofia Magdalena, and *Ulrika Catharina Koskull* (1759-1805) married to Magnus Brahe.

"*La Maconnerie des dames ou loge d'adoption*" was divided into five degrees, first the three degrees of aprentifs (apprentices), compagnons and maîtrise (master), and then the maîtres experts (high masters) and maîtres elus (selected masters). The hieroglyphs or symbols involved in the degrees were Old Testament conceptions such as the Ark, the Tower of Babel, the Rainbow, and Adam and Eve with the snake in the Garden of delights. Thus the usual symbolism of male Blue Masonry was not included, yet the lodge was held in the same rooms as male Masonry but considered as outside it, and as adopted by the brothers who were the working members. There was a male grand master called high honorable master who had to have a degree no lower than Scottish Master, just as all other working male members of the lodge: brother surveillor, brother speaker, treasurer, ceremonial master, secretary, etc.

However, during the ceremonies one Sister takes the place of director in the lodge and carries, just as the Grand Master and the Grand Mistress, a small hammer. One Masonic Sister assumes the role as introducer to oversee the foreign seeker's preparation and induction. Also, importantly, one Brother of outstanding stature and repute represents the Angel in Paradise and is called *Frère Terrible*.

First Degree of Apprentices

In the first degree, the Grand Master and Grand Mistress sit in the front of the lodge and have an altar table before them. Across from the altar there is a smaller table with a blue cloth. In the background, there lies a white cloth (tapestry) on which three paintings are placed, in this order:

Noah's Ark

Babylonian Tower **A Ladder with 5 steps**

In front of this cloth or tapestry there are two *guéridons* (lampstands) on each of which a bowl with *spiritus vini* is burning. No other light brightens the lodge.

The Sisters sit on both sides and the Brothers in between them, holding the points of their swords across each other. Brothers are clad as Scottish Masters. Sisters are clad in white.

The Candidate is led to a room where there are a candle and a Bible on the table and she is left there to contemplate.

The Introducer walks into the room and asks the Candidate if she, eager to support the aims of the Order about which she is soon to learn, and with uprightness and silence, is prepared to enter the Order. If she says yes, then the Introducer tells her: "Well, my Miss, Mistress, or Mademoiselle, then you will not refuse to take off certain parts of your clothing, which the Order sees as the first sign of your willingness to liberate yourself from the greater part of mankind's prejudiced opinions." Then she is asked to take off an earring, a *manchette* (cuff) or *engageante* (false sleeve), and one of her garters.

She is blindfolded and a trowel is put in her hand, as a sign that she does not refuse to work; then she is led to the door of the lodge, where the Introducer knocks on the door, the first two quickly, the other two slowly. This is answered by five knocks, with the question "Who is there?" To which the Introducer says: "A friend of noble heart who wants to enter our excellent society as a female Freemason."

She is led inside the hall and stood before the altar and the white cloth with images, and is placed between the *guéridons* with burning *spiritus vini*. Then the Grand Mistress says: "In this way light shows us that our secrets are not going to be concealed from you. It is only upright noble souls who reach as far as here and whom we rightly admit into our Sister and Brotherhood. We believe and wish to find such things in your heart that you now want to give us. Each of our Sisters and Brothers will encourage you to [achieve] all that you owe the Architect of the World, the King, the neighbor and yourself. Virtue is the only basis to all our works and labors and you can freely answer if you are willing to give our Order that commitment that Our Laws require." If she says yes, the blindfold is taken off so that she can see the Sisters and Brothers standing in formation. Under the arch of crossed swords, she is brought closer to the altar where the Grand Master and the *Frère Terrible* stand, with a flaming sword held above the Candidate's head as she kneels. The Grand Master recites the oath which she repeats:

"With the knowledge I have of the **Sun**, of the great construction of the world, which from a compact patch of earth have brought forth the **four elements** and thereby created the greatest art of building, I promise to keep, retain and hide all Masonic secrets in eternal silence, as well as never speak of the same, but to a Sister and a Brother, whom I after detailed research have found to be right members of this Order. I also promise in the gathering of the Order to Hear, be Obedient, to Work and to be Silent in a manner that the Laws of the Order prescribe. The Fire of the Uppermost Heaven will help me hereby and lead me on the paths that are worthy of this Order."

At that point all the Sisters and Brothers clap their hands five times. The Grand Master says: "Now you have been admitted to the Order of female Masons. From your promotion we expect and we promise Honor, from your virtues a pattern, and from your noble friendship the most permanent advantages."

The Grand Mistress clothes the recipient in a white apron with white ribbons and a triangular downward pointing piece dressed in similar ribbons. She informs her: "With our common uniform we promise, for all your lifetime, and with the inclinations of our heart and mind, that you are united with us. Its white color is an image of the Purity and Unspottedness of our intentions. You are now joined with your Brothers and Sisters and I am responsible for responding with righteous love and tenderness."

Hereupon, the Grand Mistress sets a white ribbon with a **Rose** hanging on a silver **Trowel** at her **Left** breast with these words: "Wear this symbol and tool to remind you of your labors in the Masonic Order. Industriousness and intent will lead you from this first, to the last and highest step. Learn from the Brothers, and follow the Sisters."

Then the Grand Mistress hands her the white garters with a single rose on the side and reminds her: "Always wear them when in lodge; the reason for this will not remain a Riddle." She is instructed that Sisters in this degree always wear a white dress if it is possible; always to use double white earrings and never enter the lodge without white gloves. She is given the secret handshake with the secret word, **Flix Fox**, which means The School of Virtue.[1]

Then the Grand Mistress takes the Sister and places her in a free place in the row to the right of the Grand Master and goes back to her place at the altar.

The Grand Master and the Grand Mistress clap five times with their hands, make the sign of the lodge and say: "Happily Live, Work, and be Silent, you our Sister." All present make the same claps with the hands and say the same words.

The laws are read and the Grand Mistress calls for attention to the Catechism that is then read as an explanation of the images on the cloth.

Excerpts from the *Catechism*:

Q. How come you to Masonry?
A. Through an arch of **Iron and Steel**.
Q. What does this Arch represent?
A. Strength and Permanence, which is a mark of Endurance.
Q. Where are you received as apprentice?
A. Between the Babylonian Tower, Jacob's Ladder and at the foot of Noah's Ark.
Q. What does the **Babylonian Tower** represent?
A. The haughtiness of the children of this world which you only by a self-conscious heart can loose, and which to cure is the true sign of a Mason and Masoness.
Q. What does **Jacob's Ladder** mean?
A. This ladder is full of secrets. The two ladder posts represent the love for God and the Neighbor: And between the steps are the virtues which have origin from a noble soul.
Q. What does the **Ark of Noah** mean?
A. The heart of man, which is carried and driven by passions just as the Ark by the Flood (of transgression).
Q. What are they called who are not Masons?
A. Profanes.
Q. What does the password mean?
A. The lodge is a school of virtue.
Q. What is the Mason's and Masoness' duty and responsibility?
A. To hear, to obey, and to Work and to be Silent.
Q. How is your obedience?
A. Free and without force.

Q. What do you work on?
A. To make myself Pleasant, Useful and Happy.

Then the lodge is closed with the words: "We have heard, been obedient and Worked. Let us be Silent."

Then the dinner lodge is held, at which the poor are remembered.

Second Degree of Compagnons

On the wall above the Grand Master and Grand Mistress there hangs an **Eight-pointed burning star**, whose other side is a round **globe** filled with **yellow** *spiritus vini*, which is lit.

Across from the altar, behind the Hostess, burns an illuminated picture showing the following painting:

The Garden of Eden where Adam and Eve stand by the **Tree of Knowledge of Good and Evil** and eat of the **fruit**. Around the Tree the **Snake** wriggles.

A **skull**, with crossed **bones** underneath.

In front of this representation which is lit by many lights and lamps stands a Tree on a *tabourette* with hanging fruits so naturally made they resemble real **Apples**.

In front of the altar there is a tapestry with a blue cloth divided into two parts:

A **Garden** in whose center stands The Tree of Knowledge of Good and Evil. Beneath the Tree lies **Neptune** holding a **whale** (dolphin?) under his arm from which a river flows through the Garden.

Adam and Eve being expelled from Paradise.

In front of this tapestry there is a bowl in which *spiritus vini* is burning. A Sister holds a long **chain** made of **white brass**, so long it goes around the neck and both hands.

The *Frère Terrible* has an **Olive branch** in his hand.

On the table before the Grand Master and Grand Mistress there is a bowl with **almond dough** and also a little **trowel**.

When the blindfolded candidate is led into the hall, all scream with horror and fear: "Eva! Eva!"

Then the Grand Master says: "My Brothers and Sisters! Fear not: it is not dangerous."

The Grand Master asks: "Do you feel strong enough to endure all the required terrible tests? The slightest weakness that we can sense in you would be enough to expel you from the Order and we will then be deprived of a jewel in the Order."

She assures her steadfastness.

GM: "My Brother, Let her then endure the **Fire test**."

He leads her around, during which time the Sister who holds the chain makes a great noise with it. The wandering ends at the *tabourette* where the burning *spiritus vini* stands, over which he holds her bare hand.

GM: "Has she endured the first test?"

"Yes with steadfastness, Venerable."

GM: "Let her then endure the second, and show her the state of Innocence, as well as the origin of the turpitude."

Led to the tapestry, she is directed to view the illuminated picture.

GM: "Do you see the disobedience and its consequences? Here is **the first humans' apple bite**: there the following **death**. To diminish and make milder this **punishment**, Masonry is a necessary means: as practice of virtue teaches you to endure this fatal Moment."

GM: "Let her then go from death to Life and show her the light and its guide, **The Star from the East**."

GM: "See this, my Sister, this star from the East is the enlightenment of Reason and the true light of Masonry from which we do not separate, as we through it are led to the true **felicity**."

She is shown the sign and the *Frère Terrible* holds the Olivebranch over her head, which is a sign of peace, as she kneels on a stool and is asked to say a promise:

"To let the light of Masonry, and reason, lead me. And not to eat of any forbidden fruit, as truly as my Brothers' and Sisters' confidence in my high worth is respected…"

The Grand Mistress says: "Bring me the holy Fruit!" She walks to the Tree standing on the table and takes an apple, giving it to the Candidate Sister with the following words: "My Sister. We are assured that you will keep your promise, but our Order commands that you truly prove it by eating this apple."

As soon as she does so, all the Brothers and Sisters scream: "Eva! Eva!"

Then the Grand Mistress takes a piece of the almond dough and presses it on the mouth of the candidate, saying: "Now I put the **Sigil** of Silence and Sapience on your lips. Remember to never open your mouth without speaking well of your Brothers and Sisters and also never to reveal the secrets of Freemasonry."

She hands over the Compagnon's apron of white cloth with a dark angled blue ribbon, dressed in silk and five simple roses: three above, two below.

"The blue color is a reminder of Permanence and the permanent fidelity to our Order and the unchangeable friendship you owe to the Brothers and Sisters."

At the left breast, she sets a simple rose of blue ribbon on the hanging trowel and says: "This degree does not liberate you from labor, and so now bear this instrument to show your diligence to the Sisters of the first degree." She is given blue garters and reminded on pain of severe punishment to always wear them in the lodge.

The recipient is shown the sign and the password, **Belba,** which is explained as Peace and Unanimity and which, by the striking down of the Tower of Iniquity, has been received again.

Excerpts from the *Catechism:*

Q. Are you a Compagnon?
A. Give me an apple and you will be able to tell.
Q. How are you taken as compagnons?
A. Through a sort of fruit and a ribbon.
Q. What does this fruit represent?
A. The Sweetness.
Q. What does the ribbon represent?
A. The Unity of the Brotherhood.
Q. Why do compagnons not eat the seeds of the apple?

A. Because the **Seeds** of the apple are the origin of the forbidden fruit.
Q. What did you see first in the lodge?
A. The image of seduction.
Q. How do you guard yourself against the same?
A. By a carefulness which is supported through a Masonic foundation.
Q. Who made you Compagnon?
A. My Trowel and my virtue.
Q. What do you think at the heavy word Eva?
A. It brings me to my origin and shows me what I am, and what I ought to be, in remembrance of the highest felicity.
Q. What did you see in the Garden?
A. The Tree of Knowledge of Good and Evil.
Q. What does this Tree teach?
A. That each good Mason should flee vice and seek virtue.
Q. What does the **Flood** represent?
A. The intensity and speed of human inclinations which cannot be restrained but by the Founding Rule of Masonry.
Q. What is the most noble of Masonry?
A. To Seek to make Oneself and Others Happy.
Q. How do we reach this felicity?
A. Through the Unity of Virtue.
Q. Which is the Word?
A. Belba! Which means Peace and Unity and which through the striking down of the Tower of Iniquity is now found among the Sisters and Brothers, as it was prophesied in the Fortunes of the Sibylls.
Q. What is the Mason's and Masoness' duty and responsibility?
A. To hear, obey, Work and be Silent.

Third Degree of Mistresses

The lodge is lit by **13** candles, of which **seven** stand on one side and **six** on the other. Everyone is positioned as in the other degrees.

In front of the tapestry to the right stands a Ladder or stairs with five steps.

On the left there is a mechanical **coffin** or box, on top of which lies a **Chisel**, a **Club** and a **Hammer**.

The tapestry shows paintings placed in a **Circle**.

The Rainbow
Noah's offerings
Abraham's offerings
Noah's Ark on Mount Ararat
Tower of Babel
Sodom and Gomorrah burning
Lot's wife transforming into a pillar of salt
Joseph's dream: sun, moon and 11 stars
Joseph at the well

The four parts of the world are shown on the sides and corners of the tapestry.

The Sister is led before the altar.

Question: "Has she honorably prepared herself for reception in the grade?"

Answer: "She is to be a decoration for the Order."

GM: "Then let open for her the Temple of Virtue."

Her sight is restored and she greets the whole Society with the Compagnon's sign and is greeted the same in return.

GM: "My Brother! Let this Sister step up the mysterious Staircase."

She is led up shoeless on the stairs, right foot, left foot and right foot to the third step; and then right foot and left foot to the fifth.

GM: "Is the Sister come to the highest stair of Felicity?"

"Yes, *Très Venerable*."

GM: "Happy are you who have reached this step to which many thousands strive. Step toward me and secure yourself in this Felicity, on the path of which you already see the Goal."

She falls to her knees before the altar. The *Frère Terrible* holds a sword to her neck and she recounts the following promise: "By Noah's, Abraham's and Jacob's Offerings, I promise and swear to this venerable society of Masters eternal Faith, Friendship and Silence..."

The whole Society claps five times at the last words. At the last clap there rises out of the coffin's upper opening, a heart.[2]

GM: "What has the Sister brought forward?"

"Très Venerable, a heart has been brought therefrom."

GM: "See, my Sister, that Masonry is a work for the heart. Over the heart it gives us dominion. We know how to make out of the hardest and most uncompromising the most compassionate and tender."

The Grand Mistress puts the Master's apron on her with a broad crimson-colored ribbon with 5 big double Roses of the same color: four in a square on the apron and one on the slip.

"Wear this brilliant jewel as a proof that you have stepped up on the highest step on the Staircase of Felicity through Wisdom, Sapience, Patience, Love and Labor."

Then a golden trowel hanging from a large five double Rose is set under her left breast, together with a ribbon for the hair in crimson-color with five double Rose ribbons. Then the Grand Mistress tells her never to be seen in the lodge in anything else than in **black clothes**, a black-laced corset, robe and skirt.

She is given the Master sign and the Password, **O Volzaire**, which means **The Clearly Shining Light.**

Excerpts from the *Catechism:*

Q. Are you a Master or Mistress?
A. I have stepped up on the mysterious staircase.
Q. What do the side poles mean?
A. Love for the Lord and thy Neighbor.
Q. What do the 5 steps represent?
A. Masonry's Foundation and principal parts: Wisdom, Sapience, Patience, Love and Labor.
Q. Where are you made a Mistress?
A. At the foot of Noah's Offerings.
Q. What does that Offering mean?
A. It is a recognition and **thanksgiving** after the **Flood of Iniquity**.
Q. What does the Rainbow signify?

A. The covenant that God made with Noah and his descendants. The five most noble colors therein show us the Unity of the Brotherhood.
Q. What does Abraham's offering mean?
A. Obedience and subordination to **God's will**.
Q. What does Noah's Ark represent?
A. That the human heart is fed upon and is driven by its passions.
Q. What does the Tower of Babel represent?
A. These Children of the World and their haughtiness and weakness.
Q. How is this haughtiness worked against?
A. With a right Freemasonic sign and heart, through which the foundation and law of Masonry are enlightened.
Q. What does the burning of Sodom mean?
A. Heaven's **revenge** on **perjurers**, because the **Fire** that God let fall on these ungodly towns teaches us that we shall never stray from the **path of virtue**.
Q. What does the transformation of Lot's wife into the pillar of salt teach us?
A. That not by Curiosity should we seek to search for secrets that are concealed from us.
Q. What do the Sun and Moon mean?
A. **Joseph's Father and Mother**, who recognized the honor of that Mason when he, in respect of his brothers, exercised by noble means the Laws of the Brotherhood.
Q. What do the 11 stars mean?
A. The vengeance of **Joseph's brothers**, who threw him in the pit so that he, with greater triumph, could rise therefrom and rule over all **Egypt**.
Q. What does Joseph in the pit teach us?
A. That the more you are debased, the more you are raised through virtue when you can endure, with patience, the persecutions that disturb us.
Q. What does **Jacob's dream** mean?
A. The peace and tranquility that all Masons receive in a righteous Masonic lodge.

Q. What do the 4 parts of the World mean?
A. That a right Mason, through his virtue and Good Manners, is known and loved by the whole world.
Q. Who built the Ark?
A. **Noah**, who was the keeper of all humankind.
Q. How long did the **Ark** last?
A. **100 years** which is the time a right lodge is maintained.
Q. How many levels and apartments did the Ark have?
A. Four. The lowest part was for the four-footed animals, which shall teach us to trample our desires underfoot; the second part contained domestic animals; the third, Noah and his family; and the uppermost, where the birds with their songs teach us to raise our thoughts to the praise of our highest and Greatest Master.
Q. Why did Noah cover the Ark with **Pitch**?
A. To resist the swelling of the water, which teaches us to dress our hearts with Sapience and carefulness to resist the Jealousy of the Profane.
Q. Who invented and began the Tower of Babel?
A. Nimrod.
Q. What was the foundation thereof?
A. Pride.
Q. What were the building tools?
A. Unordered inclinations.
Q. What caused the devastation of the Tower?
A. The confusion of tongues.
Q. What does this event tell us?
A. That without religion the human being is just Weakness and Nothing.
Q. What does this teach us further?
A. That without Unity and trust, as well as the concord of the senses, a Society cannot remain.
Q. What is the Master's Word?
A. O Volzaire.
Q. What does it mean?
A. The Clearly Shining Light.

Q. What is the duty of Masons and Masonesses?
A. To hear, obey, Work and be Silent.

Then the Grand Master says: "The Tower of Iniquity is fallen and Peace and Unity restored. We have heard, been obedient, Worked and been Silent."

The Lodge is closed.

This interesting Order of Friendship (*La Veritable et Constante Amitié*) took place in the Duke's chambers of the royal castle in Stockholm and lasted through the 1780s. The ritual from Swedish manuscripts in the Freemasonic archive in Stockholm abridged above has been published by Andreas Önnerfors and Johan Andersson.[3]

As for Swedenborg, his exhortation for life is "to flee evil and seek the good," but he also strongly emphasized that one cannot sincerely be in combat with evil without being in temptation first. Thus the scenario presented in the Order of Friendship would have been reflecting this spiritual truth, as it presents and illuminates temptation and its resolution into virtue on a higher plane.

In 1802, a new Order was established by Charles XIII for both men and women called the DELU (Those elected by the Eternal Light). It was held at Rosersberg castle, north of Stockholm. It was worked out by the Masonic expert Adolph Boheman, who was an emissary of Carl of Hesse in Denmark and was to have a Martinist metaphysics with a story of the primordial Fall and its ultimate restoration. It was discontinued a year later as Boheman was arrested and exiled, accused of high treason.

The participants were again the ladies in Hedwig Elisabeth Charlotta's entourage: The King and the Queen were also interrogated in the Boheman affair. For this reason, I have decided not to be the first to expose its ritual in print, but hope it will be published in the future. I believe a lot has been said above by presenting the ritual of *Vera amicitia constantia*. The brothers were not reluctant to initiate women into virtuous thought and work, except that they refused to explain to them the higher, more abstract parts of the Masonic art of building. Thus, it would be a long while before an order made entirely by and for women would appear in Sweden, for in the 18th century men still wanted to have ultimate control. But the cooperative spirit between men and women was set in motion and in this sense the movement of inner illuminism informed the Enlightenment Age in a social sense also.

1 In some lodges where one wants to avoid equivocals the word is exchanged for the word **Eva**. If asked what it means, the answer is: The origin of all living.

2 The mechanics of the coffin are so arranged that when struck on a special place, a spring drives the inside hidden heart into the air. Some lodges have the heart so illuminated that it rises burning.

3 The author's English translation of these excerpts from the degree ceremonies of *la Maçonnerie des Dames* may be compared to a full English translation found in Andreas Önnerfors, "*Maçonnerie Des Dames*: The Plans Of The Strict Observance To Establish A Female Branch," in *Women's Agency and Rituals in Mixed and Female Masonic Orders*, edited by Alexandra Heidle and Jan A.M. Snoek (Leiden: Brill, 2008), 89-218 – *Ed.*

Bibliography

Carleson, Robert. "Affären *Boheman* I ny belysning. En analys av esoteriska idéströmningar I det tidiga svenska frimurarsamhället." *Acta Masonica Scandinavica*, 13 (2010): 119-87.

Heidle, Alexandra and Jan A.M. Snoek. *Women's Agency and Rituals in Mixed and Female Masonic Orders*. Leiden: Brill, 2008.

Önnerfors, Andreas and Johan Andersson. "Kvinnligt frimureri i Sverige – en inblick i en svensk adoptionsritual från 1700-talet, Loix et statuts de la Maconnerie des Dames (Loger och statuter för kvinnors frimureri)." *Acta Masonica Scandinavica,* 9 (2006): 145-159.

Swedenborg, Emanuel. *A Hieroglyphic Key* to *natural and spiritual mysteries, by way of representations and correspondences*. (In manuscript 1741). Translated from the Latin by J. J. G. Wilkinson. London: 1847.

– . *Spiritual Diary* [1747-1765], translation from the Latin by George Bush, John H. Smithson and James F. Buss. London: 1883-1889.

The Material Culture of Freemasonry

Adam Kendall

"A man's work is nothing but this slow trek to rediscover, through the detours of art, those two or three great and simple images in whose presence his heart first opened."

– Albert Camus

During each Masonic degree, the candidate is introduced to an array of architectural symbols, and with them, is instructed in a legend concerning the construction of Solomon's Temple. The experience is often emotional and can be scarcely described by language. The initiate's subsequent attempt at an interpretation is often informed by a mixture of his own interpretation, the insight of other lodge members, and the initial impact of the symbols that impressed him most.

For over three hundred years, the ideals of the fraternity have inspired elaborate rituals and books large and small ruminating upon its true meaning or attempting to uncover its misty origins within the religious traditions of ancient cultures. From a very early period, the ceremonies required visual cues for the instruction of initiates with symbols drawn upon the floor, and later upon convenient canvases and framed boards. In addition, these same symbols were painted and printed upon aprons or fashioned into decoration for a variety of keepsakes such as jewelry, metal and stoneware, fine artworks, and other items.

In each instance the imagination and skill of the artisan was represented, as well as the Mason who commissioned the work. For example, an apron would reflect symbols important to the wearer, and its representation would reflect the skill of the maker – which was also tied to location, era, school, and, often, ethnic culture. In other words, an apron made in the Mohawk River Valley in 1800 by a Palatine German would present a list of influences easily overlooked by the untrained eye. The artifact reflects not only a local custom, but also trends popular within a specific culture, and simultaneously, within the fraternity. The same can be said about other items made for, and by, the fraternity. Even the mass-produced regalia, ritual art and *tchotchkes* (trinkets) are hallmarks of a bygone era where fraternal organizations were important components of society – particularly in the United States.

Studying the material culture of fraternal orders can lead to a better understanding of their development within a particular era in much the same manner a cultural anthropologist examines an item's importance and use within a particular civilization. Because fraternal orders have, in recent history, been considered fringe, ridiculous pastimes, and have become the subject of "alternative" and reductionist histories, the study of their material culture has languished – even within the organizations that produced them! In many cases, the survival of these items is only because they simply have not yet been destroyed by a leaky pipe, or worse, an inattentive or uninformed membership.

Camus' opening quote has a relevance to the individual Mason's initiatic quest and the use of art. This quest is a rediscovery of profundity and wonder – much like the rediscovery of the Lost Master's Word – that recalls our innocence and surrender to those forces mightier than us. As William Blake pined in his *Songs of Innocence and of Experience*:

> "How can the bird that is born for joy
> Sit in a cage and sing?
> How can a child, when fears annoy,
> But droop his tender wing,
> And forget his youthful spring?"

But the initiatic quest is long and lonely, compelling travelers to reach out in fraternity with others on a similar path. Thus, to quote the California Masonic ritual, "Freemasonry causes true friendship to exist amongst those who would otherwise remain at a perpetual distance." Commonality encourages the initiate to discover and participate in Masonic culture in order to fully appreciate its gifts of self-awareness, personal enrichment, and spiritual development. Through the detours of Masonic art and its history, we can come to understand the fraternity and our place within it.

Early Masons were cognizant of the functionality of their symbols and ceremonies, and a rich and enthusiastic material culture of decorative and literary arts developed to explain or identify this *thing* called initiation, as well as to celebrate and illustrate the benefits of participation. These were often the artist's own interpretation of key themes found in Masonic allegory, which in turn became popular and established the hieroglyphic "language" Masons still utilize in modern rituals. Even their meeting places – at first in the homes of lodge members or in taverns, and then in specially constructed halls or temples – became artistic representations of Freemasonry's initiatic subculture, which one can correctly identify as a world parallel to day-to-day existence. This sacred world was resplendent with mysterious symbols only Masons could decipher, striking awe, envy, and even dread in those who could not.

Art demands an audience, and while some Masonic art is arguably private and hidden from the eyes of the uninitiated, the reality is that from the very beginning Freemasonry relished in publicly displaying its mysterious symbols on ornate "temples" and "cathedrals," colorfully decorated aprons, sculpture, and glittering metalwork. This dual nature – public, yet private – allowed initiates to access an exclusive symbolic language of their own and display a tantalizing sense of arcane mystery to the uninitiated. In other words, Freemasonry has always played both sides of public and private to capitalize on its claims of antiquated wisdom, and to (intentionally) foster a collective sense of culture and art within the boundaries of the institution as a method of expression *and* instruction.

In the present era, there is still a rapt audience for this type of art; many potential members' first contact with Freemasonry is by virtue of its material culture. Fraternally inspired artwork appears on popular clothing and has been mined by musicians and artists seeking the next outré pop-cultural trend. The antiquated aesthetic of these artworks seems to be preserved within a pseudo-mythical age: how many of those involved in Freemasonry (or any other classic fraternal order) have been attracted to fraternal art and have become convinced that it points to an older wisdom tradition? The intangible strangeness of these objects draws immediate intrigue, and the impact of these works is undeniably visceral. Upon initiation, one might imagine these glyphs taking on an increased importance for the individual as he or she learns of their layered meanings, transforming them into something more than mysterious works of art. Nevertheless, the individuals who created them and the time periods in which they lived must be considered, otherwise interpretation remains subjective, incomplete, and ignorant of the diversity of the fraternal expression – not only of Freemasonry, but of other fraternal societies and their influence upon each other.

There is a risk of pigeonholing modern fraternal orders as insular and only for the enjoyment of a select few. How many modern initiates savor the distinction of holding membership in a secret and exclusive band of brothers? In reality, a good many of these organizations were widespread and mainstream. Even in the early years none of these groups were particularly hidden, and their bespangled members joined in frequent public processions. The hieroglyphic graphics were influenced by biblical picture books popular in the 17th century, and even the literature waxing romantic about Egyptian mystery schools and rites of Eleusis took their cues from popular cultural fascinations with the ancient Mediterranean and Near East.

But these facts should not detract from the uniqueness of such material creations – many of which are bonafide works of art. Their historical value is priceless when one considers them not only within the context of fraternalism, but as part of a broader intellectual movement. Each piece may serve as a comparative example of an entire parallel history of the last three hundred years.

The popular books of Drs Margaret Jacob and Steven Bullock, which argue for Freemasonry's deep influence on the American civic experience, certainly point to the importance of the Craft in civil society. This importance was a combination of civic life and the spiritual and philosophical; the lessons of the degrees inspired the material culture of the organization, which at once illustrated lessons well-known to a "churched" man and alluded to the purported antiquity of its philosophy. Inspired by this new age, the artists and writers of these artworks and literature were influenced by a coterie of diverse sources: the Bible, classical mythology, hermetic lore, alchemy, and so forth. The original output of these early Masons inspired others to create their own works of art, and over time the original inspirations became increasingly confused with legend and speculation. In order to foster an articulation of what it means to be initiated and participate in a fraternal organization, Masonic and fraternal art should be regarded as an historic resource with contextual value if one is to, as Camus beckons, "rediscover… those two or three great and simple images in whose presence his heart first opened," and thus obtain a balanced understanding of initiation.

During my tenure at the Grand Lodge of F. & A.M. of California and their Henry W. Coil Library & Museum, I received many phone calls and visits by earnest young men wishing to become Masons. While most inquirers knew that they had a grandfather or a distant relative who was a member, nearly all of them felt attracted to the Craft because of its popular legacy and the desire to pursue something greater than themselves. The allure of mystery the Craft evokes is a strong selling point: ancient rituals practiced within shuttered temples; arcane, occult knowledge; identification with important historical figures; a defined purpose or role in society; and self-identification as an initiate or an adept. Many of those with whom I spoke were what is now colloquially known as "Millennials," and it was certainly this popular widespread legacy of mystery and wisdom attributed to Freemasonry that attracted them, along with the recent media attention attributed to Dan Brown's books.[2]

The response of the Grand Lodge was positive, as several materials such as handbooks and DVDs were produced, not only to explain Freemasonry for the influx of potential joiners, but for those who were already members, so they could review their own experiences and, in turn, share them with their families and friends.

In contrast, during my early twenties many young Masons like myself were told that the fraternity was dying. Obviously, that was a terrible way to sell the fraternity to an eager young membership, as nearly all of us newcomers had approached our respective lodges believing Freemasonry to be a vital, if slightly diminished, educational organization. But we soldiered on, taking leadership positions and slowly gaining the trust of the long-term members by convincing them that not only were we sincere, but that Freemasonry is both a social *and* intellectual pursuit with diverse expressions; many of us reveled in traveling and experiencing Freemasonry in different cultures, and returning home with the knowledge that we were indeed a part of something that touched a multitude of hearts in a most unexplainable way. No amount of reading and waxing philosophic could ever substitute firsthand experience with the greater movement of Masonry and fraternalism.

This desire to recapture the mystery and profundity of the Craft led to the encouragement of what eventually culminated in the *Traditional Observance* (T.O.) movement. This new inspiration resulted in the creation of new lodges identifying with a canon that emphasized a quality lodge experience, a solemn approach to ceremonial work, and the serious study of Masonic history, culture and tradition. The effect was a widespread renewal of interest in Masonic education, presentations in lodges, and the support of research efforts and locally and Grand Lodge sponsored symposia.

These efforts were beneficial for changing the cultural climate, but what was most noticeable was the desire and impetus to revive and recreate a romantic semblance of Freemasonry's past. Yet these romantic overtures may often run the risk of being too subjective, especially when ill-defined but popular phrases such as "ancient mysteries" are invoked as the true origins of Freemasonry. Masons have long desired to understand their origins, sometimes delving far afield into fanciful alternative histories, along with pseudo- and neo-mysticism. This tendency has found a home within subcultures that favor a mythologized and romantic past. Despite the stream of serious scholarship from established academics and research organizations, a revival of speculative history attracted considerable attention –

especially in the wake of Dan Brown's *The Da Vinci Code* (NY, 2003) and numerous sensational documentaries on the History Channel. *Such fantasy stories refuse to be buried.*

In the library of the Grand Lodge of California, one of the most popular books is a first edition of Manly P. Hall's *The Secret Teaching of All Ages* (1928). It is a truly remarkable work if one considers Hall's tender age of 25 at the time of its writing, and the influence late 19th and early 20th century mysticism had on his life. Another popular book is Albert Pike's seminal work *Morals and Dogma of the Ancient and Accepted Scottish Rite of Freemasonry* (1871) – a massive 861-page overview of the religions of the world, both exoteric and esoteric, condensed into Pike's *new* versions of the Scottish Rite degrees for the Supreme Council of the Southern Jurisdiction. Both books have had a notable influence, not just in Masonic circles, but in conspiracy theories propagated by anti-Masons. These two books have influenced generational opinions about the (arguable) history of the "ancient mysteries" of Egypt, India, Greece and Rome. Meanwhile, the original sources of these works and the *why* have been the province of professional historians, as well as serious amateur Masonic researchers.

How do the myriad artworks, silver-bladed and ivory-handled trowels, illustrations, paintings, and gold jewels square up with the Craft's romanticized history? The newly-minted Mason is motivated to dissect the several parts of the degrees and meditate upon a galaxy of illustrated symbols and hieroglyphic charts, tracing boards, ritual tools, and regalia. The immensity of the task is tangible, yet adequate resources for proper and focused study might be lacking or even discouraged. In almost every lodge hall there is a lonely, jumbled and moldering collection of books, lodge records, and other items of potential interest crammed into a forgotten bookcase, closet, or basement. Ironically, some members clamor for education despite the incredible history – a true local history that includes primary sources – at their fingertips.

For these reasons, the maintenance and care of Masonic archives and museums is of paramount importance. Although there are plenty of subjective experiences and sources that wax poetic or esoteric about the origins of Freemasonry and its symbols, there is a historical context that can help separate fact from fiction and provide a more holistic or balanced view – or at least contextualize the information.

During my tenure at the museum, it was my conviction that for the sake of encouraging appreciation and study it just wasn't enough to display a random collection of artifacts in crowded and substandard cases. This tendency originates from a genuine desire to display a lodge (or Grand Lodge) history to visitors and for the enjoyment of the brethren. Masons might feel a certain artifact to be of great value, but not all of them are understood (or even interesting) to the public; or the display is so crammed with items that the viewer has no idea what they're supposed to see, much less understand the *why* and *who* – historical factors that contribute to the value and importance of the artifact. An institution might possess a wonderfully diverse collection of rare and historic objects, but there is a tendency to display too many at once, so that any important or inspiring piece is easy to miss. Observers will simply glance over them.

My first objective at the Henry W. Coil Library & Museum was to properly identify the intimidating number of items. Several had descriptions noted on their catalog cards, yet many were incorrect or incomplete. The greatest danger with erroneous information is that the observer might become infected with a falsehood, which will corrupt a healthy appreciation for the historical record.

As a simple example, I was dismayed to find that an otherwise beautiful apron created *c*1862 and decorated with a Star of David was labeled as being from Israel, which of course did not yet exist as a nation-state. Such an error, as innocuous as it might seem, can erode any claim to stewardship or expertise made by an institution. Identifying an object can be difficult if proper resources are unavailable but guessing should never be an option. Proper identification includes an accurate description of the object and its *provenance*, which is a record of its function within the organization, its maker, and its owner. Those who care for Masonic museums or small collections are encouraged to seek out others associated with the Masonic Library & Museum Association (MLMA), as well as other professionals who have experience with fraternal collections.

Display and context are important for the narrative, as is the arrangement of the items in a logical and uncluttered manner. Further, they should be accompanied with simple, well-designed, and informative description labels. Our artifacts were gathered into themed displays, which communicated a specific story relating to Freemasonry (and, if possible, how they related to the fraternity in California), or full-blown exhibits in which a wider theme was explored, such as the artwork of Masonic instruction (tracing boards, degree charts, and other emblematic pieces), the history of the Masonic apron, the evolution and use of the Holy Writings in Masonic ritual, anti-Masonic propaganda, and more.

We used these opportunities to feature important objects in order to create a narrative that contextualized them within a variety of traditions and time periods. Tours, or even a simple personal introduction to the displays by knowledgeable guides, were helpful to the visitors, who left satisfied that they had received quality and fascinating information. Exhibits are often the only venue any person, much less a member, will come into personal contact with many of these items. They allow the audience to view in close detail the depth and intelligence of fraternal culture, suggesting that these items should be approached and studied as genuine examples of folk art and not just as curious by-products of odd pastimes and good ol' boys' clubs.

Art and education exist in tandem as historical methods intended to instruct a Mason in the moral lessons of the Craft and the interpretation of symbolism and proportions of beauty. Exposure to Masonic material culture is essential, for these works are a gateway to the heart and soul so beautifully expressed by Camus. They are flames illuminating the entrance to the labyrinth, beckoning the initiate to travel further within. The insight gained from research unfolds like Ariadne's thread and guides the way. But it is not enough that they find beauty… they must also discover the geometry of their own hearts.

1 For an example, see: Jeremy Ladd Cross, *The True Masonic Chart or Hieroglyphic Monitor Fourth Edition* (New Haven, CT: Self Published, 1826).

2 Adam Tschorn, "Brother, You're In," *Los Angeles Times*, 18 May 2008, last accessed on 26 May 2018; articles.latimes.com/2008/may/18/image/ig-masons18.

Mysteries of Initiation in Ancient Greece, Samothrace

Greg Kaminsky

Preface

What is initiation? The term generally refers to the beginning of a process of spiritual unfoldment, usually marked by an event or ceremony that not only commemorates it in the minds of the participants, but also transmits empowerment and teachings of a secret nature. This spiritual unfoldment is characterized in Freemasonry by the journey from darkness to light and the rough stone being formed into a smooth ashlar. Throughout the ages, such illumination has been facilitated via an established link with a tradition that possesses specific beliefs and practices. The connection is also held by all those who have undergone the initiation process previously. The ceremony of initiation usually occurs at an auspicious place, time, and date and is conveyed in the name of deity. There is a crucial belief by those partaking that the initiatory process is like a key that unlocks an aspect of being that is already present, though latent, and allows one to remember the intimate connection with deity (or deities, as the case may be), all life, and the world.

The method of transformation is the ritual re-enactment of myth. By experiencing teachings in this manner, more impactful than dialectic, the initiate's mind is imprinted with an entire experience: sights, sounds, smells, sensations, and feelings. Rather than only an intellectual grasping of the world as a continuum and not as a subject in a world of objects, initiation must imply a realization of this truth through lived experience. Whether termed gnosis, illumination, or enlightenment, the resolution of mind and realization of the union of all dualities is the ultimate fruit of the initiatory process.

Aside from our personal experience, can we begin to understand how these ingredients of initiation are combined to affect transformation? One potential way is to look back at the history of ancient tradition to examine the necessary components of initiation and their function. The ancient mystery cult center at the island of Samothrace provides an excellent case study. By examining the known historical data, available archeological evidence, and expert analysis, it is possible to glimpse how the various aspects of place, deity, ritual, tradition, and mythology were integrated to bring initiates from darkness to light.

Introduction

A wild, mountainous island in the northern Aegean Sea, Samothrace was home to the sanctuary of one of the most highly regarded mystery cults of the ancient world for "perhaps as many as a thousand years … which attracted worshippers from the entire Greek and Roman world."[1] Scholars believe the cult had been in continuous existence from Neolithic times until the 4th century CE. Originally said to have been inhabited by Pelasgians, the island was later populated by Thracians. This pre-Greek mystery cult and its rites, which continued for centuries, is one of the most intriguing aspects of the study of Samothrace because one can almost perceive the shadow of primordial tradition.

Greeks arrived on the island sometime between the 8th and 6th century BCE, and then the Persians, Athenians, Macedonians and the Ptolemaic dynasty ruled but allowed the administrators of the mystery cult autonomy to operate, as they had in prior times. In modern times, knowledge of Samothrace's great gods, known as *Theoi Megaloi*, and their rites has been less accessible than those of other mystery cult centers. What is known is more than enough to serve as a worthy guide into the mists of the past, to perceive the lamp of initiation and the eternal light it casts.

The Island of Samothrace and the Sanctuary of the Great Gods
Windswept, mountainous, wild, and beautiful are just some of the words typically used to describe the remote, northern Aegean island of Samothrace. The sanctuary site includes the ruins of several very large stone structures constructed in Hellenistic and Classical style which are situated relatively close together on a hillside between a rock outcropping on the mountainside, two rivers, and the sea. The island itself, especially the site where the sanctuary was built, evokes strong feelings of the majesty of nature. One can imagine how ancient peoples, so closely connected to the land and water, would have felt

about such a magical place: they constructed one of the most prestigious mystery cult centers of the ancient world there.

Distinguished architect and scholar of ancient architecture and landscape design, Charles Griffin, annually travels to the sites of archeological excavations in Greece and Turkey. In 2015, he traveled to Samothrace to see the island and have a closer look at the ruins of the sanctuary of the great gods. According to Griffin, where the site is situated allows one to see rock outcroppings further up the slope of the mountain that resemble standing stones jutting vertically out of the mountainside. The sanctuary is surrounded on two sides by small rivers, so that passage into the heart of the site requires crossing over one of the rivers, and there is a clear view of the sea from there, as well.

In Griffin's experience, ancient temple builders were adept at selecting sacred sites and based on his analysis he is confident the site at Samothrace was selected precisely because of these geographic features. From Griffin's comments, I believe that the rock outcroppings, two closely situated rivers, and the wild and mountainous nature of the land empowered the ancient rites of initiation of Samothrace.

If we consider Griffin's analysis further, it becomes clear how the nature of a place engenders feelings of sublimity and closeness to that which is greater than ourselves. Because the ancients knew how to recognize and utilize these types of locales, they were able to channel the power of the land and water into their myth and ritual. Reverence for place is evidenced in other Greek sanctuary sites, where natural features of the landscape are incorporated into the mysteries, such as the cave entrance to Hades and the rock upon which Demeter sat at Eleusis. Photos and especially recent drone footage of the mountainous area around the sanctuary leaves little doubt that the earth itself was an integral part of the Samothracian mysteries.

In addition to the majestic natural setting, the man-made structures of the sanctuary were designed and built in Hellenistic and Classical styles to complement and enhance the features of the land and water: a large open-air amphitheater, two very large oblong square buildings, and a uniquely beautiful round structure known as the Arsinoe, named after Arsinoë II, the Ptolemaic Queen and co-regent of Ancient Egypt. Historian Walter Burkert describes his analysis of the sanctuary based on the archeological evidence:

> There are two main rectangular buildings of unusual form obviously intended for large groups of people, one conventionally called the *Anaktoron*, the other called simply *Hieron* in an inscription. The *Anaktoron* dates from Imperial times, but seems to have had two predecessors of similar form. The entrance is from the west on the long side of the rectangle; in the north there is a Holy of Holies which only *mystai* may enter; in the middle of the main room traces of carbon have been interpreted as remains of a large wooden platform; benches run along the east side. No doubt this was a room for initiations. There is further a walled precinct with a hearth altar which was perhaps superseded in its functions by the 'new temple,' the Hellenistic *Hieron*. This building has a porch with columns like a normal temple, yet on the north side; inside there is a drain to the right of the door, a hearth at the centre, marble benches along the side, and a bothros, it seems, in the apse-shaped south end. It has been assumed that the *Hieron* was the place for *epopteia* – or was it for a second act in the one night of initiation? Outside there is another altar precinct surrounded by walls. The theatre built next to it is unlikely to have had cultic functions.[2]

It is worth noting again that the extensive construction, with sophisticated architecture in a difficult but majestic natural setting, was intended to invest the place with devotion to the great gods, which was then channeled into the initiation rites, empowering its members to greatness. Burkert writes that there is evidence for religious ceremony from the 7th century BCE and the monumental construction began in the 4th century BCE.[3] Yet the cult persisted continuously until the 4th century CE. This place and the rites practised there lasted more than a thousand years and survived several ruling empires, yet retained its identity throughout. One reason for the long life of the mystery cult at Samothrace may have been the magnificence of the place and its integral nature as part of the rite.

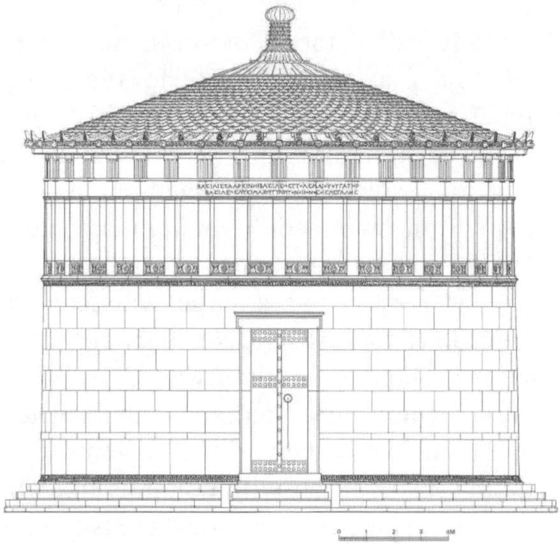

Samothracian Mythology & Deities: Great Gods / Theoi Megaloi / Kabeiroi

The great gods of the Samothracian mysteries have been identified as deities from other cultures – or similar to existing deities from other cultures – for centuries. But their identities are much more obscure than the gods and goddesses of other pantheons. The primary reason for this obscuration is that the names of the great gods were known only by the initiated. The fact that the great gods' names were not publicized suggests that the cult utilized the names of the deities for ritual and mystical purposes.

Based on comparisons with less ancient faith and esoteric traditions, the concealment of the names of the great gods of Samothrace enhanced the overall effect of the initiatory rituals, created opportunity for magical invocations, and alluded to the transcendent mystery of divinity. The gods are called "Theoi" or "Theoi Megaloi" in the inscriptions found on the island, while at other sites they were referred to as "Theoi Samothrakes."[4]

According to Burkert's *Greek Religion*, the cult of Samothrace venerated deities that were pre-Greek and associated with Hephaistos, the god of smiths and metal-working.[5] The association of fire and metals evokes a connection to the art of alchemy, which utilizes fire as the agent for purification, and the association of craftsmen and guilds evokes a connection to Freemasonry, which (possibly) originated from operative craft lodges of stonemasons. Excavations of the sanctuary have revealed two very large rectangular-shaped structures, assumed to be the site where the rites of initiation took place.[6] These facts, combined with the high regard with which ancients held Samothracian initiation and the cult's longevity, lasting into the time of Constantine, make it one of the most intriguing sites of initiation in the ancient world.[7]

The central myth which established the mysteries involved Jason and his brother Dardanos, the sons of Elektra, who sought refuge on Samothrace from a great flood, after which Jason instituted the secret rites there and subsequently Dardanos did the same at Troy.[8] Harmonia, said to have been Elektra's daughter, married Kadmos at Samothrace, and this event was entwined in the ceremonies celebrated at the sanctuary.

In addition to the general improvement of initiates as a result of undergoing this transformative experience, initiation into the Samothracian mysteries granted protection and success at sea. The cult was concerned with the origins of humanity. While the connection between an origin myth and protection of seafarers may not, at first, be clear, both are accepted aspects of the cult's rites. One is practical and immediate, the other mythical and contemplative. The ancient historian Diodorus Siculus' writings on Samothrace shed light on how these seemingly disparate ideas were connected.

> It [Samothrace] was settled by men who were sprung from the soil itself; consequently no tradition has been

handed down regarding who were the first men and leaders on the island… The first and original inhabitants used an ancient language which was peculiar to them and of which many words are preserved to this day in the ritual of their sacrifices. And the Samothracians have a story that, before the floods which befell other peoples, a great one took place among them … The inhabitants who had been caught by the flood, the account continues, ran up to the higher regions of the island; and when the sea kept rising higher and higher, they prayed to the native gods, and since their lives were spared, to commemorate their rescue they set up boundary stones about the entire circuit of the island and dedicated altars upon which they offer sacrifices even to the present day. For these reasons it is patent that they inhabited Samothrace before the flood … And while the Samothracians were living under a government of this kind, they say that there were born in that land to Zeus and Electra, who was one of the Atlantides, Dardanus and Iasion and Harmonia … But Zeus desired that the other of his two sons might also attain to honour, and so he instructed him in the initiatory rites of the mysteries, which had existed on the island since ancient times but was at that time, so to speak, put in his hands; it is not lawful, however, for any but the initiated to hear about the mysteries. And Iasion is reputed to have been the first to initiate strangers into them and by this means to bring the initiatory rite to high esteem. And after this Cadmus, the son of Agenor, came in the course of his quest for Europê to the Samothracians, and after participating in the initiation he married Harmonia … This wedding of Cadmus and Harmonia was the first, we are told, for which the gods provided the marriage-feast … Now the details of the initiatory rite are guarded among the matters not to be divulged and are communicated to the initiates alone; but the fame has travelled wide of how these gods

> appear to mankind and bring unexpected aid to those initiates of theirs who call upon them in the midst of perils. The claim is also made that men who have taken part in the mysteries become both more pious and more just and better in every respect than they were before. And this is the reason, we are told, why the most famous both of the ancient heroes and of the demi-gods were eagerly desirous of taking part in the initiatory rite; and in fact Jason and the Dioscuri, and Heracles and Orpheus as well, after their initiation attained success in all the campaigns they undertook, because these gods appeared to them.[9]

This ancient account begins with the origins of humanity (at least in this locale) and then goes into the rescue from the deluge with the help of the great gods. Both aspects of the Samothracian mysteries are accounted for in this story, but additional details about the gods and heroes, and especially the marriage of Kadmos and Harmonia, unites land and myth in a manner similar to the cult centers at Brauron and Eleusis.

When the initiates stood in the place where sacrifices were made to the great gods for their aid and experienced rites established by Jason, it must have been a powerfully evocative setting. Explicit in this mythology was a devotion to the great gods for their ready aid, a celebration of an ancient culture, the sacred union between a hero and a daughter of Zeus, and the promise of protection and success for the initiates. Implicit in this mythology was the exclusive knowledge about and use of the names of great gods. Like the initiation at Eleusis, there was the potential for what is often termed *epopteia* or "greater initiation," which may have been the fruition of the rite, characterized as beholding the glory of the gods, what we better understand as self-realization or gnosis.

Throughout history, the great gods of Samothrace have been referred to as "Kabeiroi" or "Cabiri," which traces back to a Semitic word meaning "mighty-ones." In the introduction to Susan Guettel Cole's seminal work on the subject, *Theoi Megaloi: The Cult of the*

Great Gods at Samothrace, she argues that applying the term "Kabeiroi" to the gods of Samothrace is incorrect because it associates them with the Kabeiroi of Thebes and Lemnos. Cole points out that initiation into the mysteries of the gods at Samothrace brought protection at sea, while the Kabeiroi on Lemnos were "companions of Hephaistos and associated with metalworking and wine drinking,"[10] and at Thebes there was only one Kabeiros.[11]

Aside from the fact that ancient writers believed the "Theoi Megaloi" to be synonymous with the Kabeiroi, there are other important details that undermine Cole's argument. For instance, the Kabeiros of the Thessalonians was known as a protector of the city and the great gods of Samothrace protected seafarers initiated into those mysteries, but also protected the island's inhabitants during the great flood. There is a record of the priests of the Kabeiros on Thessalonica visiting the sanctuary on Samothrace.[12] The mysteries celebrated at Samothrace, Thebes, and Lemnos all were "concerned with explaining the origins of life."[13] Additionally, a fifth century BCE drinking cup from Thebes shows ithyphallic satyrs along with the inscription "KABIROS," and coins from Thessalonica bear the image of a Hermes-like figure and the word "Kabiros" in Greek.[14]

These symbolic images are linked with the ithyphallic Hermes figures in the sanctuary at Samothrace. Although the connection between the "Kabeiroi" of Thebes, Lemnos, Thessalonika and the "Theo Megaloi" of Samothrace is not completely understood, there is clearly evidence linking them.

Historians are not always in agreement, but most sources indicate that the "Theoi Megaloi" include a great mother goddess, two other figures that are twins – either two sons or son and daughter – and another figure who was an attendant (also possibly a consort of the mother goddess and father to the twins). Mnaseas of Patara provided the only series of names that seem to be authentic Samothracian cult titles: Axeiros, Axiokersa, Axiokersos, and Kadmilos (or Kasmilos).[15] The great mother goddess was Axeiros. Axiokersos and Axiokersas were the children. Kadmilos was the attendant of the mother and perhaps father of the children. The mother goddess is often associated with the goddess Kybele due to an image with her attributes on

Samothracian coins.[16] In later times, the twins became syncretized with the Dioskouri, the twins Castor and Pollux, who were protectors of sailors.

To writers analyzing the Samothracian cult with an eye toward the Eleusinian mysteries, these three gods represent Demeter, Hades and Kore or Persephone. To those with a Roman bent, the triad is Jupiter, Juno, and Minerva. Because the names of the great gods were not publicly disseminated, scholars have felt a compulsion to recast them with more familiar identities in order to better understand and explain the myth and mysteries of Samothrace.

Kadmilos, or Kasmilos, is often described as a Hermes-like figure and the Anaktoron at Samothrace had two ithyphallic Hermes statues guarding its threshold. Hermes was portrayed as an ithyphallic god in many instances, an aspect that suggests active male sexuality, reverence for life, and possibly alluded to the mysteries of life and death (since Hermes functioned as a psychopomp, as well).

These aspects of Kadmilos are congruent with the mythology of Kadmos, the hero whose wedding to Harmonia was celebrated as part of the rite. Much of the pottery found by archeological excavation is marked with processions of festive figures, some with large phalluses, further indicating the extent to which sex and the sacred marriage festival played into the mythology of the cult.

Kadmos, who according to the myth married Harmonia at Samothrace, was reputed to have brought the first alphabet to Greek lands. The facilitation of communication is nothing if not characteristic of Hermes. Confusion over the role of Kadmilos is notable and seems significant. Is he the attendant and messenger of the great gods? Is he also one of them? Or could he be both attendant and father of the twins? Unlike the other great gods, there is not a consensus among scholars as to the role of Kadmilos, yet his part in the ritual seems to have been significant.

Kadmos was also supposed to have killed a serpent to protect his people, but afterward he suffered ill fortune and eventually was turned into a serpent himself. The famous archaic relief image said to be a portrayal of Agamemnon's initiation at Samothrace depicts three human figures and a massive snake uncoiling and rising up

toward the sky. Serpents are chthonic symbols and often represent wisdom, sex, temptation, and *kundalini* energy in eastern or non-European traditions. The connection between serpent symbolism, sexuality, and the origins of humanity can be found in other religious and esoteric contexts, eg the *Book of Genesis*, so we should not be surprised to find these motifs in the Samothracian mystery cult's mythology and symbolism.

The name Kadmos is typically understood to be based on the Semitic root word for "light" or "from the east." This is a clear reference to the sun and meaningful in light of his participation in the wedding ceremony that was symbolic of the union of sun and earth, or sun and moon, and therefore symbolic of the union of awareness

and appearance. The sun is seen in esoteric philosophy as an active principle corresponding to the phallus and procreation. Such meanings are congruent with the concepts conveyed by the Samothracian mysteries.

This concern with human origins and reproduction, illustrated by the prominent imagery of the ithyphallic god(s) and the inclusion of the marriage of Kadmos and Harmonia in the rites on Samothrace, is compelling. Burkert notes that, "Here [Samothrace] an otherwise unknown anthropogonic myth is alluded to, just as on Lemnos Kabeiros is mentioned as the first man. Anthropogony and initiation concur in the sense of a new beginning."[17]

While there is no way to know, it is interesting to consider that there may have been some form of a "hieros gamos," or sacred marriage, included as part of the ceremonies. At least one historian concluded that the experience of initiation of the Kabeiros at Thessalonika would have included a "raucous celebration" and "Dionysiac sexuality," but this opinion is by no means undisputed.[18]

In Kevin Clinton's analysis, "What is striking in the myths that have come down to us about the gods of Samothrace is the role of sexual union."[19] Thus, the idea of intervention of deity in human affairs, the origins of humanity, sex (whether explicit or implied), and wisdom through initiation were all likely components of the Samothracian mysteries.

By examining instances in which the name of deity is unspoken or unknown, it is possible to shed more light on the great gods. With such names kept secret to all but initiates, opportunities to utilize these names in ritual initiatory and magical contexts became available for those who possessed that knowledge. The use of divine names is explained by Blakely in her article "Kadmos, Jason, and the Great Gods of Samothrace: Initiation as Mediation in a Northern Aegean Context" as:

> …an imagination and imitation of "non-human language that exists prior to human articulation and comprehension," expressed in the secret names of the gods, the *voces magicae*, or 'authentic names.' The practitioner's use of the language marks his intimacy with the divine, ensures his success, and is part of a larger pattern whereby the magical specialist impersonates the gods. These ritual dynamics resonate with the Samothracian cult.[20]

This practice is one of the primary features of esotericism, so it is expected that, if the names of gods are secret, one of the reasons is so these names are available only to initiates. Exclusive knowledge of the divine names implies a familiarity that non-initiates lack, and an expectation that by knowing and using the deity's name favor would be granted. The secrecy of the names created a divide between those who knew and everyone else, giving those with knowledge not just an advantage, but a confidence to trust in their success because of it.

In addition to theosis and success, invocation or "impersonating," as Blakely puts it, provided the initiate with the understanding that he and the god or gods were inseparable. Framing the use of divine names in this manner makes it possible to apprehend the powerful nature of these initiatic rites. Burkert's commentary on the subject is appropriate to consider: "The very fact that the reactions described … are not uniform but vary between perplexity and exaltation indicates that this is … a … *sympatheia* of souls and rituals, some form of resonance which does not come in every case but which, once it is there, will deeply move or even shatter the constructs of reality."[21]

Samothracian Rites of Initiation

The rites consisted of several known and some speculated aspects. We know that initiates had to travel by sea to the island in the northern Aegean Sea. Candidates are believed to have undergone purification prior to the initiation ceremony. Special garb was used in the ceremony and rings were given to the new initiates, who were thought to gain protection at sea.

All the greatest rulers of the ancient world sought initiation at Samothrace. The primary benefit was "salvation from drowning at sea and successful voyages."[22] According to the myth, the first seafarers, the Argonauts, underwent initiation there. There is evidence of great monuments of ships and, of course, the statue of the goddess Nike with wings spread, landing on the prow of a ship and erected to celebrate a victory at sea. The cult at Samothrace was an established initiatory institution for more than a thousand years.

The known elements of the rites are effectively summarized as follows:

> There was an annual festival to which festal envoys, *theoroi*, would come from far and wide. Yet personal initiation, *myesis*, could evidently be procured at other times, too, on a chance visit. As in Eleusis there are … those who came back to watch the ceremonies again. About the initiation ritual three remarkable details are known. First, the priest asks the initiand what is the worst deed that he has ever committed in his life. This question is intended, it seems, not so much to elicit a confession

> of sins as to establish complicity, thereby securing unbreakable solidarity. Second, the initiates wind a purple sash around their bodies; this presupposes undressing and probably a bath. In accordance with this, as it is said, Odysseus stripped off his clothes during the tempest and wearing the veil of Leukothea jumped into the sea which could no longer do him any harm. Third, the initiates wear iron rings thereafter. A ram sacrifice must, moreover, have been a prominent feature in the cult. Initiations took place at night.[23]

We must also consider the more speculative aspects of the initiation rite. First, there are claims that the candidate plays the role of the servant/consort Kadmilos and that this involves a ritual death and resurrection. As outlined by Masonic historian A.E. Waite:

> We hear … of a ceremonial observance which was called the Kabiric Death, celebrated … amidst darkness and sorrow, but afterwards in rejoicing and gladness. It was in commemoration of the mystical death and restoration of Kasmillos, the youngest of the Kabiric gods. I have failed to discover on what authority the Candidate for the Mysteries of Initiation is said to have taken the part of Kasmillos, suggesting that in the course of his experience he also was slain figuratively by the gods, that is by the officiating priests, and was thereafter restored to life.[24]

Waite's analysis is not inconsistent with ancient initiatory rites, and therefore certainly plausible. Other unconfirmed interpretations of what occurred during the initiation claim that the candidate, playing the role of Kadmilos, servant to the gods, goes through the rite, including the resurrection, and then is brought to an alcove covered by a veil. He is told to prepare to meet the great god, face-to-face. When the veil dropped, the initiate was confronted by an altar with a mirror upon it reflecting the initiate's face. This moment of beholding was intended for the initiate to realize he was a god gazing upon himself, triggering *epopteia* or *gnosis*.[25]

Philosophical Speculation on the Meaning of the Great Gods of Samothrace

Friedrich Schelling was a prominent Romantic and Idealist German philosopher, who trained in classical studies and was concerned with religion, metaphysics, mythology, ancient history, and the revelation of divinity over time. Schelling delivered an address to the Bavarian Academy of Sciences in 1815 entitled *The Deities of Samothrace*, which was an important milestone in the development of his philosophy. This treatise was sympathetic to the Samothracian cult and its mythology because Schelling believed it fit into the philosophy he later articulated fully in *The Ages of the World*. Notably, he found that the meanings of the names of great gods resulted in a hierarchy that, while speculative, provided greater context for the Samothracian mysteries.

Schelling's analysis is far more sophisticated and subtle than most scholarly writing on the subject, albeit developed before the modern archeological research and subsequent analysis was available. For example, Schelling determined that the mother goddess' name, Axieros, meant "seeking" or "yearning," and thus he connected her with Demeter.[26] Axiokersa was related to Persephone and can be best understood as a sorceress, or the quality of magic in the world.[27] Axiokersos was one who overcame the magic of Axiokersa and was identified with Hades-Dionysus.[28]

Schelling saw Kadmilos as the mediator between the highest and the lowest, like Hermes, but also related etymologically to the angelic name Kadmiel.[29] "Kadmiel" literally means "he who goes before the god," and again, according to Semitic usage, this means nothing else than "the harbinger," "the herald of the coming god." To that extent, Kadmilos, being derived from Kadmiel, is related to the unknown god, just as the so-called "angel of the presence" (or "countenance") is related to the Old Testament Jehovah … one who foretells the deity, who, in preceding it, announces its coming."[30]

Schelling also conveyed an important idea about the reconciliation of multiplicity and unity in relation to the wholeness of God. In doing so, he places Kadmilos at the top of the hierarchy of the great gods.

> Naturally the sensible researcher has the inclination so far as possible to comprehend everything human in a humane way; therefore in researching the ancient mythology it is natural to seek a means whereby the multiplicity of divine natures may be harmonized with the humanly necessary and indelible idea of the unity of god. But it is neither suitable and clear in itself to represent the diverse gods as merely emanations of One into them, as a primal power propagating itself into diverse rays; nor can its determinateness and boundlessness be compatible well with the determinateness and sharpness of the outlines of every individual form, as also with the limited number of these forms. For whoever elevates "Once" to the thought of

> One highest being from which all other natures are merely radiations, will scarcely direct his reverence to these radiations… It is an entirely different matter if the various gods be not downward-proceeding, ever more self-attenuating emanations of a highest and superior deity; if instead they be gradations of a lowest power lying at the basis, which are all finally transfigured in One highest personality. Then they are as links of a chain ascending from the depths into the heights, or as rungs of a ladder, the lower of which cannot be bypassed by one who wants to climb the higher ones. Because for a human being they are mediators between him and the highest divinity, though only as messengers, proclaimers, heralds of the coming god, the worship of them acquires a lustre which even endures for the higher humanity. This fact alone explains how the honor rendered to the multiple gods strikes roots so deep and almost ineradicable, how it can maintain itself for so long. Therefore the notion of emanation seems suited neither for the interpretation of ancient mythology in general, nor for the interpretation of the Samothracian mythology in particular. Here it founders on the correctly understood concept of Kadmilos … Kadmilos is not subordinated to the other three, but rather stands above them … Over nature and the spirit world is Kadmilos or Hermes who has both subordinate to him, as well as mediating between them and the transcendent. Beyond all these is the demiurge, the god who stands free over against the world.[31]

In Schelling's interpretation, we may perceive a sense of the initiate, Kadmilos, mediating between the earthly and transcendent: not subordinate, but superior to the gods. This same sense of the eternal can be perceived in the outline of the Samothracian resurrection rite, sacred marriage, and rumored revelation of the god.

Concluson

There are several important points that should be re-emphasized regarding the initiations at Samothrace. The rites had similar aspects as modern initiatory rites, including purification or vetting of the candidate, the use of secret names or words, resurrection themes, and the potential for awakening greater potential within the initiate. Similarly, the Samothracian cult's deep connection with the land and the myth – these were inseparable and crucial to the empowerment of the cult and their rites. As we celebrate 300 years of official Freemasonry, we might consider the foundations of a mystery school that lasted more than a thousand years in the ancient world. Connection to land and myth to empower initiatory ritual is not only historically significant, but important for the longevity initiatory traditions.

Finally, as Masonic initiates we must accept the task of building the temple, which is the work that must follow the initiation. To complete our work, we must ever seek more light and follow its wisdom. We should consider the process begun by initiation to be completed when the temple "not built with hands" is constructed and the angel of the presence dwells within – for enlightenment is the ultimate purpose of the ancient initiatic art.

As initiates we honor tradition, ourselves, deity, and all beings by working toward gnostic awakening. Like in ancient times, we must return to self-realization and gnosis as the standard by which we judge our esoteric traditions.

Then, like Kadmilos, we will realize our place not only in the earthly or transcendent, but also in a bridging of the two.

1 Guettel Cole, Susan, *Theoi Megaloi: The Cult of the Great Gods at Samothrace* (Leiden: Brill, 1984), 1.

2 Walter Burkert, *Greek Religion* (Malden, MA: Blackwell Publishing Ltd. and Harvard University Press, 1985), 282-3.

3 Ibid., 282.

4 Cole, *Theoi Megaloi*, 2.

5 Burkert, *Greek Religion*, 281.
6 Ibid., 282-3.
7 Ibid., 282.
8 Cole, *Theoi Megaloi*, 3.
9 C. H. Oldfather, trans., *Diodorus Siculus, Library of History, Vol. V*, accessed May 13, 2015, http://www.theoi.com/Text/DiodorusSiculus5B.html.
10 Cole, *Theoi Megaloi*, 2.
11 Ibid.
12 Helmut Koester, *Paul & His World: Interpreting the New Testament in Its Context* (Minneapolis: Fortress Press, 2007), 57.
13 Cole, *Theoi Megaloi*, 2.
14 Koester, *Paul & His World*, 40.
15 Cole, *Theoi Megaloi*, 3.
16 Ibid.
17 Burkert, *Greek Religion*, 282.
18 Koester, *Paul & His World*, 58. The conclusion was from Jewett's *The Thessalonian Correspondence*, 130-31. Koester also remarks, "It is noteworthy that these conclusions are based on Witt's interpretation of the famous 5th-century BCE Kabiros kylix from Thebes. Moreover, the cult of the Kabiroi at Thebes had been subject to a thorough Greek reinterpretation as early as the classical, or even the archaic, period and was by no means representative for the kabiros cult on Samothrake and in Macedonia."
19 Kevin Clinton, "Stages of Initiation in the Eleusinian and Samothracian Mysteries," *Greek Mysteries: The Archaeology and Ritual of Ancient Greek Secret Cults* (New York: Routledge, 2003), 68.
20 Sandra Blakely, "Kadmos, Jason, and the Great Gods of Samothrace: Initiation as Mediation in a Northern Aegean Context," *Electronic Antiquity* XI, no. 1, Nov. (2007): 85, http://scholar.lib.vt.edu/ejournals/ElAnt/V11N1/pdf/blakely.pdf.
21 Burkert, *Greek Religion*, 114.
22 Ibid., 284.
23 Burkert, *Greek Religion*, 283.
24 Arthur Edward Waite, *A New Encyclopedia of Freemasonry Vol. I* (New York: Cosimo, Inc., 2007), 427-8.
25 Mer-Amun, "Samothrace: Sanctuary of the Mighty Ones," http://dreaminghades.com/articles/hekate-articles/samothrace-sanctuary-of-the-mighty-ones, accessed January 12, 2018.
26 Robert F. Brown, trans., *Schelling's Treatise on the Deities of Samothrace* (Missoula: Scholars Press, 1977), 18.
27 Brown, *Schelling's Treatise*, 20-21.
28 Ibid., 21.
29 Ibid., 2.
30 Ibid.
31 Ibid., 23-24.

Bibliography

Blakely, Sandra. "Kadmos, Jason, and the Great Gods of Samothrace: Initiation as Mediation in a Northern Aegean Context." *Electronic Antiquity*, Vol. XI, No. 1, Nov. 2007. Accessed 18 April 2015. http://scholar.lib.vt.edu/ejournals/ElAnt/V11N1/pdf/blakely.pdf.

Brown, Robert F., trans. *Schelling's Treatise on "The Deities of Samothrace."* Missoula: Scholars Press, 1977.

Burkert, Walter. *Greek Religion*. Malden. MA: Blackwell Publishing Ltd. and Harvard University Press, 1985.

Clinton, Kevin. "Stages of Initiation in the Eleusinian and Samothracian Mysteries," in *Greek Mysteries: The Archaeology and Ritual of Ancient Greek Secret Cults*. New York: Routledge, 2003.

Gasparro, Guilia Sfameni. "Soteriology and Mystic Aspects in the Cult of Cybele in Attis." Leiden: The Netherlands, Brill, 1985. Accessed 18 April 2015. https://books.google.com/books?id=EqCyeOD8spEC&printsec=frontcover#v=onepage&q&f=false.

Griffin, Charles. Personal conversation with Mr Griffin regarding his visit to research the ruins and island of Samothrace in summer 2015. Meeting occurred at Mr. Griffin's residence in Newburyport, MA on 27 December 2017.

Guettel Cole, Susan. *Theoi Megaloi: The Cult of the Great Gods at Samothrace*. Leiden, The Netherlands: Brill, 1984.

Koester, Helmut. *Paul & His World: Interpreting the New Testament in Its Context*. Minneapolis: Fortress Press, 2007.

Kripal, Jeffrey J. *The Serpent's Gift: Gnostic Reflections on the Study of Religion*. Chicago: The University of Chicago Press, 2007.

Lehmann, Phyllis Williams. "Samothrace." *Grove Art Online. Oxford Art Online*. Oxford University Press. Accessed 18 April 2015. http://www.oxfordartonline.com.ezp-prod1.hul.harvard.edu/subscriber/article/grove/art/T075552.

Mackey, Albert G. *The Symbolism of Freemasonry: Illustrating and Explaining Its Science and Philosophy, its Legends, Myths and*

Symbols. 1882. Accessed 18 April 2015. http://www.sacred-texts.com/mas/sof/sof33.htm.

May, Herbert G. and Metzger, Bruce M., eds. *The New Oxford Annotated Bible with the Apocrypha*. New York: Oxford University Press, 1977.

Mer-Amun, "Samothrace: Sanctuary of the Mighty Ones." Accessed 12 January 2018. http://dreaminghades.com/articles/hekate-articles/samothrace-sanctuary-of-the-mighty-ones.

Versnel, H.S. "Mercurius Amongst the Magni Dei." *Mnemosyne*, Vol. 27, Iss. 2, 1974. Accessed 18 April 2015. http://booksandjournals.brillonline.com/content/journals/10.1163/156852574x00845.

Waite, Arthur Edward. *A New Encyclopedia of Freemasonry*. New York: Cosimo, Inc., 2007. Accessed 14 May 2015. https://books.google.com/books?id=Mo55gdJ1o8QC&pg=PA428&lpg=PA428&dq=kasmillos&source=bl&ots=UZ_e5r8uIQ&sig=AjJDcs_YNaV6K8AX5qAPzt6MTUU&hl=en&sa=X&ei=l9ZUVaLaMoqLNsSBgagM&ved=0CCgQ6AEwAg#v=onepage&q=kasmillos&f=false.

René Guénon: Initiation and the Question of the Christian Sacraments[*]

Timothy Scott

'...in our present state of affairs (and indeed for quite a long time now) we can no longer in any way consider Christian rites to have an initiatic character...'

(René Guénon, 'Christianity and Initiation')[1]

Introduction

René Guénon was born in Blois in 1886.[2] He grew up in a Catholic environment and was schooled by Jesuits. He moved to Paris to take up studies in mathematics. In 1905 he abandoned his academic studies and submerged himself in French occultism, becoming a leading member in several societies – theosophical, spiritualistic, masonic and "gnostic." These groups tended to be marked by the repudiation of bourgeois ideologies and the institutions of modernity. They turned to the archaic past in search of authentic spiritual values, often emphasizing the spiritual writings of the East. During this time Guénon came to serious study of Islam, Taoism and Hinduism, with particular focus on the *Advaita* school. He was later to disown the philosophical and historical assumptions of these secret societies contrasting their "counterfeit spirituality" with what he came to see as genuine expressions of esotericism.

Guénon's life entered a new phase in 1912 with his marriage to a devout Catholic. His thought had undergone a major shift away from occultism to an interest in the sapiential traditions within the frameworks of the great religions. He became interested in the possibility of a Christian esotericism within the Catholic tradition. However, personal circumstances, which included the death of his wife in 1928, led to his disillusionment with the Church. This coincided (to some extent) with Guénon's adoption of Islam. One should not think that his disillusionment with Christianity led to a conversion to Islam, for Guénon's acceptance of Islam appears perfectly coherent with his personal spiritual archetype.[3] Rather what we should note here is the way that his disillusionment with the Christianity of his early life appears to have left him with an intellectual myopia where certain understandings of Christianity are at issue, in particular his understanding of the Christian sacraments. A series of fortuitous circumstances saw Guénon leave France on a three month visit to Cairo. He remained there until his death in 1951.

In Cairo Guénon was initiated into the Sufi order of the Shadilites. He remarried and lived a modest and retiring existence. He maintained correspondence with readers in Europe and published extensively on questions concerning initiation into authentic esoteric traditions. Guénon explored traditions such as Freemasonry and the *Fedeli d'Amore* before concluding that the possibility for initiation was only available to the Occident (at least at the time he was writing) through either of the 'genuine western initiatic organizations,' which he felt to be the Compagnonnage and Masonry.[4] Along with these he allowed for initiation within the Eastern Church, and more specifically, within the tradition of Hesychasm.[5] However, shortly before his death he concluded that there was no effective hope of an esoteric regeneration within either Masonry or Catholicism.

***

René Guénon is recognized, along with Ananda Coomaraswamy and Frithjof Schuon, as one of the founders of what is often referred to as the "Traditionalist School." In fact, Guénon rejected the terms "traditionalist" and "traditionalism," preferring instead to be seen as an exponent of the *sophia perennis*.[6] Some followers of Guénon have tried to specifically associate the terms "Traditionalism" and "Traditionalist School" with Schuon, although this procrustean exercise is highly problematic in itself. In his landmark survey of "Traditionalism," Kenneth Oldmeadow observes the political and sentimental accretions associated with the terms "tradition," "traditionalism" and "traditionalist"; nevertheless, he concludes that 'as these writers would concede the need for some kind of generic label for their thought most would find "traditionalism" the least unsatisfactory.'[7]

This granted we must recognize that Guénon, Coomaraswamy and Schuon were not in harmony on all points. Still, it is safe to say that the essential elements of their combined *opus* present a united front against the understandings (or lack thereof) of the modern world. Nevertheless, certain followers of these luminaries are all too intent on engaging in polemic over elements that are often altogether peripheral, choosing to highlight the differences between these three thinkers, rather than recognize the benefits of their works taken as a whole. In saying this we should not ignore differences, where they appear, for the sake of trying to maintain a false harmony, for in such cases we are entitled, if not obliged, to question and challenge the ideas of these thinkers; not to do so speaks of a lack of intellectual curiosity and discernment and risks sycophancy, traits which were deplored by all of these thinkers alike. It should be obvious that where one concludes error or weakness this is an altogether different matter from dismissing the worth of that thinker's essential message.

A key disagreement between Guénon and Schuon occurs with the question of initiation and the status of the Christian sacraments. The debate has generated a sizable secondary literature. The primary sources, of course, are Guénon's various writings on initiation and Schuon's direct criticisms offered in *René Guénon: Some Observations*, a collection of critical comments based on personal notes not originally intended for publication but eventually published some 30-odd years after Guénon's death. In this work Schuon pays tribute and offers "unfailing gratitude" to Guénon for 'the presentation, both precise and profound, of crucial ideas, and thus indispensable truths'[8]; nevertheless, recognizing that 'there is no right superior to truth,' he presents a criticism of some of Guénon's ideas and of certain elements of the man himself. On the whole these are not unjustified: one cannot in good faith deny, for example, that Guénon was in fact 'somewhat slipshod in scholarship,' as Whitall Perry once observed.[9] A balanced study requires that we first attempt an analysis of Guénon's teaching on initiation. With this in hand we may consider the implications of Guénon's argument for the Christian sacraments.

Guénonian Initiation

Guénon approached the topic of initiation in two ways: in principle and specifically. In the first case he developed conclusions based on metaphysical principles, only drawing on specific traditions where apposite; in the second case he discussed specific traditions assessing their historical importance and validity, and explicating their particular symbolisms. The series of essays that make up his books *Perspectives on Initiation* and *Initiation & Spiritual Realization* are primarily, but not exclusively, of the first type. Of his other works that treat of initiation we have *The Esoterism of Dante*, *Studies in Freemasonry and the Compagnonnage,* and the enigmatic *The King of the World*; these are primarily of the second type. The posthumous *Insights into Christian Esoterism* is comprised of two parts: Part Two is made up of essays on Dante, the *Fedeli d'Amore*, the Holy Grail, and the Holy Land: these are primarily essays focusing on specific "Christian" organizations and symbolisms. Part One comprises two essays, 'On Sacred Languages' and 'Christianity and Initiation.' The first is a short rumination on Christianity's lack – in Guénon's opinion – of a sacred language. Guénon's argument and conclusions here are problematic. Schuon offers arguments against Guénon's view in *René Guénon: Some Observations* and also his essay, 'Communion and Invocation.'[10]

In 'Christianity and Initiation' Guénon clarifies his position on Christian initiation and the status of the Christian sacraments in light of 'rather unwelcome confusions [that] had made their way into the mind of a sizable number of our readers.'[11] He notes his surprise at learning that some of his readers considered *Perspectives on Initiation* to be more or less directly and extensively concerned with Christianity. As I have remarked, this work is essentially general and "theoretical."[12] Nevertheless certain ideas developed in *Perspectives on Initiation* do lead to conclusions on the status of Christianity and it is these that Guénon seeks to clarify in 'Christianity and Initiation.'

In summary: Guénon claims that Christianity was originally esoteric and initiatic but that at some time before Constantine and the

Council of Nicaea it became a purely exoteric – which for Guénon is synonymous with "religious" – organization. He believes that this "descent" into the exoteric had a "providential character" in being a "redressal" of the modern Occidental decline, in perfect agreement with cyclic laws.[13] Guénon concludes that, due to this state of affairs 'and even from a very remote time, one can no longer consider, in any way, the Christian rites as having an initiatic character,' saying that 'this is what we shall have to insist upon with greater precision.'[14] The sacraments are thus "reduced" to the purely exoteric domain, although he recognizes that the sacraments can have an esoteric character or usage, but only for those who have already received initiation in another form, in which case the sacraments are for such people 'transposed, as it were, onto a different level, in the sense that these initiates will use them as supports for the initiatic work itself.'[15]

In saying that initiation was available in another form, Guénon felt that the possibility for initiation was only available to the Occident through either the Compagnonnage or Masonry, or through the Eastern Churches, and more specifically, Hesychasm. However, he remarks, 'the sacraments cannot produce such effects by themselves, their intrinsic efficacy being limited to the exoteric domain.'[16]

An obvious difficulty and source of confusion in all this arises in admitting that the word "initiation" has a breadth and depth of meaning that goes beyond Guénon's specific usage. Guénon's precision is, in general, a mark of his genius; however, he is occasionally guilty of monopolizing the "true meaning" of words where this is not necessarily justified, either etymologically or in terms of common usage.[17] That said, Guénon offers sufficient definition to clarify his use of the word "initiation." His definition is both *précising* and *stipulative* – which is not surprising given his mathematical background; it is this definition that we shall concern ourselves with here, only taking issue where his definition is guilty of squirreling the argument.

For Guénon, initiation is essentially a "transmission," where this can be understood in two different senses: 'on the one hand, transmission of a spiritual influence, and on the other, transmission of a traditional teaching.'[18] In talking of "traditional teachings"

Guénon does not mean bookish learning or a didactic program. Instead these teachings are methods aimed at the realization of the "initiatic work," which is itself the actualization of "states of being" that are opened up to the qualified initiate via "spiritual influences": 'What can be taught are only the preparatory methods for obtaining these states; what can be furnished from the outside in this respect is only an aid, a support, that greatly facilitates the work to be accomplished, and also a control that dispels those obstacles and dangers that may present themselves.'[19]

At the outset we must ask: What does Guénon mean by "spiritual influences?" What are the "states" that these open the initiate to? What "qualification" does the initiate require? And, in turn, who is qualified to offer initiation? Finally: What is the process of the "initiatic work?"

Spiritual Influences

For Guénon initiation is the transmission of spiritual influences to a qualified initiate by means of filiation with a traditional organization that is itself orthodox and regular; these spiritual influences give the initiate spiritual illumination sufficient to develop, in conjunction with the active efforts of the initiate's interior work, the possibilities that precisely constitute their qualification. This initiatic process presents itself in three hierarchic conditions: potential, virtual, and actual. The final goal of the initiatic work is for the initiate to transcend individuality in achieving Deliverance, which is the state of Supreme Identity with the Reality. Guénon:

> …initiation implies three conditions that present themselves successively and correspond respectively to the terms "potentiality," "virtuality," and "actuality"; (i) "qualification," consisting in certain possibilities inherent in the nature of the individual …; (ii) transmission, by means of filiation with a traditional organization, of a spiritual influence giving to the individual the "illumination" that will allow him to order and develop those possibilities that he carries within himself; and (iii)

> interior work by which ... this development will be gradually realized as the individual passes stage by stage through the different degrees of the initiatic hierarchy and is led to the final goal of "Deliverance" or "Supreme Identity."[20]

Guénon is quick to distinguish the transmission of "spiritual influences" from simple bookish learning and profane didactic teaching, and needless to say, he dismisses the idea of initiation on the "social" or "moral" order.[21] It appears that what he has in mind when he refers to "spiritual influences" is what Islamic tradition calls *barakah* ("blessing"), although he does not specify this as such;[22] he does recognize that these spiritual influences are what Christian tradition designates by the power of the Holy Ghost.[23] According to Guénon, a spiritual influence is 'essentially transcendent and supra-individual,' although this does not prevent it 'from acting according to different modalities and in equally different domains,' that is to say, to produce secondary effects that are themselves not necessarily of the same transcending order of the spiritual influences.[24]

What he is describing here is the concept of a mediating principle, both transcendent and immanent; in the Islamic tradition this has its source in the *barzakh*, the isthmus between the "two seas": 'It was He who sent the two seas rolling, the one sweet and fresh, and the other salty and bitter, and set a rampart between them as an insurmountable barrier.'[25] Seyyed Hossein Nasr, discussing the *Hayy ibn Yaqzān* of Ibn Sina, says of the *barzakh* that it is 'the *intellectus materialis*, or *al-'aql al-hayūlānī*, which with respect to the intelligible forms acts as *materia prima*.'[26] This informs Guénon's view of initiation as being a process of 'bringing the being back to a state of undifferentiated simplicity comparable ... to that of *materia prima*.'[27] Thus the initiate requires the *barakah* to be reintegrated into the *barzakh*, where these are essentially of the same ontological status. This is, *mutatis mundis*, the Christian doctrine of the *Logos*, both uncreated and created.

Guénon further clarifies the idea of "superior states," that is to say supra-individual states, saying that these must not be confused with that which is simply extraordinary, such as psychic states, 'for the psychic states have nothing "superior" or "transcendent" about them.'[28] In comparison he observes that when it is a question of communication of superior states 'what is involved … is something that is in its very essence "incommunicable" since it concerns states that are realized inwardly.'[29] Moreover, 'mere communication with superior states cannot be regarded as an end but only as a point of departure. If this communication must be established at the very start by the action of a spiritual influence, it is only to permit the prospective initiate effectively to take possession of these states and not simply, as in the order of religion, to have "grace" descend upon him, a "grace" that does link him to these states in a certain way but does not grant him entry to them.'[30] This last quote is somewhat problematic, for Guénon does not clarify why "grace" should not in fact grant entry into the superior states, in the sense that one might be "lifted" thence by God. However, for Guénon the answer lies in the idea of the "active" nature of initiation.

The communication with superior states via the transmission of spiritual influences is experiential and unitive rather than dialectic. This experience constitutes what Guénon calls the "initiatic secret": 'the "initiatic secret" … is such because it cannot but be so, since it consists exclusively of the "inexpressible," which consequently is necessarily also the "incommunicable."'[31] He is quick to distinguish this idea from mere profane secrets which are so by a matter of contrivance. Moreover, he recognizes that properly speaking, 'what is transmitted by initiation is not the secret itself, since this is incommunicable, but the spiritual influence that the rites vehicle and that makes possible the interior work by means of which, with the symbols as base and support, each one will attain that secret and penetrate it more or less completely, more or less profoundly, according to the measure of his own possibilities of comprehension and realization.'[32]

Similarly, he says:

> Obviously, a teaching that concerns the inexpressible can only suggest it with the help of appropriate images, which

> then become the supports for contemplation; ... This was always and among all peoples one of the essential characteristics of initiation into the mysteries, whatever name may have been given it, and we can therefore say that symbols, and particularly myths when the teaching is conveyed by words, truly constitute, according to their primary purpose, the very language of initiation.[33]

***

The idea of the "incommunicable" leads Guénon to recognize the "most profound" meaning of the term "mystery" as being "silence" in the sense of that which is "strictly inexpressible." In this context he recognizes the initiatic quality of the ancient "Mysteries," although when used in the context of "mysticism" he denies this most profound sense and allows only the most passive quietism. As I have alluded to earlier, Guénon's argument against mysticism is unsatisfactory, being for the most part *ad hoc* and based on a procrustean definition of this phenomenon.

There are two main reasons why Guénon denies mysticism access to the superior states of the being. In the first place, he feels that mysticism is entirely passive, involving no interior spiritual work; "mysticism" is characterized by "passivity," whereas, in contrast, he describes initiation as "precise" and "positive."[34] Guénon: 'mysticism ... pertains exclusively to the religious or exoteric domain ... the mystical path differs from the initiatic path in all its essential characteristics, which difference is such as to render the two truly incompatible.'[35] This quote recognizes a further problem arising from a question of definition, for Guénon's use of the terms "religion" and "exoteric" are again *précising* and *stipulative*. Leaving this difficulty aside, let us observe that the generalization that mysticism is purely passive quite simply suggests that Guénon's knowledge of mystical theology was severely limited.[36] Again, according to Guénon, 'in mystical union individuality as such subsists.'[37] Meister Eckhart, who is often utilized to refute Guénon, says: 'If we fail to find God it is because we seek in semblance what has no resemblance

… On merging into the Godhead all definition is lost'; again, 'When I go back into the ground, into the depths, into the well-spring of the Godhead, no one will ask whence I came or whither I went.' It is hard to see how these imply a state of being that maintains individuality; moreover, there are any number of references to "mystics" of various traditions that would suffice to refute Guénon's opinion.[38]

Guénon's second criticism is more potent, namely: mysticism lacks the transmission of spiritual influences that is guaranteed by filiation to an authentic initiatic organization, therefore mysticism cannot access states that transcend individuality. It must be admitted that much of what is labelled mysticism did in fact take place in the context of, or with some association to, organizations that Guénon would recognize as initiatic, albeit that these were also "religious"; in such cases he would argue it would not have been the mysticism but the initiation that allowed access to superior states. Here there is the problem of distinguishing between what constitutes mystical practice or activity – for whatever Guénon may say, this is an active path[39] – and what constitutes initiatic practice, and to what degree they coincide – which challenges Guénon's claim that these two are "truly incompatible."

Whether one wishes to defend Guénon, attempting thereby to maintain some idea of infallibility (which he himself never claimed), or whether one wishes to defend the complexity of mysticism, the question of mysticism and Guénon's understanding thereof, is, in the end, peripheral to the issue of initiation and must await a detailed treatment of its own.

Superior States of the Being

The spiritual influences involved in initiation are supra-individual. They belong properly to the metaphysical domain. Nevertheless, Guénon says that they can enter into the individual state via initiatic transmission, thus opening these superior states up to the initiate. In his book, *Man and his Becoming according to the Vedānta*, Guénon offers the following summary of the states of the being:[40]

Universal	The Unmanifested Formless Manifestation
Individual	Formal Manifestation Subtle state Gross state

He remarks that 'religion considers the human being exclusively in his state of individuality and does not aim to bring him beyond it but rather to assure him of the most favorable conditions in this state, whereas the essential aim of initiation is to go beyond the possibilities of this state and to effect a passage to the superior states, and even finally to lead the being beyond every conditioned state of whatever kind.'[41] To this he adds the following note: 'Here of course, it is a question of the human state envisaged in its [*sic*] integrality, including the indefinite extension of its extra-corporeal prolongations.'

A thorough consideration of Guénon's theory of the "multiple states of the being," valuable and highly interesting as it is, would take us too far beyond the scope of the present study. This is not to say that a deeper understanding of this is irrelevant to the topic of initiation, and the interested reader is encouraged to see Guénon's *The Multiple States of the Being* and *Symbolism of the Cross*. It suffices to appreciate two key points: firstly, that the spiritual influences are supra-individual but capable of effect in the individual domain; and secondly, that for Guénon it is only through initiation that the individual can take possession of these spiritual influences in a manner that will allow them to transcend the individual state.

When Guénon talks of the "most favorable condition" of individuality as opposed to the transcending of "every conditioned state of whatever kind," he is alluding to the distinction between "salvation" and "Deliverance." Guénon first explicated this distinction in *Man and his Becoming*;[42] he alludes to it in *Perspectives on Initiation*,[43] and returns to it in more detail in chapter eight of *Initiation & Spiritual Realization*.[44] According to Guénon, salvation is the highest achievable condition of the individual state and constitutes "preservation" of the human state; thus one who gains salvation is 'fixed ... in the prolongations of the human state as long as this state itself subsists in manifestation – which is equivalent to perpetuity or an indefinite time.'[45] The benefit of this is that the individual is thereby guaranteed 'the central position occupied by man in the degree of existence to which he belongs'[46] and protected, thereby, against the "dangers" of a more peripheral condition 'comparable in our world to those of animals or even vegetables,' which would constitute a serious disadvantage from the point of view of spiritual development.'[47]

Guénon's argument rests on the distinction between Non-Being and Being, and in turn, between Being and Existence. Being is the principle of manifestation, whereas Universal Existence 'will then be integral manifestation of the ensemble of possibilities of manifestation, implying the effective development of those possibilities in a conditioned mode.'[48] 'A state of a being is then the development of a particular possibility contained in such a degree [of existence], that degree being defined by the conditions to which the possibility is subject insofar as it is envisaged as realizing itself in the domain of manifestation.'[49]

In *Symbolism of the Cross* Guénon develops a brilliant and complex geometric representation of the states of the being and the degrees of existence; for our purposes it will do to offer a simplified explanation. The degree of existence to which human individuality belongs may be envisaged as a horizontal plane of existence; the center of this plane of existence is occupied by the conditioning principle, which is in this case the principle of the human state; each individual is only human qua human insomuch as they participate in the center, just as by analogy radii of a circle participate in the geometric center. The purpose of this degree of existence is to realize the center, from whence the being can possibly "progress" vertically. It is only through being human that a state of being can "move" "inwards" along the horizontal radii that, in a sense, defines them; moving into the center from which "the being" (for it is no longer proper to speak in terms of the individual) transcends to superior states.

This vertical ascent is likewise envisaged as a movement back into the realm of pure Being, which would here be envisaged as the center of a sphere, of which the plane of human existence is but one horizontal cross-section. Realization of the center of the plane of human existence constitutes the state of what the Chinese call True Man (*chen jen*) and what the Semitic traditions designate by Primordial Man; this is the state of being described by "salvation," as Guénon envisages this term.[50] Realization of the state of pure Being constitutes the state of Transcendent Man (*chün jen*), what Semitic traditions designate by Universal Man; this is the state indicated by Deliverance. Now this is of course a simplification, but one hopes that the basic distinctions are evident.

Salvation is the state of being "preserved," although this begs the questions: preserved from what and for what? The simple religious answer would be: preserved from "sin" until the "End of Time" or "Final Judgement." The "individual" who has achieved Deliverance has, in effect, transcended time and any concept of judgement. The question as to the difference between the being who has achieved Deliverance here and now, and the person who is judged "worthy" at the end of time is not addressed by Guénon, who is primarily concerned with questions of initiation rather than eschatology. For Guénon, Salvation preserves one from falling away from the human state. He does not explain why we should wish not to be human, that is to say, why we should not wish to belong to a condition 'comparable … to those of animals or even vegetables,' except to say that this would be disadvantageous to spiritual development and alluding to "oriental texts" that say that 'human birth is difficult to obtain.'[51]

Of course, Guénon is not alone in his emphasis on the favorability of the human condition, for this is a universal maxim which can be recognized in the pericope: 'God made man in His own image.' The primacy of the human condition is a central theme of Schuon's work, where man's objectivity is the defining element: 'When we speak of man, what we have in mind first of all is human nature as such, that is, inasmuch as it is distinguished from animal nature. Specifically human nature is made of centrality and totality, and hence of objectivity; objectivity being the capacity to step outside oneself, while centrality and totality are the capacity to conceive the

Absolute.'[52] Centrality, totality, objectivity: these qualify the human condition.

Here we must acknowledge two points. First: that Schuon took issue with Guénon's account of the relationship between the Self and the ego, but a full consideration of this would take us beyond the boundaries of this essay.[53] Second: in describing the transition through states of the being and degrees of existence, Guénon is considering the idea of transmigration, which raises numerous difficulties but principally the question of reincarnation. Again, a full consideration of this area lies beyond the scope of this essay, but I will note that Guénon talks of "states of the being" emphasizing that what he intends is the idea of the "one and only transmigrant," to use Coomaraswamy's phrase.[54]

Qualification

The question of qualifications is problematic because we are here in the realm of individuality and thus, subjectivity. As Guénon remarks, the first and primary condition of initiation is initiatic "qualifications":[55] 'these qualifications belong exclusively to the individual domain … the individual must necessarily be taken as a means and a support of initiatic realization, and thus must possess the necessary aptitudes for this role, which is not always the case.'[56] The orthodoxy of the initiatic organization is thus essential to provide an objective guarantee by which to measure the qualification of the prospective initiate.

Still here there is the difficulty that arises with one orthodox initiatic organization seemingly applying different criteria for qualification than another. In fact Guénon observed to a seeker that 'an Islamic initiation is, broadly speaking, easier to get than a Hindu initiation.'[57] This, of course, is specifically connected to questions of caste; however, Guénon notes similar difficulties, *mutatis mundis*, in obtaining initiation in the Hesychast tradition,[58] which is not constrained by the question of caste. And, in fact, many Christian followers of Guénon took the "easy" (to use Guénon's word) option of becoming Muslims, thus allowing them to seek initiation into a Sufi *tarîqa*.[59]

The conditions that constitute initiatic qualifications, as Guénon describes them, may be summed up as: initiative, acceptance, receptivity, and discrimination. Initiative: 'In the case of initiation … the individual is the source of the initiative toward "realization," pursued methodically under rigorous and unremitting control, and normally reaching beyond the very possibilities of the individual as such. We must not fail to add that this initiative alone does not suffice, for it is quite evident that the individual cannot surpass himself through his own efforts.'[60] This last point highlights the need for acceptance: 'the individual must not only have the intention of being initiated but he must be "accepted" by a regular traditional organization that is qualified to confer initiation on him … it must be a strictly initiatic organization, to the exclusion of any other kind of traditional organization.'[61]

Receptivity can been seen as "natural aptitude": 'this aptitude, forming what some call "initiability," properly constitutes the requisite "qualification" demanded by all initiatic traditions.'[62] Guénon remarks that in order to be truly profitable, 'initiatic teaching naturally requires a "receptive" mental attitude,' while stressing that '"receptivity" is not at all a synonym for "passivity."'[63] Any informed description of mysticism might well argue in exactly the same way, which shows the difficulty in guaranteeing an unequivocal argument here. In fact, the receptivity of the potential initiate can only be assessed by the initiatic organization, which returns us to the difficulties of assessing the orthodoxy of said organization and, in turn, the difficulties of assessing the criteria they demand for qualifying to gain initiation. Of course here it will be argued that such assessments cannot be made in a manner that is dialectic and profane, that it is a matter of experience; in the final analysis I am in agreement, but if we were to leave things there the initiate would have no means by which to distinguish between psychological experience and pseudo-initiation, and what Guénon, on the other hand, takes to be authentic spiritual initiation. Therefore, we arrive at the need for discrimination.

There are two areas wherein the initiate requires the capacity for discrimination. In the first place the potential initiate needs to be able to recognize the orthodox and regular nature of the initiatic organization. In the second place, observes Guénon, initiation requires doctrinal preparation necessary for discrimination among "influences,"[64] indicating by this that along with spiritual influences the process of initiation and the initiatic work opens one to the dangers of psychic influences, which can be detrimental if not recognized as such. Of course, for Guénon, "doctrinal knowledge" is distinct from outward instruction or profane "knowledge," as we have noted already.

The idea of "qualifications" raises the modern specter of elitism. We need not go into the denial of hierarchy envisaged by modern egalitarianism. Let us just note Guénon: 'It goes without saying that the essential qualification, which takes precedence over all the others, is that of a greater or lesser "intellectual horizon."'[65] He envisages precisely an "intellectual elite" – a pleonasm, according to Guénon; however, we must be aware that he is using the term "intellect" more in line with scholastic usage, and really as a cognomen for the *Logos* or, in the Hindu tradition with which he is more familiar, the *Buddhi*.[66] As such he observes that 'the eminence that characterizes the elite by very definition can only be effected from "on high," that is, in respect of the highest possibilities of the being.'[67]

Guénon is quick to point out that 'initiation is not a sort of special religion reserved for a minority.'[68] Neither is the elite a matter of numbers: 'number counts for little here … It is evident that in all that relates to the elite, only "quality" must be envisaged, not "quantity."'[69] 'In the final analysis,' says Guénon, 'the elite as we understand it represents the totality of those who possess the qualifications required for initiation, and who naturally are always a minority among men; all men are in a sense "called"[70] by reason of the "central" position the human being occupies among all the other beings founding this same state of existence.'[71]

Initiatic Organizations

In talking of qualifications, we recognized the need for the ability to discriminate with respect to the orthodoxy of a particular initiatic organization. By way of clearing the ground let us first note that affiliation must be "real" and "effective," as opposed to "ideal." Here Guénon wishes to guard against syncretic pseudo-initiatic organizations, the likes of which were evident in French occultist circles at Guénon's time and which generally speaking present themselves as "theosophists" today. A mark of such "ideal" organizations is their often spontaneous origin, frequently accompanied by "revealed" links with any number of fantastic traditions, of which they may claim to be a "reconstitution."[72] In contrast a "real" initiatic organization must be "regular" and effected according to definite laws.[73] These "definite laws" act as a measure of orthodoxy, where the "necessary and sufficient condition" of orthodoxy, as Guénon puts it, is the 'concordance of a conception with the fundamental principle of the tradition.'[74] This means that initiation must be regular: 'initiation is essentially "regular," having nothing to do with anomalies';[75] this regularity, says Guénon, 'excludes pseudo-initiatic organizations.'[76] For Guénon, "regularity" is defined by attachment to an orthodox traditional center:[77] 'the link to the supreme center is clearly indispensable for the continuity of transmission of spiritual influences from the very origins of present humanity (or, rather, from beyond these origins, since what is involved is "non-human") and throughout the entire duration of its cycle of existence.'[78]

This last point recognizes that the transmission of spiritual influences is transcendent in origin. Guénon: 'it is necessary that an organization truly be the repository of a spiritual influence if it is to be able to communicate this influence.'[79] Initiatic organizations are effectively the "chain" that binds one to the transcendent: 'a succession that ensures the uninterrupted transmission [of spiritual influences].'[80] 'Outside of this succession,' says Guénon, 'even the observance of ritual forms is in vain.'[81] Guénon sees "succession" as the essential element in the efficacy of initiation. This "unbroken chain" is recognized variously as *shelsheleth* in Hebrew, *silsilah* in Arabic, *parampara* in Sanskrit.[82]

When Guénon says that 'outside of this succession even the observance of ritual forms is in vain' the immediate implication is that this is by definition a question of human transmission – leaving aside the original "non-human" transmission;[83] in fact this appears even more so to be the case when Guénon emphasizes that this must be "oral" transmission. However, he also says that relics 'are precisely vehicles of spiritual influences';[84] similarly temples, images, and ritual objects must be "vivified" by consecration.[85] In this last case we might suggest that these objects receive the spiritual influences, so as to vivify them, but do not then have the power to transmit them onwards; however, this seems to go against traditional teachings on the purpose of symbols as vehicles for spiritual influences. In fact, Guénon remarks: 'The true foundation of symbolism is the correspondence that exists among all orders of reality, that links one to another, and that therefore extends from the natural order taken in its entirety to the supernatural order itself. By virtue of this correspondence all of nature is itself only a symbol, that is to say it receives its true meaning only if seen as a support to raise us to the knowledge of supernatural or "metaphysical" (in its proper and etymological sense) truths, which is precisely the essential function of symbolism as well as the fundamental purpose of all traditional science.'[86] That is to say that the function of all symbols, as Guénon defines them, derives from their "linking" the hierarchy of states in a manner that allows them to "raise us" to superior states of the being.

This suggests that symbolic forms (both human and non-human) may act to transmit spiritual influences opening access to higher states of the being, and this would suggest that ritual forms, which are after all primarily symbolic, are anything but "in vain." In the case of relics these are "vehicles" precisely, transmitting the spiritual influences. This, at least, would seem to allow for non-human transmission of spiritual influences, which, according to Guénon's definition, allows for initiatic transmission through ritual forms, such as one might suggest is the case with the Christian sacraments. Thus the ritual form, given that it was orthodox and regular, would constitute the element of succession itself.

Certainly Guénon is not as dismissive of ritual as might appear from the above quote. 'Ritual,' as Guénon remarks, 'is not something to be played with; it is and always remains something serious and truly efficacious, even when those taking part in it are unaware of this.'[87] Moreover, he emphasizes that spiritual influences do in fact intervene in exoteric rites as well as initiatic rites.[88] However, 'unlike initiatic rites, exoteric rites do not in fact have as their goal the opening of the being to certain possibilities of knowledge for which all cannot be qualified.'[89] The goal for exoteric rites, according to Guénon, must be restricted to the individual order, 'having "salvation" as its finality.'[90] Still, granted that both ritual forms and initiation entail the transmission of spiritual influences, we are left to ask just how they differ.

We might suggest that these influences are simply of different orders. Yet if this were the end of the explanation, it would do nothing but render the term "spiritual influences" meaningless. A stronger argument develops with the idea that the spiritual influences are hierarchic so that it makes sense to talk about spiritual influences of this or that order. However, the difference, as we have it with Guénon, between the spiritual influences that are transmitted by religious rites and the spiritual influences transmitted by initiation resides in his *a priori* definition of them as such. No explanation or argument is offered.

It might also be suggested that these influences are of the same order but that only a qualified person can access the higher states. This would imply that the measure of "initiability" is the initiate's receptivity, which is to say that the measure resides, in the first place, in the individual and not the initiatic organization. Of course, as we have noted, the receptivity of the initiate, which constitutes the requisite "qualification," can only be guaranteed by the authority of the initiatic organization and then this receptivity can only be vivified by the initiatic transmission of the spiritual influences. If this were not the case then the influences vehicled by a specific ritual form might spontaneously vivify one's receptivity, which Guénon denies can be the case.

As an argument for the superiority of initiation – as Guénon envisages initiation – over religious rites this is flawed. It is a self-sealing augment. Put simply: spiritual influences transmitted by initiation in an initiatic organization are greater than the spiritual influences transmitted by a religious rite because only a qualified person can access the influences transmitted by initiation and the only way to be qualified is to undergo initiation. Thus it seems that the role of the guaranteeing organization is not an argument *against* ritual forms vivifying receptivity *per se* but is rather a guarantee of the authenticity of this within initiation. The latter does not necessarily deny the former.

Guénon's argument – such as it is, for to do him justice he is not in fact concerned with semantics – rests upon the essential element of human transmission. This in itself is not contingent on the officiant having understanding of the rite of initiation: 'the necessary and sufficient condition is that the officiant should have regularly received the power to accomplish the rite, and it makes little difference if he does not truly understand its significance and even if he does not believe in its efficacy, for this cannot prevent the rite from being valid if all the prescribed rules have been properly observed.'[91] Again: 'the efficacy of the rite accomplished by an individual can be independent of the true merit of the individual as such, something that is equally true of religious rites. We do not intend this in any "moral" sense, which would clearly have no importance to an exclusively "technical" question, but in the sense that even if the individual lacks the degree of knowledge necessary to comprehend the profound meaning of the rite and the essential reason for its diverse elements, that rite will nonetheless be fully effective if the individual is properly invested with the function of "transmitter" and accomplishes it while observing all the prescribed rules and with an intention that suffices to determine his consciousness of attachment to the traditional organization.'[92] In contrast, 'a profane person who knew all the rites from having read their descriptions in books would still not be initiated in any way, for it is quite evident that the spiritual influence attached to these rites would in no way have been transmitted to him.'[93]

When Guénon emphasizes "oral" transmission there are two fundamental aspects he has in mind. The first is the sound of the voice, which is linked to the existential nature, that is to say the primordial vibration field (*nāda*), the sound of the sacred monosyllable, *OM*.[94] In nearly every mythology of the world the cosmogenesis is symbolized by either sound or light, or a combination of the two symbolisms. Both describe the idea of vibration as the principal descriptor of creation. The second aspect is the *prana*, the "breath of life," the Hebrew *nephesh*, that God blew into the nose of Adam to make him a living being (*Genesis* 2:7), which is also identified with the Spirit or *ruah* (*Genesis* 6:17).[95]

A final point about initiatic organizations is that these are not necessarily "organizations" in the modern sense of the term. They are not defined by profane and formalistic structures, although they may have these. Rather, they are "organizations" according to two senses: that they are "organic" from the Greek *organikos*, which in turn derives from *organon*, which means "instrument" revealing that these are instruments in the process of "Return to God"; and that they form an organic or unified whole, which refers to their link to the supra-human source, the Centre. This is enough to appreciate that, theoretically, a single living human could form the corporeal manifestation of an initiatic organization; in fact we should say *the* initiatic Organization, for in truth there is only one God, one Organism, one unified Whole, so that there can only really be one initiatic organization. Guénon explicitly recognizes this when he says, 'Since in principle there is but one unique Tradition from which every orthodox traditional form is derived, there can only be one initiation, equally unique in its essence although present under diverse forms and with multiple modalities.'[96]

This shows that what he is referring to by initiation is an existential change that cannot be reversed or undone: 'once one has been admitted into an initiatic organization, whatever it may be, one can never by any means cease to be attached to it … initiation is necessarily conferred once and for all and possesses a strictly ineffaceable character.'[97] Again: 'initiation of any degree represents for the being who receives it a permanent acquisition, a state that virtually or effectively it has reached once and for all and that nothing can ever take away.'[98] This type of hypothesis is sometimes used to argue against the notion that repetitive rites, such as the Eucharist, can be initiatic. However, this is to be ignorant of what Guénon means by "multiple modalities" and of the truth that, in essence, there is only one unique Eucharist.

The Initiatic Work

The above distinction between "virtual" and "effective" initiation requires consideration. Guénon states that attachment to a regular initiatic organization is sufficient for "virtual initiation."[99] 'Virtual initiation,' he says, is 'initiation understood in the strictest possible sense of the word, that is, as an "entering" or a "beginning."'[100] In contrast 'the interior work that comes afterward properly pertains to effective initiation, which in the final analysis is, in all its degrees, the development "in act" of the possibilities to which virtual initiation gives access.'[101] Attachment to a traditional organization 'could of course never exempt one from the necessary inner work that each must accomplish for himself; it is, rather a preliminary condition for such work effectively to bear fruit.'[102] Again: 'entering on the path is virtual initiation; following the path is effective initiation.'[103] The aim is "Realization."

Guénon refers to virtual initiation as a "first initiation" saying that it is a passage from the profane to the initiatic order.[104] This description might seem to contradict what he said concerning the idea of there only being "one initiation." However, this "one initiation," as he observes, while being unique in its essence, is 'present under diverse forms and with multiple modalities.'[105] In fact the initiatic changes are, according to Guénon, "indefinite,"[106] insomuch as they correspond to the indefinite states of the being that comprise a degree of existence. At the same time 'the initiatic degrees ritually conferred, whatever the traditional form may be, can thus correspond only to a sort of general classification of the principal stages to be traversed.'[107]

The idea that there is but one unique initiation present under diverse forms and multiple modalities mirrors the act of creation, which is entirely appropriate, for initiation is a "new creation" or a "re-creation." The idea that creation is an eternal act is wonderfully expressed in the words of the *Srimad Bhagavatam* (11.10): 'The atoms of the universe may be counted, but not so my manifestations; for eternally I create innumerable worlds.' The phases of initiation, remarks Guénon, 'reproduce those of the cosmogonic process … the aptitudes or possibilities included in the individual nature are, in themselves, first of all only a *prima materia*, that is, a pure potentiality, where nothing is developed or differentiated … Thereafter, and by virtue of this [spiritual] influence, the spiritual possibilities of the being are no longer the simple potentiality they were before but have become a virtuality ready to be made actual with the various stages of initiatic realization.'[108]

Virtual initiation is symbolically a "second birth" or a "psychic birth": 'The "second birth," understood as corresponding to the first initiation, is … what can be properly called a psychic regeneration, that is to say in the order where the subtle elements of the human being are found … But these phases do not constitute a goal in themselves, for they are still only preparatory to the realisation of possibilities of a higher order, by which is meant the spiritual order in the true sense.'[109] The first birth denotes physical birth into the corporeal state; the second birth, which is equally a "first death" – for as Guénon says, 'new birth necessarily presupposes death to the former state'[110] – denotes a "psychic birth"; the third birth – which is a "second death" – denotes a "spiritual birth," which is represented by the idea of "resurrection."[111]

Summarizing Guénon on Initiation

For Guénon, initiation is the transmission of spiritual influences to a qualified initiate by means of filiation with a traditional organization that is itself orthodox and regular; these spiritual influences give the initiate spiritual illumination sufficient to develop, in conjunction with the active efforts of the initiate's interior work, the possibilities that precisely constitute their qualification. The initiatic transmission must be oral, thereby including the two cosmogonic elements: sound and breath. The initiatic process presents itself under three hierarchical conditions: potential, virtual, and actual. There is one unique initiation which is present and developed under diverse forms and with multiple modalities. What this means is that the transition from virtual to actual involves indefinite changes or "initiations." At the same time these indefinite changes can only be ritually conferred according to a sort of general classification of the stages to be traversed. The final goal of the initiatic work is that the initiate transcend individuality in achieving Deliverance, which is the state of Supreme Identity with the Reality.

The Question of the Christian Sacraments

Guénon's assessment of the Christian sacraments rests on conjectures that, for the sake of simplicity, we can sum up as follows: Christianity is a "religion" and *ipso facto* it is incompatible with initiation; similarly, the sacraments are public or popularist and *as such* are incompatible with initiation. A third argument that is not explicit in Guénon's work but is typically used by "guénonians" to claim that the sacraments cannot be initiatic is the idea that initiation is unique and cannot be bestowed more than once, which, in their minds, argues against the idea that a rite such as the Eucharist, which is enacted periodically, could be initiatic.

***

Debate over Guénon's thesis on Christian initiation has generated a sizable secondary literature.[112] Jean Borella's *Guénonian Esoterism and Christian Mystery* provides, perhaps, the best critical examination. Borella recognizes that there are two kinds of refutation that need to be addressed: a direct refutation that considers the internal logic of the thesis considered, and an indirect refutation where, 'the thesis as such is no longer taken into account, but we consider the subject dealt with, and explaining this subject for itself, we establish *by this means* that the thesis in question is unaware of it in its own and positive reality.'[113] I agree with Borella when he writes:

> Now, for reasons that stem from the very "mathematical" nature of his intelligence, from his distrust of the history of religions, and from the circumstances of his life and times, we are convinced that it was not granted to Guénon to "see" what Christianity was. And so, not having grasped its essence, he did not have the authority to speak

> in such a global and peremptory manner – which does not exclude that, on numerous particular points, he was able to communicate valuable information.[114]

Hence, a direct refutation is insufficient and ineffective. The internal logic of Guénon's thesis on Christianity is essentially sound, according to the parameters that he sets. The problem is that his argument against Christian esoterism is a strawman argument.[115] Guénon rejects the initiatic status for the sacraments because *his* conception of the sacraments does not conform to *his* conception of initiation. Therefore I accept Guénon's definition of initiation but find his understanding of Christianity and the Christian sacraments unsatisfactory. It follows to consider if his thesis applies to the Christian sacraments considered in terms of their "own and positive reality."

Borella shows that an orthodox conception of the sacraments is far more complex than Guénon conceives or, maybe, allows. What is needed, says Borella, is a 'displacement of the problem *into its rightful place*.'[116] This is what he sets out to do in his book. In Part I (*Nature of the Esoteric Perspective*) Borella traces the historical development of the term esoterism and the ideas associated with this. In Part II (*René Guénon and Christianity: A Critical Examination*) Borella challenges Guénon's vision of the history of Christianity and his application of *his* esotericism to it. It is worth observing that Guénon's "argument" about the obscurity of early Christianity is reliant on an untenable historical interpretation and, moreover, proceeds from conclusion to premise. The greater part of Borella's book (chapters 6 to 10) is devoted to expounding the Christian doctrines of the sacraments, initiation and mystery *in and of* themselves. Considered thus these doctrines counter Guénon's description of Christianity as being purely exoteric. In terms of a detailed study of the Christian doctrines one is well served by Borella's book. My principle aim, for what it is worth, is to present an account of Guénon's writings on the Christian sacraments. We will also consider the symbolism of Baptism and the Eucharist to a small extent.

***

Guénon treats the term "exoteric" as synonymous with "religious," envisaging esoterism and exoterism as distinct entities, so that esoterism and religion must also be distinct. Esoterism, he says, 'is not the "interior" aspect of a religion but is essentially something other than religion, even when its base and support are found therein.'[117] Again he remarks that esoterism and initiation have 'nothing whatsoever to do with religion but rather with pure knowledge and "sacred science."'[118] This second statement is not a necessary qualification, as one can see by reference to the previous point about religion acting as a base and support for esoterism; rather Guénon is emphasizing the essentially autonomous and sufficient nature of esoterism considered in and of itself.

The distinction between esoteric and exoteric is also found in Schuon's thought. It is worth considering this because it brings Guénon's vision into focus. Esoterism, says Schuon, 'is not, in its intrinsic reality, a complement or a half; it is so only extrinsically and as it were "accidentally." This means that the word "esoterism" designates not only the total truth inasmuch as it is "colored" by entering a system of partial truth, but also the total truth as such, which is colorless … Thus esoterism as such is metaphysics, to which is necessarily joined an appropriate method of realization.'[119] Equally exoterism 'does not come from esoterism; it comes directly from God. This reminds one of Dante's thesis according to which the Empire comes from God and not from the papacy. "Render unto Caesar the things that are Caesar's, and unto God the things that are God's."'[120]

For Schuon, esoterism, 'in its intrinsic reality,' is not a manifestation of the exoteric or spatiotemporal realm. Insomuch as esoterism does penetrate the exoteric domain it is "colored" by Relativity or by its "appropriate method of realization." 'Thus,' says Schuon, 'it is necessary to distinguish … between an esoterism more or less largely based upon a particular theology and linked to speculations offered to us *de facto* by traditional sources … and another esoterism springing from the truly crucial elements of the religion and also, for that very reason, from the simple nature of things; the two dimensions can be combined, it is true, and most often do combine in fact.'[121] Again: 'the esoterism of a particular religion – of a particular exoterism precisely – tends to adapt itself to this religion and thereby enter into theological, psychological and legalistic meanders foreign to its nature, while preserving in its secret center its authentic and plenary nature, but for which it would not be what it is.'[122] Insomuch as esoterism penetrates this world it is, in a sense, the center of an exoteric manifestation, which is in turn its appropriate method of realization.

For Guénon 'esoterism is not the "interior" aspect of a religion but is essentially something other than religion.' Here Guénon's definition is something like Schuon's esoterism "in its intrinsic reality," the total truth as such. Guénon describes the relationship between esoterism and religion by saying, 'What the spirit is to the body, so truly is esoterism to religious exoterism.'[123] There is a sense whereby the spirit/body relationship might be envisaged as one of interiority and exteriority, but equally so the spirit and the body are separate entities. Schuon would no doubt agree with both of Guénon's remarks, granted that we were referring to esoterism *qua* metaphysics, as distinct from the esoterism of a particular theology. While Schuon recognizes "particular esoterisms" he is primarily interested in "esoterism in its intrinsic reality." Thus he does not tend to talk of manifestations as essentially esoteric or exoteric in nature, rather manifestation *per se* is *a posteriori* evidence of the penetration of the esoteric into the exoteric.

There is a difficulty in distinguishing between these two types of esoterism, which are intrinsically related. Guénon recognizes the difficulty of describing esoterism and exoterism, viewed in terms of their 'most precise sense,' as if these were two separate spatiotemporal manifestations.[124] Nevertheless, he suggests that 'for the sake of convenience we could divide traditional organizations into the "exoteric" and the "esoteric."'[125] He allows this for the purpose of defining the idea of "initiation." Thus, he says, 'it will suffice to understand by "exoteric" those organizations that in certain forms of civilizations are open to all without distinction, and by "esoteric" those organizations reserved for an elite that admits only those possessing a particular "qualification." Only the last are initiatic organizations…'[126]

This is a crucial moment in Guénon's consideration of initiation and in his description of Christianity as being "exoteric." Guénon's description of esoterism suggests a transcendent or "non-human" reality; but then, 'for the sake of convenience,' he uses this term to refer to organizations that are particular spatiotemporal entities. His use of "esoteric" and "exoteric," in reference to organizations, is not out of place; but it is not then consistent with his description of "esoterism." The unfortunate result is the sense of privileging certain organizations with a status that is not properly theirs, at least according to Guénon's description of esoterism. An organization that is reserved for "an elite" – where this term indicates reference to a particular group of "people" – is still a particular spatiotemporal entity, which is to say, it is distinct from metaphysics or esoterism *per se*. Moreover, the description of religious organizations as purely "exoteric" seems to contradict the fact that the body cannot live without the spirit.

Guénon has here redefined "esoteric," within the context of his thesis, as a description of *an organization reserved for a qualified elite*, and "exoteric" as a description of *an organization that is open to all without distinction*. However, his earlier description of esoterism does not justify this. It is not necessarily incorrect to describe an organization reserved for a qualified elite as "esoteric," in the sense that what is reserved is "hidden" – in a spatiotemporal or "human" sense; but this is not the same as saying that this elite is privileged by sole access to the esoteric or "non-human" realm, which in the end is what Guénon implies.

By the equivocal use of the word "esoteric," Guénon rightly or wrongly gives the impression that those organizations which are reserved for a qualified elite are thereby somehow essentially "non-human," while those that are open to all without distinction are somehow cut off from this transcendent element. On the one hand, Guénon states that the nature of being open to all without distinction disqualifies an organization from being esoteric; here the term "esoteric" is used in the sense of "that which is hidden." On the other hand, Guénon claims that organizations that are reserved for a qualified elite are *ipso facto* esoteric, where "esoteric" now indicates a non-human element.

***

According to Guénon, 'initiation in the true sense of the word implies particular "qualifications," and thus cannot be of a religious order.'[127] The element of qualification he has in mind is that of *receptivity*. This is receptivity to "spiritual influences,"[128] which are essentially non-human and supra-individual. He emphasizes that "receptivity" is not a synonym for "passivity,"[129] which he sees as characteristic of religion and particularly mysticism. Guénon:

> What must be taken into account is that, in a religious organization like Catholicism, only the priest actively accomplishes the rites, whereas the lay people participate in them only in a "receptive" [passive] mode; on the contrary, activity in the ritual is always and without any exception an essential element of every initiatic method...[130]

It is doubtful whether many Christians, particularly of a Catholic or Orthodox tradition, would think of their participation in the rites as "passive" given the active rigor of confession. Moreover, to suggest that the lay people only participate passively ignores the volitional, and thus *active*, nature of receiving, properly understood and practiced.

Guénon does allow that there are "qualifications" required for priestly ordination, but claims that, '...in that case it is only a matter of exercising certain particular functions while in [initiation] the "qualifications" are necessary not only for exercising a function in an initiatic organization, but for receiving the initiation itself, which is something completely different.'[131]

The distinction between the qualification to exercise certain functions and the qualification to receive initiation is well made. However, Guénon does not support or justify his allusion that priestly ordination does not in fact require receptivity to spiritual influences. Such a claim inexplicably ignores the Imposition of Hands and passing on of apostolic Grace, which both require the precise receptivity that Guénon argues is necessary for initiation. Certainly these cannot be said to be simply a matter of "qualifying" to perform a function.

For Guénon, the conditions that constitute initiatic qualification are initiative, acceptance, receptivity, and discrimination.[132] The first three conditions are immediately evident in Ordination. However, the question of discrimination is more difficult. Guenon says that initiation requires doctrinal preparation necessary for discrimination. There is no doubt that Ordination requires doctrinal preparation; however, how much this is simply didactic – and then how much of this is actually "understood," which is to say existentially assimilated – might well be questioned. But if profane knowledge was all that was at stake then the same criticism could be levelled at certain people who claim what we might call "guénonian initiation." This is not to deny either initiation but to recognize that what is at issue is something other than bookish learning and profane teaching (as Guénon stresses) and that in both instances it is a question of receptivity to spiritual influences.

Guénon does not deny the existence of spiritual influences in Christianity, recognizing that these are what Christian tradition designates by the "power of the Holy Spirit."[133] However, he is not willing to allow the power of the Holy Spirit the same capacity in the order of religion as spiritual influences have in an "initiatic organization." In the first place he argues that the Holy Spirit, and for that matter all spiritual influences, may intervene in exoteric rites as in initiatic rites, but that the effects produced 'could never be of the same order in the two cases, for otherwise the very distinction between the two corresponding domains would no longer exist.'[134] Here he intends that religious rites may be affected by the Holy Spirit but that because they are religious the effect cannot be initiatic.

To wit: The sacraments are a religious rite. Are the sacraments initiatic? To be initiatic, a rite must involve the transmission of a spiritual influence. There is a transmission of a spiritual influence in the sacraments. Therefore, the sacraments conform to our definition of initiatic. However, *because* the sacraments are religious the effect of this transmission cannot be initiatic.

Guénon further claims that in the order of religion, the "grace" of the Holy Spirit may descend upon a person and thus link him to higher states 'in a certain way,' but it does not grant him entry to them.[135] For Guénon it cannot do this because it is bestowed at the order of religion which, in his opinion, lacks the requisite element of qualification. The element of qualification underpins Guénon's critique of organizations that are open to 'all without distinction.' In Christianity 'as it exists today,' he says,

> …all rites without exception are public; everyone may be present at these rites, even at those rites which would have seemed to demand "restriction," such as the ordination of a priest or the consecration of a bishop, or, with all the more reason, baptism or confirmation. Now this would be inadmissible in the case of rites of initiation, which normally can only be accomplished in the presence of those who have received the same initiation; there is an obvious incompatibility between what is public, on the one hand, and the esoteric or initiatic on the other.[136]

Similarly, he says of the Christian sacrament of baptism that even though it is a "second birth" – a concept he identifies with initiation[137] – it can have nothing in common with an initiation because it is open to all.[138] This argument is strangely at odds with the idea of qualification. Suffice to say something can be "hidden" in public view; an organization may be open to all without sacrificing the quality of its rites and symbols. Here it is not the character of the rite that is in question but the preparation – the *qualification* precisely. In the words of William Blake, 'a fool sees not the same tree that a wise man sees.'

Nevertheless, the idea of preparation highlights the difficulty of the question of infant baptism or paedobaptism. Paedobaptism is a well-known source of contention among the denominations of Christianity. The Roman Catholic Church, to which Guénon is mostly responding, sees paedobaptism as 'an immemorial tradition of the Church.'[139] For the Roman Catholic Church baptism is a sacrament involving the transmission of Grace, which is to say, spiritual influence. This is a view shared by the Eastern Orthodox Church, Orient Orthodoxy and the Assyrian Church of the East. Nevertheless, for Guénon it was a given that, in the earliest stages of Christianity, baptism required a preparation that excluded the possibility of paedobaptism: 'we do at least know that at the very beginning [of Christianity] rigorous precautions surrounded the conferring of baptism, and that those who were to receive it were subject to a long preparation.'[140]

Paedobaptism is usually justified by referral to biblical references such as Acts 16:15, Acts 16:31-33 and 1 Corinthians 1:16. These speak of individuals and their "whole household" being baptized, where "household" is seen to include small children and infants. Moreover, paedobaptists point to the weight of ecclesiastical tradition. However, scholars such as Stanley J. Grenz argue that exegesis 'has netted the conclusion that the inclusion of infants in such baptisms, while possible, is remote.'[141] What we do know is that the earliest extra-biblical directions for baptism occurs in the *Didache* (*c*100) and seems to envisage the baptism of adults, rather than young children, since it requires that the person to be baptized should fast: 'Before the baptism let the baptizer fast, and the baptized, and whoever else can; but you shall order the baptized to fast one or two days before.'[142] Writings of the second and early third century indicate that Christians baptized infants too.[143] As noted, Guénon claims that Christianity became exoteric 'some time before Constantine and the Council of Nicaea' (AD 325). Whether or not paedobaptism was practiced in the first two centuries of Christianity is, in fact, an accidental (and even irrelevant) point in terms of an argument for its metaphysical veracity. Here, as Guénon stresses, the main issue is the lack of preparation, on behalf of the participant, which paedobaptism entails.[144]

The objection was put to Guénon that paedobaptism may be seen to convey a "virtual initiation" of the type that Guénon had himself recognized. As we recall, Guénon defines virtual initiation as 'initiation understood in the strictest possible sense of the word, that is, as an "entering" or a "beginning."'[145] Virtual initiation is a "first initiation," a passage from the profane to the initiatic order.[146] This sounds remarkably similar to the Roman Catholic Church teaching on baptism as being 'the gateway to life in the Spirit (*vitae spiritualis ianua*), and the door which gives access to the other sacraments.'[147] Guénon specifies that 'entering on the path is virtual initiation … [but] following the path is effective initiation.'[148] Certainly this sounds like the teachings of the Roman Catholic Church on paedobaptism. Yet Guénon rejects the idea of infant baptism – indeed, of the sacraments as a whole – as a form of virtual initiation:

> If Christianity still possessed a virtual initiation, as some have envisaged in their objections, and if in consequence those receiving the Christian sacraments, even baptism alone, no longer needed to seek any other form of initiation whatsoever, how could one explain the specifically Christian initiatic organizations that incontestably existed throughout the Middle Ages, and what could have been their raison d'être if their particular rites were in a sense useless repetitions of the ordinary Christianity rites?[149]

Guénon's argument feels unusually forced. His description of initiatic organizations allows for virtual initiation and the subsequent work that constitutes effective initiation. But in assessing the validity of paedobaptism, or even baptism in general, as virtual initiation he treats it as a different beast altogether, his argument based on the idea that it needs no subsequent effective initiation. Within the Roman Catholic Church, and other churches, baptism might be said to be made "effective" in a number of "initiatic rites" such as Confirmation and, even more so, the lifelong participation in the Eucharist. In fact, as Borella observes, the sacraments of Baptism, Confirmation and the Eucharist 'were often conferred at a single time and were considered … to be part of the baptismal rites.'[150]

Guénon then turns his argument on its head when he says that there were, in fact, initiations required after baptism, a point that fits precisely with the idea of baptism as virtual initiation. However, Guénon simply ignores this option and moves to argue that the initiatic organizations of the Middle Ages refute baptism as being virtual initiation by their very existence: 'what could have been their raison d'être if their particular rites were in a sense useless repetitions of the ordinary Christianity rites?' One *might* counter Guénon with the suggestion that baptism, or even the sacraments *per se*, do constitute virtual initiation and that the organizations, which he refers to, then served to offer effective initiation. This counters Guénon's claim as it is presented here. However, neither Guénon nor Christianity could be satisfied with this.

Let us start with Guénon. While Guénon begins in the above passage by appearing to present an argument against baptism as a virtual initiation, his appeal to the 'raison d'être' of those initiatic organizations of the Middle Ages is nothing less than a claim that these organizations offered something "other" – and even greater – than the 'ordinary rites of Christianity.' He denies the sacraments may even be seen as virtual initiation because he takes it that the initiatic organizations of the Middle Ages where self-sufficient, offering both virtual and effective initiations separate and distinct from the sacraments. Yet these organizations were 'specifically Christian' so one should realize that any rites were based upon inherently Christian "realities," such that any rite, no matter how unique in appearance, could only be a means to realize the Christian Truth, which is, in the final analysis, the Realization that Guénon argues to be the aim of initiation.

This returns us to why Christianity could not accept the suggestion that the sacraments be viewed as virtual initiation with the necessity of effective initiation offered by distinct initiatic organizations. To say this would be to attribute greater status to the initiatic organizations, which came from Christianity, than to the religion itself. As often noted, the greater cannot come from the lesser.

So how then might one explain the existence of the initiatic organizations of the Middle Ages? According to Guénon, if they are not something other than Christianity then, effectively, they are redundant. Because he takes it that these organizations were not redundant, he concludes that ordinary Christianity cannot be initiatic. One *might* simply object that they were, in fact, redundant, but a more sympathetic (and, in my opinion, more satisfactory) response would be that they satisfied a particular human margin; that is, they address particular human temperaments and paths. Within the Ecclesia the vocational nature of Ordination presents a "living" or effecting of the spiritual influences transmitted through the sacraments. For the laity this living of the sacraments has been reinforced within the types of initiatic organizations of the Middle Ages that Guénon alludes to. These were, moreover, on the whole craft organizations, that is, vocational. Like Ordination, these do not replace those sacraments that are "essential" for Realization: Baptism and Eucharist. Rather they provide a support in which to engage with the grace bestowed by the sacraments. These frameworks are not *necessary* but rather act as mercies through which God accommodates the diversity of human dispositions.

***

To return to paedobaptism. Guénon claims that 'it is only too clear that a rite conferred upon new-born infants, without any means being employed to determine their qualifications, could not have the character and value of an initiation, even if it were reduced to a mere virtuality.'[151] As noted above, Guénon says that attachment to a regular initiatic organization is sufficient for "virtual initiation" and refers to virtual initiation as an "entering" or a "beginning." Baptism is precisely the entering of Christianity. If one disregards Guénon's *a priori* definition of a religious organization as *ipso facto* not being initiatic, then, according to the conditions by which Guénon defines initiation, Christianity is a regular initiatic organization. As such Baptism, the entering of and attachment to a regular initiatic organization, would *seem* to satisfy Guénon's definition of a virtual initiation. However, the issue is more complex than it may seem.

In the case of paedobaptism the quality of discrimination – one of the four conditions that constitute initiatic qualifications, the others being initiative, acceptance, and receptivity – is taken on by the parent, godparent and Church body *in parentis loci*. This is effectively no different to Guénon's conception, for discrimination in the guénonian sense serves the dual purpose of recognizing the orthodox and regular nature of the initiatic organization and protects against "psychic influences."[152] This discrimination may well be made *in parentis loci*.

As to receptivity, this is according to Guénon "natural aptitude" and forms 'the requisite "qualification" demanded by all initiatic traditions.'[153] To talk of natural aptitude is at one level to talk of the individual, which, it appears, is what Guénon has in mind; however, at a deeper level it is to talk of that which is inherent in the human condition. This, it might well be said, is most unaffected by the processes of birth, individualization and nurture, at the time of infancy. Here Guénon might counter that *this* "receptivity" is nothing more than "passivity," a condition that he denies as having any profitability in initiation.[154] Guénon's problem with passivity in the general context of the Christian rites rests upon a flawed appreciation of the volitional nature of these rites. Guénon directs a similar criticism at what is his idiosyncratic concept of "mysticism." As with his understanding of the Christian rites in general, Guénon's error when conceiving of mysticism was to inexplicably deny the volitional nature of the renunciation of selfhood that underpins mysticism in its deeper sense.

In the case of paedobaptism the volitional aspect goes straight to the heart of the lack of initiative and acceptance on the behalf of the infant. Here the infant *is* passive in the sense that Guénon criticizes. In the case of paedobaptism this criticism carries more weight, for the receptivity of an infant does not entail a volitional element, which is to recognize that it lacks both initiative and acceptance. This is a criticism that is far from unique to Guénon being shared by Christian groups such as Baptists, Churches of Christ, Mennonites, Amish, and most Pentecostals. I do not think that we may reconcile Guénon's vision of initiation with the sacraments as practiced in paedobaptism, at least not on the surface. But this is not to completely reject Guénon's vision nor paedobaptism.

The volitional character evident in mysticism proper and in adult participation in the sacraments entails both initiative and acceptance. This is initiative *towards* and acceptance *of* the submission and negation of one's self in the face of the only Reality. In the final analysis, and from a certain point of view, the state of supreme submission or extinction that is coincident with Realization may be said to be a state of "no submission" because there is no longer any self that need submit.[155] In the case of an infant we are in the presence of the human state which most closely mirrors this lack of self.

Guénon's initiatic qualifications precisely qualify the initiate to receive the transmission of spiritual influences in a manner either virtual or actual, and then made actual by effective integration of said influences. His objection to passivity is that it is a passivity *of* the self. In the case of paedobaptism there is effectively no self,[156] so that the infant's receptivity is that of an empty vessel, precisely the condition that initiative and acceptance aim at. Understood at this deepest level we see that paedobaptism does satisfy the qualifications that Guénon sets out as essential for initiation.

***

Within Christianity initiation is most immediately associated with the rite of Baptism, while Union is associated with the Eucharistic communion. Like Baptism, the Eucharist is understood to entail a 'transmission of spiritual influences to a qualified initiate.' The participant must demonstrate initiative, acceptance, receptivity, and discrimination, even if these are not perfect, which is to say, even if one's participation is "only" at a level that might be considered to be a virtual initiation. Nevertheless, the Eucharist demonstrates the key guénonian criteria to be recognized as an initiatic rite, quite apart from the fact that it is a religious rite.

We have observed that, for Guénon, initiatic transmission must be oral, founded on the cosmogonic elements of sound and breath. These are the twin elements of a sacred language, the initiatic "words." For Guénon, Christianity lacks a sacred language, another argument against the sacraments being initiatic. Here he is quick to distinguish between a sacred language and one that is simply liturgical. It is somewhat astounding that Guénon, who was such a master of symbolism, simply ignores the fact that, for the Christian, the sacred language *par excellence* is not the liturgical languages of Greek and Latin, but the 'Word made flesh.' It is precisely the flesh and blood of the Word that is transmitted orally to the participant in the Eucharist.[158]

As noted above, some guénonians have claimed that the Eucharist cannot be initiatic because it is enacted periodically, which, in their minds argues against it being "unique."[159] Yet, as Guénon explains, there is one unique initiation, present and developed under diverse forms and with multiple modalities, meaning that the transition from virtual to actual may involve indefinite changes or *initiations*. The periodic enactment of the Eucharist is not multiple "eucharists" but the participation in the unique and eternal Eucharist.[160] In the rite of the Eucharist the participant enters into Union with God; they thus enter into the Eternity of God, which embraces all time and existence in total simultaneity (*tota simul*).

This answers another argument against the initiatic status of the Eucharist. Initiation, according to Guénon, requires regular filiation and transmission of spiritual influences. In Sufism this is said to be guaranteed by the sequential chain of spiritual ancestry; likewise, Christianity claims apostolic succession. However, not all Christian denominations accept the doctrine of apostolic succession. Nevertheless, understood at its deepest level the Eucharist is not transmitted sequentially, from priest to initiate; rather, the Eucharist is always transmitted directly by Christ to the participant in the Eternal Now (*in illo tempore*) of the unique Eucharist.

As Borella remarks, in some forms of Christianity Baptism and the Eucharist are not two separate rites but one initiatic mystery. That these have "separated" in many forms of Christianity does not diminish their unity – or, might we say, *the* unity of *the* initiatic Mystery – for the blessing it confers is itself beyond time and space: it is in fact the Centre and the Origin, from which all things originate anew.

1 Guénon, R., 'Christianity and Initiation' in *Insights into Christian Esoterism* (Ghent, NY: Sophia Perennis, 2001), 9.
2 This short biographical introduction to Guénon is drawn almost directly from Harry Oldmeadow's *Traditionalism: Religion in the Light of the Perennial Philosophy* (Colombo: The Sri Lanka Institute of Traditional Studies, 2000).
3 Schuon questioned whether Guénon would have entered Islam as a "way" if he had not settled in an Islamic country, given that he had already received an Islamic initiation in France without practicing the Muslim religion: 'When he accepted the Shdhil initiation, it was thus an initiation that Guénon chose, and not a "way"' (Schuon, F., *René Guénon: Some Observations* [Hillsdale, NY: Sophia Perennis, 2004], 6). Nevertheless, Guénon did settle in a Muslim country and to all intents and purposes conformed to a traditional Muslim life. Schuon, on the other hand, has been criticised precisely because his "material" practice of the Islamic way seemed, to some, to be heterodox (see for example Ringgenberg, P., 'Frithjof Schuon – Paradoxes and Providence,' *Sacred Web* 7 (Vancouver: Sacred Web Publishing, 2001).
4 Guénon, R., *Perspectives on Initiation* (Ghent, NY: Sophia Perennis, 2001), 34, n.6. See Guénon's *Studies in Freemasonry and the Compagnonnage*, and *The Esoterism of Dante*, both (Ghent, NY: Sophia Perennis, 2005).
5 Guénon, *Insights*, 18.
6 On Guénon's usage of these terms see *The Reign of Quantity & The Sign of the Times* (New York: Sophia Perennis et Universalis, 1995), 251-52.
7 Oldmeadow, *Traditionalism*, x.
8 Schuon, *René Guénon*, 49.
9 Perry, Whitall, 'Coomaraswamy: The Man, Myth and History,' *Studies in Comparative Religion 11.3* (1977), 160.
10 Originally published in *Etudes Traditionnelles*, May (1940); recently republished in Patrick Laude, *Prayer without Ceasing: The Way of Invocation in World Religions* (Bloomington, IN: World Wisdom, 2006).
11 Guénon, 'Christianity and Initiation' in *Insights into Christian Esoterism*, 13.
12 From a position of principles, which is far from suggesting that Guénon's conclusions were not rooted in actual spiritual experience.
13 Guénon, 'Christianity and Initiation,' 16-17.
14 Ibid., 15.
15 Ibid., 22.
16 Ibid., 22.

17 His procrustean criticism of "mysticism" (see *Perspectives on Initiation*, 9) is a perfect example of this.
18 Guénon, *Perspectives*, 194.
19 Ibid., 26.
20 Ibid., 27.
21 Ibid., 17.
22 In *Initiation and Spiritual Realization* (123, n.2) Guénon implicitly recognizes that this is what he intends.
23 Guénon, 'Christianity and Initiation,' 15.
24 Guénon, 'Christianity and Initiation,' 15.
25 Sürah 25, *al-furquan*.
26 Nasr, *Islamic Cosmological Doctrines* (London: Thames & Hudson, 1978), 269. Nasr observes that the use of the Aristotelian language of form and matter is here transposed into the spiritual domain to symbolize the inner experiences of the traveller.
27 Guénon, *Perspectives*, 27.
28 Ibid., 18.
29 Ibid., 25-26.
30 Ibid., 20.
31 Ibid., 84.
32 Ibid., 85.
33 Ibid., 123.
34 Ibid., 7.
35 Ibid., 9.
36 Schuon remarks that Guénon had a 'curiously poor regard for Neoplatonism, and … admitted that he had never read Meister Eckhart' (*René Guénon*, 49).
37 Guénon, *Initiation*, 48.
38 Guénon was influenced by both Shankara and Ibn al-'Arabi and even recognized their writings to have a "properly initiatic character" (*Initiation*, 33) so it is highly informative to recognize the parallels of both thought and expression that exist between these two thinkers and Meister Eckhart, as demonstrated in Reza Shah-Kazemi's excellent book, *Paths to Transcendence According to Shankara, Ibn Arabi, and Meister Eckhart* (Bloomington, IN: World Wisdom, 2006).
39 I will not say "undeniably an active path" because obviously certain people do deny this, Guénon for one; nevertheless, one wonders how anyone with any knowledge of "mysticism" could maintain this denial.
40 Guénon, R., *Man and his Becoming* (New Delhi: Oriental Books Reprint, 1981), 34.
41 Guénon, *Perspectives*, 20.
42 Guénon, *Man and his Becoming*, chs.22-24.
43 Guénon, *Perspectives*, 107.
44 Chapter 18 of Guénon's *The Great Triad* discusses the distinction between "True Man" and "Transcendent Man" which are not unrelated here.
45 Guénon, *Initiation*, 47.
46 Ibid., 47.
47 Ibid., 47.

48 Guénon, *Multiple States*, 27.
49 Ibid., 28.
50 Marco Pallis questions this restriction of the word "salvation" to the individual domain noting that while it might be so restricted in the minds of the majority this does not mean that it is so in principle: 'It must be remembered that "salvation" is the term Christians have always used: its authority goes back to Scriptures and to Christ Himself. It would be surprising indeed if it implied any restriction of finality in an absolute sense' ('The Veil of the Temple' in *The Sword of Gnosis*, ed. Needleman, J. [Baltimore: Penguin, 1974], 94).
51 Guénon, *Initiation*, 47.
52 Schuon, *To Have a Centre* (Bloomington, IN: World Wisdom Books, 1990), 39.
53 Schuon, *René Guénon*, 32-37.
54 The reader should see Coomaraswamy's essay 'The One and Only Transmigrant' in *Selected Papers Vol.2 'Metaphysics,'* ed. Roger Lipsey. (New Jersey: Princeton University Press, 1977).
55 Guénon, *Perspectives*, 91.
56 Ibid., 91.
57 Guénon, Letter to Vasile Lovinescu, September 29 (1935).
58 Guénon, *Le Dossier H* (1997), 283.
59 One must be careful not to see Guénon's description of this path as "easier" as being in any way a dismissal or lessening of the path.
60 Guénon, *Perspectives*, 11-12.
61 Ibid., 32 & n.5.
62 Ibid., 22.
63 Ibid., 224.
64 Ibid., 9.
65 Ibid., 93.
66 See Guénon, *Man and his Becoming*, ch.7.
67 Guénon, *Perspectives*, 270.
68 Ibid., 20.
69 Ibid., 271, n.7.
70 Matthew 22:14: 'For many are called, but few are chosen.'
71 Guénon, *Perspectives*, 271.
72 Guénon, *Reign*, 291-304.
73 Guénon, *Perspectives*, 28.
74 Guénon, *Man and his Becoming*, 15.
75 Guénon, *Perspectives*, 25.
76 Ibid., 48.
77 Ibid., 65.
78 Ibid., 60.
79 Ibid., 32.
80 Ibid., 48.
81 Ibid., 48.
82 Noting the onomatopoeia of these names (*shelsheleth*, *silsilah*, *parampara*), which are themselves "chains" of sounds.

83 Guénon, *Perspectives*, 54, 75.
84 Ibid., 53, n.11.
85 Ibid., 54, n.12.
86 Ibid., 127.
87 Ibid., 105, n.2.
88 Guénon, 'Christianity and Initiation,' 14.
89 Guénon, *Perspectives*, 106.
90 Guénon, 'Christianity and Initiation,' 16.
91 Guénon, *Perspectives*, 105.
92 Ibid., 53.
93 Ibid., 75.
94 According to the *Chāndogya Upanishad* 1.1.1-3: The essence of all beings is earth, the essence of earth is water, the essence of water is the plants, the essence of the plants is man, the essence of man is speech, the essence of speech is the *Rg Veda*, the essence of the *Rg Veda* is the *Sāmaveda*, the essence of the *Sāmaveda* is the *Udgīta* (which is *OM*). That *Udgīta* is the best of all essences, the highest, deserving the highest place, the eighth.
95 Guénon refers to both the sound and the *prana* in *Perspectives*, 54.
96 Guénon, *Perspectives*, 65.
97 Ibid., 76.
98 Ibid., 107.
99 Ibid., 174.
100 Ibid., 193.
101 Ibid., 174.
102 Ibid., 25.
103 Ibid., 193.
104 Ibid., 173.
105 Ibid., 65.
106 Ibid., 173.
107 Ibid., 173.
108 Ibid., 26 & 27.
109 Ibid., 174.
110 Guénon, R., *Fundamental Symbols* (Cambridge: Quinta Essentia, 1995), 110.
111 Guénon, *Perspectives*, 174.
112 Criticisms are presented by Frithjof Schuon, *René Guénon: Some Observations*; Jean Borella, *Guenonian Esoterism and Christian Mystery*; Martin Lings, 'Answers to Questions About the Spiritual Master' (Appendix B) in *The Eleventh Hour*; and Marco Pallis, 'The Veil of the Temple: A Study of Christian Initiation' in Jacob Needleman (ed.), *The Sword of Gnosis*, and 'Supplementary Notes on Christian Initiation,' *Sophia* 6:2, 2000; *et al.* Defense is offered by Michel Vâlsan, 'l'initiation chrétienne,'response à Marco Pallis, *Étude Traditionnelles* numbers 389-390, May-August,1965; Florin Mihescu 'Christianity and Initiation,' *Oriens* 1.1, 2004, 'René Guénon, Frithjof Schuon, Vasile Lovinescu and Initiation Parts I, II, & III,' *Oriens* 1.2-4, 2004; Mircea Tamas, 'Initiation and Spiritual Realisation,' *Oriens* 2.5-6, 2005; *et al.* It is worth noting that Ananda Coomaraswamy also considered this area in his

discussion of whether Buddhist ordination could be equated with initiation (see his essay 'Some Pali Words,' s.v. *Dikkhita*).

113 Borella, J., *Guénonian Esoterism and Christian Mystery* (Hillsdale, NY: Sophia Perennis, 2004), 90.
114 Ibid., 90.
115 Schuon likens Guénon's arguments on the Christian sacraments to 'a tilting at windmills' (*René Guénon*, 14).
116 Borella, *Guénonian Esoterism*, 90.
117 Guénon, *Perspectives*, 20.
118 Ibid., 68.
119 Schuon, F., *Survey of Metaphysics and Esoterism* (Bloomington, Indiana: World Wisdom, 2000), 115.
120 Schuon, F., *Spiritual Perspectives and Human Facts* (Middlesex: Perennial Books, 1987), 80.
121 Schuon, *Survey*, 117.
122 Ibid.,117.
123 Guénon, *Perspectives*, 70.
124 Ibid., 50.
125 Ibid., 50.
126 Ibid., 50.
127 Ibid., 69.
128 Ibid., 194.
129 Ibid., 224.
130 Ibid., 99.
131 Ibid., 69, n.5.
132 Ibid., 9.
133 Guénon, 'Christianity and Initiation,' 8.
134 Ibid., 8-9.
135 Guénon, *Perspectives*, 20.
136 Guénon, 'Christianity and Initiation,' 15-16.
137 See Guénon, *Perspectives*, 172; Guénon, 'Christianity and Initiation,' 14-16
138 Guénon, *Perspectives*, 156.
139 *Catechism of the Catholic Church* 1252
140 Guénon, 'Christianity and Initiation,' 15.
141 Grenz, S. J., *Theology for the Community of God* (Grand Rapids, MI: Eerdmans, 2000), 528. Grenz refers to Beasley-Murray, *Baptism in the New Testament*, 306-86.
142 *Didache* 7.6 (tr. Lightfoot).
143 For example, Irenaeus, *Against Hereses* 2.22.4; Origen, *Homilies on Leviticus* 8.3.11; *Commentary on Romans* 5.9; and *Homily on Luke 14.5*; *The Apostolic Tradition of Hippolytus of Rome* 21.4-5. Tertullian argues for delay in baptism until the individual is ready (*On Baptism,* 18), specifically mentioning infant baptism. Borella observes that 'it is the most Platonic of the Fathers who provide the firmest authority in favour of paedobaptism: Clement, Origen, St Ambrose, St Augustine, etc.' (Borella, *Guénonian Esoterism*, 388).
144 Guénon, 'Christianity and Initiation,' 15.

145 Guénon, *Perspectives*, 193.
146 Ibid., 173.
147 *Catechism of the Catholic Church* 1213.
148 Guénon, *Perspectives*, 193.
149 Guénon, 'Christianity and Initiation,' 16.
150 Borella, *Guénonian Esoterism*, 362.
151 Guénon, 'Christianity and Initiation,' 15.
152 Guénon, *Perspectives on Initiation*, 9.
153 Ibid., 22.
154 Ibid., 224.
155 From a certain point of view because, as we find in the Islamic tradition, extinction (*al-fanā*) is also subsistence (*al-baqā*), a truth not unrelated to the Christian doctrine of the resurrection of the flesh.
156 We are a long way here from denying an infant personality, which is an issue of an altogether different level to that which we are discussing.
157 See Guénon, 'Concerning Sacred Languages' in *Insights into Christian Esoterism*.
158 See Schuon, F., 'Communion and Invocation' originally published in *Etudes Traditionnelles*, May (1940); republished in Laudes, P., *Prayer without Ceasing: The Way of Invocation in World Religions* (Bloomington, IN: World Wisdom, 2006).
159 Personal correspondence with the author.
160 I have discussed this in more detail in my 'Towards a Definition of "Initiation,"' *Sacred Web* 23 (2009), 127-137; see also my 'Remarks on the Cosmological Symbolism of the Eucharist,' *Sacred Web* 37 (2016), 25-42.

PART II
The Art of Initiation

Meeting a Philosopher

Joscelyn Godwin

This memoir was sketched in 1988 in order to capture the memory of a crucial encounter and shared with a handful of others who had been present at the same events. Lightly edited and framed, its present purpose is to show that initiation can take forms that owe nothing to institutions, traditions, religions, or orders.

In the Fall of 1968, a year that had already made political and cultural history, I first walked into the American Brahman Bookstore on State Street in Ithaca, New York. It was a shabby store, looking more as if someone was moving out, with a few shelves against the walls filled with books on yoga, mysticism, Zen Buddhism, and other subjects then coming into vogue. At a table two men sat hunched over what appeared to be a horoscope. One of them looked up as I came in: a striking Mediterranean type in his late forties, with a very dark and beady pair of eyes which he fixed on me as he invited me to look around. I found little there to satisfy my unformed appetite for literary odds and ends, but when his companion left, I could not resist asking the proprietor whether he actually believed in astrology. In a strong Brooklyn accent, he informed me that it wasn't a case of believing, but of knowing what astrology was and what it wasn't. I left the store with two books: P. D. Ouspensky's *In Search of the Miraculous,* which looked intriguing, and Paul Brunton's *A Search in Secret India,* which I remembered having read some years ago, and which the proprietor said I would enjoy.

It was a painter friend who had told me about this new bookstore, and I was eager to share her impressions of the astrologer, who called himself Tony.[1] Sitting among the canvases in her Cornell University studio, we agreed that he was someone quite out of the ordinary and worth seeing more of. Apparently he was holding evening classes in the bookstore; so there we went. Before two weeks had passed, I believed in astrology myself, and in much more. Things that I had dabbled with in my teens, like Theosophy, the idea of reincarnation, and C. G. Jung on flying saucers, came flooding back with a new meaning. The Oriental art I had loved from childhood began to reveal its spiritual roots. Most of all, I realized that Tony Damiani was a teacher such as my privileged education had never provided.

Tony remembered this first meeting, too. He indiscreetly told one of my fellow students that when I appeared in the bookstore he said to himself: "Here he is again" – the implication being a link from the past, and not without a certain ambivalence.

I spent January 1969 working on my dissertation in New York City, with Paul Brunton's *The Wisdom of the Overself* for company.[2] This book was regarded with holy awe by the coterie that had formed around Tony's classes, and I was not sure that I should be reading something so advanced, so soon. Actually, it was so consonant with my own needs and convictions that I absorbed it like a sponge and formed a lifelong attachment to its author and his philosophy. I liked the photograph of Brunton that hung in the bookstore: such a handsome and aristocratic profile, with a slightly Indian cast to the features that was entirely appropriate. Later I learned that I had been admiring a photograph of Krishnamurti, and that Brunton was the bald man with the *impériale* beard and the lopsided smile who hung next to him. I forthwith grew a small beard and moustache.

As the winter wore on, I discovered more about Tony. When the evening classes came to an end, he would put on a gray uniform and leave to work fifty miles away on the New York State Thruway, taking tickets on the night shift at the Waterloo exit. With him he would take a box of books, in which I remember seeing the original folio volumes of Thomas Taylor's translations: *The Works of Plato* (1810) and *The Six Books of Proclus, the Platonic Successor, on the Theology of Plato* (1816).

Tony's home was an old farmhouse on Seneca Lake, to which he kindly invited me and my painter friend. There we met his wife, Ella May Damiani, and five of his six sons. The family was all vegetarian. They had lived in Brooklyn until quite recently; Tony had managed a large "occult" bookstore in Manhattan that I was later to know well as Weiser's. Some of the books in the Ithaca bookstore were, in fact, sacrificed from the rich esoteric library that Tony had collected during that period. I wish I had had the sense to buy more of them, although even today Proclus is beyond me.

Tony was a memorable raconteur, and we heard of other things in his past that became the stuff of legend. For some years he had been a longshoreman "to teach my body who's boss." During the same period he had shaved off all his luxurious black hair, having decided that he was too attached to his appearance. He had worked on the New York subway, taking tickets at night – not many of them, for his station was next to a graveyard – and using the time for study and meditation. "I knew I was deeply in when I didn't hear the trains go by," he said. Once he was held up at gunpoint and had quietly handed over the cash before his consciousness registered what had happened. One winter's day, he sat down on a bench in Central Park and began to meditate; hours later, he found himself under six inches of snow.

These were the kind of stories he would tell to us neophytes; but he told them as if they were of another person, far away and aeons ago. What Tony's inner life had been like, I could not begin to imagine, and I still can't.

As time went on, more people were lured by the astrology classes at the bookstore. Tony was a master astrologer, his intuition being at its height when interpreting planetary aspects and the Sabian Symbols. Once he used my horoscope as the example for a class. That analysis has stuck with me ever since as a guide to objective self-knowledge. Yet astrology of this personal type was only a lure, for what Tony wanted us to learn was Philosophy, the "love of wisdom." For that there were classes on Brunton's works, which would branch off into Tony's favorite studies of Neoplatonism, Vedanta, Buddhism, and Jungian psychology. At first I fumbled for reference points in my own discarded Christianity, but mention of that tradition was usually squashed. Many of the classes would end with silent meditation, following a few directives on the unfamiliar task of watching one's own thoughts as they arise. For further instruction we were referred to Paul Brunton's works, especially *The Secret Path* and *The Quest of the Overself.*

Some of us could not get enough of Tony's mind and presence. Not content with dropping into the bookstore most afternoons and sitting in class several evenings a week, we started to go out to his house on Sundays. Ella May would make a lunch that encouraged us to persist in our new vegetarian diet, then everyone would sit around and listen to Tony, until the sun began to set through the big window overlooking Seneca Lake. Not many people helped with the dishwashing, though those who did would discover that Ella May was herself a mystical philosopher, though her life had left her no time, and perhaps no need, for the intellectual path that had seized our imaginations. Many of us were attached to Cornell University or Ithaca College as graduate students, young faculty or staff, but our new teacher spared us none of his disdain for universities, scholarship, academic philosophy, and anyone with a Ph.D. I duly inscribed at the end of my dissertation the Latin words DISSERTATIONE CONFECTA INCIPIT PHILOSOPHIA VERA ("Dissertation finished, true Philosophy begins"), confident that no one would read it carefully enough to query them.[3]

Tony's own higher education – and again, I relate anecdotes, not biography – had begun and ended in the space of a few weeks. While other teenagers were worrying about sports and dating, the young Damiani was tormented by the question: "How do I perceive a world?" Where would one go for an answer to this burning question? A university, naturally, where all wisdom is kept, and in particular to the Department of Philosophy. So Tony enrolled in Freshman Philosophy, I believe at Columbia. After a few lectures, as his problem was no closer to being solved, he went up to the professor and enquired when the class would be taught how we perceive a world. "That's epistemology – not until the third term," muttered the dignitary; and that was enough for Tony. He would find out for himself.

Not long after, Tony saw a display in a bookstore window of Paul Brunton's works, and, curiously attracted, tried reading them. Immediately he found his question being answered, as academic philosophy had never been able to answer it. More than that, he found the epistemological explanation connected to a whole way of life, a whole reason for living. In gratitude to this author, Tony wrote to him in care of the publisher, hoping that his letter might reach Brunton in some Himalayan or jungle retreat. But Brunton happened, just then in 1946, to be in New York City, and there Tony met him. He had found his master, though one who never claimed such a role, describing himself as no guru but "just a student of these matters."[4]

Tony's teaching was a carefully calculated blend of positive and negative touches. I remember going at sunset to find seclusion by an attic window and imagining his great love for me and for all those he was helping streaming across Cayuga Lake. But the love which enabled him to put up with us was for our Overselves, not for our childish egos. Since my ego was currently vested in the music and art of the avant-garde, I found Tony's taste for loud romantic music rather passé, while as far as I could tell, he had no taste at all in art. I wanted to have my own connoisseurship appreciated, but he was certainly not going to play along with that; nor, to my disappointment, was he the slightest bit interested in my own history and personality. Later I understood that a teacher of his kind cannot possibly get involved with the ego-problems of his students, least of all when his teaching has to do precisely with liberation from the ego. As he wrote to me when I was beginning to appreciate his method, "You may have seen that the stance I subscribe to, is to regard the I-bound soul objectively, concretely and not to experience it subjectively. This comes from growth; not books…"[5]

Deep philosophy has seldom worn such casual clothing. Tony's conversation was so familiar and colloquial in style as sometimes to seem crude. His words, easy to understand, were often hard to accept, for they aimed at our pet delusions and felt out every chink in our psychological armor. He was one of those who have taken heaven by storm and wrested the truth from the wreckage of the ego. By no means all of his students, especially the women among them, were moved to emulate him. Everyone tried, or pretended, to read Plotinus or Malkani's *Philosophy of the Self*,[6] but few could keep at it all night.

Obviously there was another side to Tony, or he would have repelled all but the hardy few.

As far as I know, his only relaxation was music, in which his preference was for deep, melancholy, meditative pieces (Bach's and Beethoven's slow movements, Chopin's Nocturnes) or for the exultant monuments of later Romanticism (Wagner, Mahler, Scriabin). He had no enthusiasm for the more objective music of earlier and later periods. In full-blooded Romanticism, perhaps he experienced in pure form the emotional energies that enabled him to keep going, against all obstacles, first as a student and later as a teacher. There was behind his intensity – and it can easily be sensed in his recorded conversations – a reservoir of impersonal compassion for human ignorance such as fuels the efforts of every genuine spiritual teacher. There was never any doubt in our minds that we had known him before, and that, if we did not abandon the Quest, we would meet him again.

It was concern for Tony's family, suffering the continual invasion of their home and feeding dozens every weekend, that gave some of the "questers" the idea of building a separate center for meditation and philosophic study. They put up a large log cabin on part of his land, which was henceforth known as "Wisdom's Goldenrod Limited," or "The Center." The "Limited" was a discreet statement that the core of students had now formed, and that, while others would be welcomed if they wished to take the initiative, no further outreach would be made, no 100-level courses offered, as it were. Several people bought or built houses near to the Center, so that a close community formed. One or two "monks" lived in small rooms in the meditation building and took care of the property which was beautifully landscaped and maintained. A venerable Swedish lady took up residence in her own cabin on the Wisdom's Goldenrod land. It was she who decided that it was inappropriate to call our teacher by a familiar name; Tony found himself promoted to "Anthony," and so he has remained.

The locals on Seneca Lake regarded the Center with some suspicion and had to be reassured that it was not a cult, with all that that implied. Public recognition of a spectacular kind came in 1979.

By then, some of Anthony's early students had gravitated to Tibetan Buddhist circles and visited the Fourteenth Dalai Lama in Dharamsala, India. The exiled leader accepted the invitation to visit Wisdom's Goldenrod during his coming American tour, and to open the new library that had just been built. While it came as no surprise to those who already recognized Anthony's worth, the Dalai Lama's three-day visit did put a stamp of approval on his teaching which few could gainsay.[7] It was also the beginning of Ithaca's development as a center for Tibetan Buddhism: the city now houses the Dalai Lama's official North American Seat.[8]

By the time the Wisdom's Goldenrod Center was built I had left Ithaca and felt little part in that increasingly focused community. Nor – and not for want of trying – could I understand "Astronoesis," the system-of-all-systems that occupied Anthony's mind and those of his closest pupils.[9] My only attraction to Tibetan traditions came through an encounter, in the winter of 1978-79, with the non-institutional Dzogchen. Most of all, I was set on building bridges between the academic and esoteric realms, convinced that each could benefit from the better parts of the other. The academy needed to break through the restrictions of the scientistic mentality, formed in reaction to religious dogma; the New Age that was then appearing as the public face of esotericism needed more rigorous and self-critical methods. (Some hope, I can hear Anthony saying!) Encounters with Brunton himself had already confirmed that I must go my own way, as did Anthony's last "fraternal" communications.

The last time I saw Anthony was in 1984. I had been asked to come and talk to the students about the Traditionalist philosopher René Guénon. My translation of his *Multiple States of Being*[10] had just come out, and they wanted to know about the untranslated works, especially *The Great Triad.*[11] After my presentation, Anthony made some remarks about Guénon's incredible arrogance and that of all the Traditionalists (no matter that my discovery of them had come through him[12]). Talk turned to the future. Anthony's view was very bleak. "Just so long as President Reagan keeps those missiles pointed against Russia" were his words. This was election year, and everyone else I knew was against Reagan and his aggressive policies. I went cold. But then I didn't know that Anthony was already suffering from lung cancer, nor how the 1980s would turn out. He died in October 1984, leaving Wisdom's Goldenrod without anyone remotely resembling a successor. Thus the institution was spared the indignities and rivalries that so often follow the founder's demise.[13]

In the previous year, 1983, Anthony had given a series of talks, or rather conversations, to a circle of students in Sweden. These were gathered, after his death, into a book called *Looking into Mind.*[14] The dialogue form recalls what survives of Socrates' teachings; and the comparison is not a casual one, for the Athenian stonemason and the New York toll-collector had many things in common. Both came of humble backgrounds and began to teach, neglecting their families, because of a sacred sign that left them no alternative. (In Anthony's case, it was a revelation following a heart-attack in 1967.) Both were spellbinding talkers, but neither could or would write his philosophy down. Socrates' discourse was captured by Plato, or so the latter would persuade us; a fragment of Anthony's was recorded, more reliably, on tape. Both had conservative political opinions that disconcerted some of their listeners. Neither was a feminist in the slightest degree. But that is irrelevant to the theme of *Looking into Mind,* which begins with the question of Anthony's boyhood obsession – "how do I perceive a world?" – and ends with the dissolution of that world in the One which is, paradoxically, the only true reality.

Much later I saw the whole enterprise in the context of the spiritual movements that have arisen in Upstate New York. Of these, the Shakers, Mormons, Spiritualists, Adventists, Oneida Perfectionists, and Jane Roberts' "Seth Material" (exactly contemporary with Anthony's work) are the best known among a host of others.[15] But there is, to my mind, a great difference between their religious, social, or at best mystical goals and the independent, philosophical path into which Anthony initiated us.

While some may argue over how to define initiation, I know from this encounter that it can come without a ritual, a degree, or a title. It can seek you out, rather than being sought, but need not enroll you in its club or cult. Fifty years later I see it as a fundamental rearrangement of the soul that removes certain obstacles to its development. The technical details of how it is done are unknown to me, but the consequence is that a door opens, or even just a window, that can never be closed again. From then on, the path is open to solving the particular "equation" with which each of us is born, until all its factors are reduced to zero.[16]

1 The founder and proprietor of the American Brahman Bookstore was actually Tony's eldest son, Stephen Damiani. His memoir clarifies many circumstances that were unclear to me at the time: http://www.wisdomsgoldenrod.com/index.php/about/160-american-brahman-bookstore (accessed 16 October 2017).

2 Paul Brunton, *The Wisdom of the Overself* (New York: Dutton, 1943).

3 No one did: my dissertation on "The Music of Henry Cowell" (Cornell, 1969) was banned from publication until the composer's widow died in 1995. In retrospect, this also seems part of the initiatic process.

4 Letter to the author, 12 May 1970.

5 Letter to the author, circa 1975.

6 Ghanshamdas Rattanmal Malkani, *Philosophy of the Self, or A system of Idealism based upon Advait Vedanta* (Amalner: Indian Institute of Philosophy, 1939).

7 See Judith Horstman, "Wisdom's Goldenrod: Damiani's center for dialogue," *Ithaca Journal,* 3 November 1979, 5.

8 See the website of Ithaca's Namgyal Monastery: http://www.namgyal.org/. Moreover, it is now announced that Paul Brunton's "entire archive will soon be housed and available to read at the Cornell University Kroch Library, Division of Rare and Manuscript Collections."
https://www.goodreads.com/topic/show/18944847-paperback-version-needs-updating. (Both websites accessed 16 October 2017.)

9 Published as Anthony J. Damiani, *Astronoesis: Philosophy's Empirical Context; Astrology's Transcendental Ground* (Burdett, NY: Larson Publications, 2000).

10 René Guénon, *The Multiple States of Being,* tr. Joscelyn Godwin (Burdett: Larson Publications, 1984).

11 Guénon's collected works have since been published in English by Sophia Perennis in Hillsdale, NY.

12 Among his own specially bound copies which I bought in the bookstore were Julius Evola's *Rivolta contro il mondo moderno* (Milan: Bocca, 1951), *La tradizione ermetica* (Bari: Laterza, 1948), and René Guénon's *Initiation et réalisation spirituelle* (Paris: Éditions Traditionnelles, 1952) and *Aperçus sur l'initiation* (Paris: Éditions Traditionnelles, 1953).

13 See the Center's website for its history and current activities: http://www.wisdomsgoldenrod.com/; also the Paul Brunton Philosophic Foundation (http://www.paulbrunton.org/) which grew out of it. (Both accessed 16 October 2017.)

14 Anthony Damiani, *Looking into Mind: How to Recognize Who You Are and How You Know* (Burdett, NY: Larson Publications, 1990). A second book of dialogues followed: Anthony Damiani, *Standing in Your Own Way: Talks on the Nature of the Ego* (Burdett, NY: Larson Publications, 1993).

15 See Joscelyn Godwin, *Upstate Cauldron: Eccentric Spiritual Movements in Early New York State* (Albany: State University of New York Press, 2015), especially 295-301.

16 An allusion to Julius Evola's mathematical metaphor: that each person enters life with a "personal equation" – symbolized in Damiani's system by the natal horoscope – that they are challenged to "solve."

Raised in His Image: The Death and Non-Resurrection of Hiram Abiff in the Life of a Master Mason

Jeffrey S. Kupperman

Initiation, we are told, is the term used by the Romans to indicate admission into one of the mystery cults. Further, the word is derived from the Latin *initia*, which refers to the first principles of a science.[1] It is also defined as meaning "to begin,"[2] and so it is not at all surprising to find themes not only of birth, but of death and resurrection to be common to initiation rituals. In his *Morals and Dogma*, for instance, Albert Pike connects initiation with death and/or rebirth no fewer than seven times.[3] In Freemasonry, the central figure to the story of the candidate's death and resurrection is Hiram Abiff. However, Abiff, much like Christian Rosenkreutz, poses a difficulty in the death and resurrection initiatory narrative because even though Hiram Abiff dies, and the candidate is raised, Hiram Abiff is not.

This essay examines the myth of Hiram Abiff and how it is applied to the life of a Freemason, and especially a Master Mason. It will show how the lessons which are perfected in Hiram Abiff are foreshadowed in the Entered Apprentice and Fellowcraft degrees. These lessons are in turn used to transform the Master Mason into a living image of Hiram Abiff who is resurrected not in the Master Mason degree ritual but *through* the newly raised Master Mason. It will further survey what kind of person Grand Master Abiff was, and so what kind of person a Master Mason should become before finally examining the entire science of the Freemasonic initiatory system in light of Platonic theurgy.

The Death of Hiram Abiff and the Raising of a Master Mason

As recounted in the famous exposé *Duncan's Masonic Ritual and Monitor* published in the mid-19th century, the Masonic legend of Grand Master Hiram Abiff is told to the candidate during his raising to the sublime degree of Master Mason.[4] However, as A.E. Waite recognized, there are elements within a ritual of initiation that cannot be explained through instruction but must be experienced firsthand.[5] As such, before the death of Abiff is described to the candidate it is first experienced through symbolic reenactment.[6]

Hiram's death at the hands of three men working on the construction of Solomon's Temple, described as ruffians, who wanted the Master's Word before they had earned it is brutal, though the candidate's experience of it is somewhat less so. The first ruffian, Jubela, slashes Hiram across the throat, the second, Jubelo, slashes Hiram's breast, and the third, Jubelum, crushes his skull with a setting maul, killing him.[7]

Once Hiram's body is found, and the culprits punished, three attempts are made to raise Hiram's body so it may be transported for proper burial. Three attempts are also made to raise the symbolically slain candidate, who here is still a surrogate for Hiram Abiff. The first two attempts, using the grips of an Entered Apprentice and Fellowcraft, fail. It is only the third grip, that of a Master Mason, which is able to raise up Hiram/the Candidate. The reason the first two grips fail is due to the putrefaction of Hiram's body, who has now been dead for over two weeks; the skin of his hand falls off and the body slips from the grip. The third grip circumvents this and Hiram is successfully raised.

Key to this part of the ritual is that once the candidate is brought to their feet the narrative immediately changes perspectives: before the raising the candidate was referred to and treated as Grand Master Abiff, once raised the candidate is again themselves. That is, while Hiram and symbolically the candidate die, it is only the candidate who is resurrected. Certainly, the body of Hiram is raised up, but the animating spirit is gone.

The candidate has now been raised as a Master Mason and is given the Master's Word, or at least its substitute. But what is the significance of this resurrection of the candidate, but not of Hiram? I will argue that this transforms the newly raised Master Mason into an *eikon*, or living image, of the deceased Hiram Abiff. Although this image is perhaps perfected in the third degree, its creation does not occur all at once at the moment of raising. Instead, the process of becoming like Hiram begins as an Entered Apprentice and continues as a Fellowcraft.

Foreshadowing: The Due Guards and Penalties

Before looking at the nature of the Hiramic *eikon*, this Hiram Abiff made manifest in the Master Mason, there is cause to step back to see how the image is developed in a Freemason. The degree of Master Mason instills the final lessons of Ancient Craft Masonry, the last push of transformation, and so serves to perfect the image of Hiram Abiff. However, this degree is not the first time the candidate is introduced to, even if veiled, Hiramic symbolism.

One of the initial ways the candidate is introduced to this symbolism is through the due guards and penalties associated with each of the three degrees, which are amongst the first things taught to the newly initiated Mason. The due guards are related to the three blows Hiram receives from the ruffians: to the throat, breast, and head. Two of these blows form the basis of the due guards taught in the initiation rituals and which any duly entered, passed, and raised Freemason will recognize. These are called due guards because they bring to mind the symbolic penalties for knowingly violating one's obligations as a Mason and so guard our actions.[8] While the due guards may allude to the blows taken by Hiram, they also directly refer to the oaths made by the ruffians while hiding in the mountains of Israel. Each describes a rather horrific death that they wish they had received to prevent them from killing Hiram.

These declarations connect the due guards of the three degrees to the three blows dealt to Hiram by Jubela, Jubelo, and Jubelum, who proclaim them as befitting their unworthiness for having "consented to the death of so good a man as our Grand Master Hiram Abiff." While the penalties, and corresponding due guards, are taught in their respective degrees it is only now that the candidate learns of their origins. However, even without knowing their origins, these due guards, when properly considered in relation to their corresponding obligations and symbolic penalties, help keep the Mason walking the upright path.

This initiatory foreshadowing is important. Through these ritual elements the candidate is being made, or remade, in the image of Grand Master Abiff. Even before receiving a single blow from one of the ruffians the Entered Apprentice and Fellowcraft have already heard the words of the ruffians after they slayed their own Grand Master. Furthermore, the candidate hears these words coming from their own mouth, as though echoing backwards from the third degree to the first.

Since the due guards and penalties are found in all three of the Masonic degrees we can infer something important: The Masonic initiatory system is not one of three distinct and unrelated degrees but, ultimately, a single and continuous process of three stages. Each stage builds upon the last until a complete *eikon* of Hiram Abiff, the symbolically perfect Freemason, is formed in, and of, the Master Mason.

The Measure of a Mason: The Cardinal Virtues

We are given almost nothing by way of a biography for the Grand Master architect in the third degree ritual, and so most of the details of his life are lost to us. Biblically, he appears only twice, in 1 Kings 7:13-14 and 2 Chronicles 2:13-14. We are told he is from Tyre, a widow's son, and a cunning and skillful worker in metals, stone, wood, dyes, etc.[9] This tells us nothing of his moral nature, so how can we know what kind of person he was? This question must be answered if we are to act in such a way as the Grand Master might have approved, and if we are to be found worthy of receiving the true Master's Word. The third degree once again gives us a clue, for each of the ruffians tells us that Hiram was a good man. Further, we know that he was the kind of man who would die rather than betray his oaths or give something as important as the Master's Word to those who are not worthy. That is, Hiram was a just and upright man.

This implies a profoundly ethical life but does not necessarily give us enough specifics to emulate him. Fortunately, the degree of Entered Apprentice does give us enough information to begin our development of a "Masonic ethic." This takes the form of a description of the four cardinal virtues: temperance, fortitude, prudence, and justice. Unfortunately, the descriptions of these virtues are brief. Where thousands of pages have been written on these subjects only a paragraph is given to each in the degree. Fortunately, we need not limit ourselves to the degree material, which we may take as a starting point on the subject, not the final word.

These virtues, well known to every Mason, have their source in the writings of Plato, most especially the *Republic*, and can be found explicated in the writings of later Platonists such as Iamblichus. The crown of the virtues is prudence, φρονήσεως, which is practical wisdom. It is knowing a subject well enough to be able to give good advice about it and then giving that good advice when necessary. Prudence allows us to know what things are noble so we may live noble lives.[10] Just as a Freemason is not to judge another based on outward trappings but on inward nobility, prudence focuses not on material value but immaterial and spiritual dignity. Prudence is the guide to all human behavior.[11]

Fortitude, ἀνδρείας, is built upon the foundations of prudence. Once one knows what is noble one is to do exactly that, regardless of consequences, good or bad.[12] That is, once the prudent course of action has been determined, do that no matter what.[13] Plato describes this as knowing what is to be feared – things of an eternal and spiritual nature, such as the state of one's soul – and what is not – things of a temporal and impermanent nature, such as popular opinion.[14]

Relying upon fortitude is temperance, σωφροσύνης, literally "sound-mindedness." A temperate person is a master of themselves.[15] This is because through temperance we are able to organize and prioritize our desires, allowing prudence to rule over them and using fortitude to overcome baser desires even though they may be more outwardly attractive than the nobler sorts.[16]

The final virtue is justice, διχαιοσύνης. Plato describes justice as the "residue" of the other virtues because a person can only act justly when the other three virtues are present within them.[17] Justice is the doing of one's own business but also includes feelings of community and working toward its betterment through the improvement of its people as well as oneself and acting justly regardless of consequences.[18] By combining the doing of one's business with feelings of community we must extend our notion of our own business. My neighbor's wellbeing is as much my business as my own. As a Freemason I do not try to only improve myself, but to improve those around me, even if only by example.

Each of these virtues are found in the actions of Hiram presented in the Master Mason degree. According to *Duncan's Masonic Ritual and Monitor*, Hiram, when confronted by Jubela and asked for the Master's Word, responds thus: "It is neither a proper time or place; but be true to your engagement, and I will be true to mine. Wait until the Temple is completed, and then, if you are found worthy and well qualified, you will unquestionably receive the secrets of a Master Mason; but, until then, you cannot."[19]

Here, the Grand Master is displaying prudence and justice. He is prudent because he is giving his expert opinion on a subject over which he is master, that of a Master Mason's secrets. His response includes justice; when at the proper time and place, and if found worthy, then the Master's secrets will be imparted to Jubela. This is justice because it ensures Jubela will get what he deserves, but only once he truly deserves it. If Hiram were to give the secrets to an unworthy person that person could go on to defraud others while posing as a master of the craft, causing harm to the community and to himself through self-deception.

The ruffian's reply is also telling: "This does not satisfy me! Talk not to me of time or place, but give me the secrets of a Master Mason, or I will take your life!"[20] This shows a distinct lack of virtue on the part of Jubela, as well as his brothers who respond similarly. Here Jubela ignores Hiram's prudent advice and reasoning; Jubela is not led by reason but by his desire for knowledge illicit to him. In wanting what he does not deserve and threatening to kill Hiram for justly not giving it to him, he displays a severe lack of justice and a preponderance of its opposite. In all this the ruffians fail to use their fortitude to wait until they have met the requirements to earn the Master's secrets and so lack temperance, for even though Hiram's response is reasonable, he is met with "This does not satisfy me!"; Jubela's desire is stronger than his reason.

Jubela's response not only provides an example of a person devoid of virtue but also allows us to see Hiram's other virtues in action. Hiram displays fortitude in his denial of the Master's Word to the ruffians, even though they threaten to kill him, a threat Hiram has every reason to believe they mean in earnest. This also displays Hiram's temperance. It would be easy to let his desire to live overtake his desire to act justly. However, by knowing what is to be feared and what is not he is able to properly order his own desires, letting them be ruled by reason and prudence.

What kind of man was Hiram Abiff? He was a man of prudence and fortitude, temperance and justice. What's more, Hiram is placed alongside two other important men: King Solomon and Hiram, King of Tyre. The wisdom and justice of Solomon is well known. In Masonic tradition King Hiram is also a person of wisdom, at one time the Grand Master of all Masons, and, much as is often said of Solomon, given to mystical and philosophical leanings.[21] Placed among these great and wise rulers, Hiram Abiff is here described as what Plato referred to as a "philosopher king." In describing such kings, Plato says,

> Unless … either philosophers become kings in our states or those whom we now call our kings and rulers take to the pursuit of philosophy seriously and adequately, and there is a conjunction of these two things, political power and philosophical intelligence, while the motely horde of the natures who at present pursue either apart from the other are compulsorily excluded, there can be no cessation of troubles … for our states, nor … for the human race either.[22]

The role of a philosopher sovereign is precisely what it sounds like: to rule the people through the use of philosophy, especially in the realm of ethics. Such a ruler acts for the good of the people, helping them to improve their own lives and ethical natures, only truly becoming happy and satisfied once the people have achieved their individual and corporate potentials.[23] This role of wise governance is found also in the description of the Worshipful Master, who, like the sun rising in the east, rises to open and govern his lodge.[24] That in late Platonic writing the sun, or its presiding deity, is often used as a sign for the Demiurge, the Craftsman and Great Architect of the Universe, is not a coincidence.

The Master Mason as an *Eikon* of Hiram Abiff

We now have an idea as to what sort of person was Hiram Abiff. This allows us to understand what sort of person, as Freemasons, we are supposed to be. The movement of perspective, from the candidate representing Hiram to becoming himself upon being raised by the officer representing King Solomon, signals this. Hiram is dead and decaying, but the new Master Mason is full of life and has the Master's Word echoing in their ear. That the Freemason is raised by no less than King Solomon, the epitome of wisdom, piety, and sovereignty, signifies the Mason's movement from the life of a laborer as a Fellowcraft to that of one who oversees all such labor. Much as King Solomon himself, and just as Hiram Abiff before him, the Master Mason becomes a philosopher sovereign. Such a Masonic philosopher sovereign is one whose life is always upright and plumb and who is always on the level with those over whom they might have authority.

What is the work of the Master Mason in whom such a living image dwells, what is the purpose of an *eikon*? The Platonist Proclus points us in the right direction in his discussion of ensouled statues in his commentary on Plato's *Parmenides*:

> The ensouled statue, for example, participates by way of impression in the art which turns it on the lathe or polishes it and shapes it in such and such a fashion, while from the universe it has received reflections of vitality which even cause us to say it is ensouled; and as a whole

> it has been made like the god whose statue it is. For a telestic priest who sets up a statue as a likeness of a certain divine order perfects the *symbola* of its identity with reference to that order, acting as does the craftsman when he makes a likeness by looking to its proper model.[25]

An ensouled statue, which can also be described as a divine shrine, becomes an *eikon* of the deity which it represents through its spiritual likeness to that deity.[26] A properly and duly raised Master Mason, living an ethical life after the cardinal virtues and following in the spiritual life of a man so great as Hiram Abiff, does the same. Further, the Mason, like the statue, is not simply living in the likeness of some higher form, but perfects what is within them that partakes of the nature of that higher form. In this work they act to perfect themselves but also move to take an interest in the wellbeing and perfection of others, those whom the Freemason serves as leader.

There must, however, be something beyond this identification with Hiram Abiff. One cannot become the living image of a person who never really lived. Certainly, it is possible Hiram existed; portions of the Bible do have the function of history. But the Hiram presented in Masonic lore is largely a creation of Masonry itself. A Hiram Abiff may have existed, but we have no good reason to believe he was anything like the Masonic Hiram, and *that* is the Hiram after which we're modeling ourselves. Whose living image are we really trying to become? That of the Great Architect of the Universe. To understand this, we must first understand the nature of theurgy and its relationship to Masonic initiation.

Demiurgy: Freemasonic Initiation as Theurgy

Theurgy, θεουργια, means "divine activity." This is ritual activity performed in imitation of the gods or God.[27] The innovator of late Platonic theurgy, Iamblichus, defines it as: "present[ing] a double aspect. On the one hand, it is performed by men... but on the other, it controls divine symbols, and in virtue of them is raised up to union with the higher powers, and directs itself harmoniously in accordance with their dispensation, which enables it quite properly to assume the mantle of the gods."[28]

As such, theurgy may be understood as activities in which humans imitate the actions and behaviors of the divine and, in doing so, raise themselves up to the divine while simultaneously manifesting divine munificence in the world. When we emulate the work of the Great Architect of the Universe and thereby engage in a life pleasing to Him, we are engaging in a kind of theurgy known as demiurgy, the work of a divine being called by Plato the "Demiurgos," a word meaning "Craftsman."[29] Pagan Neoplatonists understood this to be any number of Greek deities, such as Zeus or Helios. In the Christian Platonic writing of Pseudo-Dionysius, however, the Demiurgic figure is well identified with Jesus, especially as Logos.[30] Such connections can be found in other religions as well.[31]

How is Masonic work a form of theurgy? There are several ways in which this can be considered. For instance, even though the dramas within Masonic initiation rituals are not quite imitations of events found in scripture – which is seen by theurgists as being divine in nature and thus a possible source of theurgic activity – scripture is frequently cited and used as a bolster, along with prayer, for the candidate and can be understood as a form of theurgy. Significantly, the three stages of Masonic development found in the three initiation rituals parallel those of Neoplatonic theurgic apotheosis: the purification, elevation, and perfection of the soul.[32]

In traditional theurgy, purification comes through rituals of catharsis and especially the living of an ethical life. The Entered Apprentice learns, and begins to live, the cardinal virtues, and so enters the ethical life. This means the Apprentice is beginning to live in imitation of Hiram Abiff and is beginning to purify their soul. The purification of the candidate is also symbolized by the common gavel as understood in speculative Masonry.[33]

The Legend of the Spiral Staircase, found in the Fellowcraft degree, dramatizes the stage of elevation or illumination. The staircase represents the Fellowcraft's moral self-improvement, mental illumination, and long climb towards the divine realm, "which none but Craftsmen ever saw," symbolized by the stair's top landing.[34] The use and recitation by the candidate of the due guards and penalties in each degree can also be understood as the symbolic slaying of the ruffians who symbolize the lower, impure parts of the candidate's psyche.

The third degree, of course, sees the death of Hiram Abiff and the resurrection of the new Master Mason. This ritually symbolizes the death of the Mason to their old life and their birth into the full life of a Master Mason.[35] In each degree the Mason is shown the working tools of operative masonry and given their symbolic meaning in speculative Freemasonry, with each set of tools being said to "belong" to the grade. In the third degree all the working tools are given to the Master Mason. The trestle board, upon which the master writes the plans for their workers to follow, is one of the Master Mason's tools which is introduced in this degree. The speculative trestle board is the one a Master Mason follows to build their spiritual temple as laid down by the Great Architect of the Universe, traditionally through the medium of the Book of Sacred Law.[36] Significantly, in the third degree ritual, after the murder of Hiram at the hands of the ruffians, the masons working on the Temple are found in disarray because there are no plans upon the trestle board.[37] Here we fully see the Grand Master representing the Great Architect. As the Master Mason is raised in the image of Hiram Abiff, and Hiram is himself an image of the Great Architect, the Master Mason, who has successfully purified and elevated themselves through the use of their working tools, must also be an image of the Great Architect of the Universe and their work an image of His work.

This is the ultimate goal of the Masonic science of initiation, the transformation of the Mason into an image of the divine Craftsman. Such an image is not a static thing; a craftsman builds, and so too does the Freemason. The structures built by such a Mason are not built with bricks of stone but with those of light and grace. The edifice they perfect is not one which houses any human but is humanity itself.

1 Mackey, *Mackey's Revised Encyclopedia of Freemasonry*, 336.
2 Cicero and Cicero, xv.
3 Pike, 353; 373; 386-88; 392; Kupperman, "Towards a Definition of Initiation: Emic and Etic Views of Initiation in the Western Mystery Tradition," 72.
4 Duncan, 122-125.
5 Waite, 394.
6 Duncan, 102-20.
7 Ibid., 103-05.
8 Mackey, *Mackey's Revised Encyclopedia of Freemasonry*, 551; Waite, 295.
9 Mackey, *Mackey's Revised Encyclopedia of Freemasonry*, 455-56.
10 Plato, *Republic* VI.501b-c; Iamblichus, *The Letters* L4.
11 Mackey, *Encyclopedia of Freemasonry*, 595.
12 Iamblichus, *The Letters* L10, fr. 2.
13 C.f. Mackey, *Mackey's Revised Encyclopedia of Freemasonry*, 364.
14 Plato, *Republic* IV.442c1.
15 Ibid., IV.430e.
16 Iamblichus, *The Letters* L3, frs. 3; 4; Mackey, *Encyclopedia of Freemasonry*, 762.
17 Plato, *Republic* IV.433b-c.
18 Ibid., IV.433a-b; Iamblichus, *The Letters* L2, fr. 2; Mackey, *Mackey's Revised Encyclopedia of Freemasonry*, 513.
19 Duncan, 103.
20 Ibid., 104.
21 Mackey, *Mackey's Revised Encyclopedia of Freemasonry*, 459.
22 Plato, *Republic* V.473c-d.
23 Kupperman, *Living Theurgy*, 64-65.
24 Duncan, 15.
25 Johnston, 454.
26 Kupperman, *Living Theurgy*, 208.
27 Ibid., 264.
28 Iamblichus, *De Mysteriis* IV.2, 207.
29 Kupperman, *Living Theurgy*, 23.
30 Kupperman, "The Anagogic Role of Sunthemata in the Sacramental Liturgy of Pseudo-Dionysius," 9; 10-11.
31 Kupperman, *Living Theurgy*, 119.
32 Iamblichus, *De Anima: Text, Translation, and Commentary* VII.35; cf Pseudo-Dionysius CH III.2.165C., EH VI.5.536D.
33 Mackey, *Encyclopedia of Freemasonry*, 601.
34 Ibid., 650-53.
35 Ibid., 601.
36 Ibid., 798.
37 Duncan, 109.

Bibliography

Cicero, Chic, and Sandra Tabatha Cicero. *Self-Initiation into the Golden Dawn Tradition*. Llewellyn Publications, 1995.

Duncan, Malcolm C. *Duncan's Ritual of Freemasonry*. David McKay Company, Inc., 1976.

Iamblichus. *De Anima: Text, Translation, and Commentary*. Society of Biblical Literature, 2002.

– . *De Mysteriis*. Translated by Emma C. Clarke et al., Society of Biblical Literature, 2003.

– . *The Letters*. Society of Biblical Literature, 2009.

Johnston, Sarah Iles. "Animating Statues: A Case Study in Ritual." *Arethusa*, vol. 41, no. 3, 2008, 445–77.

Kupperman, Jeffrey. *Living Theurgy*. Avalonia Books, 2013.

– . *The Anagogic Role of Sunthemata in the Sacramental Liturgy of Pseudo-Dionysius*. Apostolic Johannite Church Conclave, Harrisburg, PA.

– . "Towards a Definition of Initiation: Emic and Etic Views of Initiation in the Western Mystery Tradition." *Esoterica*, vol. VI, 2004, 67–80, http://www.esoteric.msu.edu/VolumeVI/Initiation.htm.

Mackey, Albert. *Encyclopedia of Freemasonry*. Vol. 2, The Masonic History Company, 1921.

– . *Mackey's Revised Encyclopedia of Freemasonry*. Edited by Robert Clegg, vol. 1, The Masonic History Company, 1923.

Pike, Albert. *Morals and Dogma*. L. H. Jenkins, Inc., 1944.

Plato. *Collected Dialogues*. Edited by Edith Hamilton and Huntington Cairns, Princeton University Press, 1980.

Pseudo-Dionysius. *The Works of Dionysius the Areopagite*. Veritatis Splendor Publications, 2013.

Waite, Arthur Edward. *A New Encyclopedia of Freemasonry*. Weathervane Books, 1970.

Contemplation and Ritual Initiation

C. R. Dunning, Jr.

A Pennsylvania Mason attests:

> Because of a contemplative approach, my initiation into Freemasonry was a powerful life-changing experience. The brothers of the lodge and myself all came together on that night with sincerity and open hearts. In the weeks before, they had carefully prepared themselves for their roles. They had also prepared me for mine, advising me to spend time each day in reading, meditation, and prayer. The ritual was beautifully done, the lodge room truly felt like a sanctum, and I experienced the whole thing as an act of brotherly love like nothing I had ever known. Even though the ritual formally ended with the strike of a gavel, in many ways it has never stopped. It set me on a path in which every moment of my life has the potential to reveal more Light, and for me to share more Light with others.[1]

What aspiring new seeker or seasoned ritualist wouldn't hope for such a meaningful experience of their tradition's initiatic possibilities?

In some initiatic societies, contemplative practice in one or more forms is regarded as essential to understanding their customs and tenets. Such inner work is deemed vital to the initiate's self-awareness and to their spiritual, philosophical, and psychological development.

Yet in today's most popular initiatic organizations, a significant percentage of members may be totally unaware of their tradition's contemplative dimension. Even those who are aware can regard it as a relatively unimportant element that attracts a small number of their associates. Because of these unfortunate circumstances, this essay examines the value and means of integrating contemplative practice and the experience of Masonic initiation.[2]

The Significance of Contemplation in Speculative Masonry

The meaning of *contemplation* varies according to source and context. We are using it in its broadest sense of representing states or operations of consciousness believed to help one attain depth of insight and clarity of understanding. Mackey's *Encyclopedia* addresses the meaning of the *contemplative* by identifying the word's origin:

> To contemplate is, literally, to watch and inspect the Temple. The augur, or prophet, among the Romans, having taken his stand on the Capitoline Hill, marked out with his wand the space in the heavens he intended to consult. This space he called the *templum*, the Latin word for a designated or marked-off area. [...] The watching of the templum was called *contemplating*; and hence those who devoted themselves to meditation upon sacred subjects assumed this title. [...] Among the Freemasons, the word *speculative* is used as equivalent to *contemplative*.[3]

In fact, when the English word *contemplation* first appeared (*c*1200) it meant "religious musing."[4] In the term *musing* we see Mackey's connection with *speculation*, both words suggesting an attempt to arrive at new insight or possibility of meaning.

This definition of *contemplation* is evident in its use in Masonic ritual. One of the most influential Masonic lecturers of the 18th century, William Preston, references contemplation more than a dozen times in his *Illustrations of Masonry*. Several of these references have become common elements of Masonic ritual and monitorial instructions across many jurisdictions. The following are two examples emphasizing the rightful place of contemplation in the Craft.

> Knowledge is attained by degrees, and cannot every where [*sic*] be found. Wisdom seeks the secret shade, the lonely cell designed for contemplation. There enthroned she sits, delivering her sacred oracles. There let us seek her, and pursue the real bliss.[5]

> It [Speculative Masonry] leads the contemplative to view with reverence and admiration the glorious works of creation, and inspires them with the most exalted ideas of the perfections of the Divine Creator.[6]

Speculative Masonry's own literature promotes the value of contemplation for unlocking the fullest experience of the tradition. We thus turn our attention to exploring *how* this unlocking can be achieved.

Integrating Contemplative Practice and Initiatic Experience

Every Mason spends some amount of time in contemplation of the tradition's tenets and customs. At the very least, one does so because the ritual itself is designed to focus attention on its symbolic words, actions, and images. In the process, the ritual explains how these things serve as allegories for social and moral development and urges participants to continue seeking insight and understanding. Even outside of ritual, a Mason naturally slips into contemplation during any pause to think about the meaning of the symbols.

Our present concern is not about bringing something new into Masonic experience but rather about intentionally and comprehensively *practising* contemplation to make the most of Masonic initiation. Contemplative practices include ways of opening or focusing awareness, such as mindfulness, reflection, dialogue, and study.[7] As we shall see, all four of these practices connect with and support each other, and they are put to good use in conjunction with initiatic experience.

Four Cornerstones of Initiatic Contemplative Practice

Mindfulness

A California Mason reports:

> At one of my favorite lodges, all the brothers line up in silence outside the door before the opening ceremony and then process into the room in silence. When the Master says we are free from restraint – a time when the candidate is being prepared to enter the room to start the ceremony – all the "sideliners" remain seated in a silent contemplative state. This is not a passive, uninvolved state, but a deeply engaged one. There is an amazing powerful atmosphere created by this – a truly sacred space that envelops the candidate from the moment he enters the lodge room.

This quote illustrates the importance of contemplative practice in establishing an optimal atmosphere during Masonic rites. The most basic of all contemplative practices for anyone in a lodge is simply to be as mentally present as possible, attending to whatever is happening in the moment. This kind of attentiveness has become popularized with the term *mindfulness*, which is the first cornerstone of initiatic contemplative practice.

Mindfulness is enhanced by the practice of silence, but not a detached silence in which one drifts off along unfocused tangents of thoughts and perceptions. Instead, silence facilitates mindfulness when it is part of minimizing internal mental distractions and external environmental distractions. Note that the quote above mentions how every member in attendance has a significant role in the practice of mindfulness, not just those performing the ritual. No matter how much the candidate may be contemplatively engaged, the atmosphere of the room and the qualities of the ritual's performance are determined by the ritualists and audience. By quietly and consistently redirecting their senses and thoughts to the actions and intentions of the ritual, everyone in attendance directly contributes to its proper performance and the desired effects upon the candidate.

When ritual is mindfully rehearsed, ritualists are more likely to remember or discover the implications of even its most subtle elements, including those in their speech and actions and the attitudes that naturally accompany them. In this way, they refine their ability to effectively communicate everything the ritual has to offer. While delivering the initiatic experience, mindful ritualists are apt to perceive the effects of their performance. This empathic awareness inspires ritualists to make helpful adjustments, such as slowing down or changing the loudness of their voices, as well as note particular moments they can revisit with the new initiate after the ritual has concluded. Mindfulness can play a similarly significant role with regard to the awareness of and intentional interaction with subtle energies like chi, prana, or those associated with planets and constellations, the sefirot of the Kabbalah, or the classical elements.[8]

Of course, mindfulness is also vitally important for candidates to practice during ritual initiation. A Mason from Oklahoma recalls:

> A couple of weeks before I received the Master Mason degree, one of my mentors asked what going through the first two degrees was like for me. I told him I had missed some things because I was still thinking about the last thing that happened. I also admitted it was hard not to be wondering about the people and things I couldn't see. So he told me about mindfulness, and suggested I immediately start practicing it from time to time during my usual activities. I got a lot more out of the third degree because of that! I was much more aware of details, like feelings in the brothers' voices. But, since I didn't let myself get lost in those details, didn't try to figure them out at the time, I was able to remember the whole thing much more clearly. The practice of mindfulness stuck with me because of that experience.

This reminds us that, while many aspects of ritual serve to draw and keep the candidate's attention, one can easily be overwhelmed by the quantity and unfamiliarity of the sensory experiences, ideas, and emotions that arise. A lodge could address this issue by informing candidates about how common information overload is during the degrees, and by preparing them to practice mindfulness. Candidates would learn a valuable skill for recognizing and engaging opportunities to apply Masonic teachings in their everyday life.

Reflection

Ritual initiation is best understood as a potentially powerful form of experiential learning. Educational theorist David A. Kolb describes such learning as a "process whereby knowledge is created through the transformation of experience."[9] He suggests all experiential learning includes four elements:[10]

> an actual concrete experience;
> observing and reflecting on the experience;
> forming abstract concepts based on reflections;
> testing the new concepts.

The delivery of an initiatic ritual provides the element of concrete experience, and in Masonry it is designed to do so primarily through the senses of hearing, touch, and sight, each providing its own type of information. By providing this rich experience, and especially when the different types of sensory input complement each other, initiatic ritual effectively anchors its information in the mind. The candidate's observation of these sensory inputs, or mindfulness of them, leads into Kolb's second element, which is fully engaged by the practice of reflection after the experience.

Like mindfulness, reflection – which is the second cornerstone of initiatic contemplative practice – is enhanced by reducing internal and external distractions. One establishes a more meditative atmosphere for contemplative reflection by setting aside time and space to engage the process as deeply as possible. Contemplative reflection may focus on a single part of the ritual, or become a search for recurring elements, or even an attempt to mentally recreate the entire experience from beginning to end. Such reflections include not only what was perceived through the physical senses, but also the candidate's recollection of the thoughts and emotions that arose along the way. For example, during ritual, participants may mindfully note synchronicities between elements of the ritual and other recent experiences in their lives, taking time afterward to more thoroughly explore the implications.

As with mindfulness, the lodge can facilitate the process of reflection for its candidates. Most jurisdictions require candidates to learn a catechism, a series of questions and answers about the ritual, which is indeed a formalized reflective process. There are also lodges, even entire jurisdictions, that require initiates to submit a reflective essay before being allowed to receive the next degree. Not only does this help solidify a candidate's memories of the initiatic experience, but it also provides opportunities to begin forming one's own abstract concepts about it, which is the third element of experiential learning. In Masonry that element is engaged by speculating on possible meanings of one's experience in addition to those suggested during the ritual and catechism.

A Texas Mason reflects:

> When I was learning the questions and answers for my EA degree, one of the brothers would sometimes ask questions like: "What do you remember from that time in the ritual? What were you thinking or feeling then? What do you think that answer means? What might be a completely different way to answer that question? How can you use this in your life?" Questions like those actually became part of Masonry for me, and I've applied them to all the other degrees and installations I've received or performed. By asking those questions of myself and other Masons, I not only learned more about what being a Mason means to me, I have a better understanding of how to perform our rituals than if I had only done the memorization.

In addition to affirming the value of personal reflection, this quote touts its benefits for others. Reflecting on the experience of one's initiations, and on performances one has either witnessed or given, magnifies the technical and empathic benefits previously noted for the practice of mindfulness in rehearsing and delivering ritual.

Dialogue

To examine dialogue as the third cornerstone of initiatic contemplative practice, we must observe that three of the four personal accounts already provided in this essay mention influential discussions that occurred either before or after the initiatic experience. Masonic ritual directly addresses the importance of conversation, as in this statement from the Fellow Craft degree on hearing:

> By it we are enabled to enjoy the pleasures of society, and reciprocally to communicate to each other our thoughts and intentions – our purposes and desires; and thus our reason is rendered capable of exerting its utmost power and energy. The wise and beneficent Author of Nature intended, by the formation of this sense, that we should be social creatures, and receive the greatest and most important part of our knowledge from social intercourse with each other.[11]

Steven Wirth, the founder and executive director of the Centre for Contemplative Dialogue, suggests that, as a contemplative practice, dialogue "develops a consistent ability to relate with and to the collective mind of a group."[12] This understanding sheds light on Masonry's traditional teaching about the cement of brotherly love, "which unites us into one sacred band, or society of friends and brothers, among whom no contention should ever exist, but that noble contention, or rather emulation, of who best can work and best agree."[13]

The aim is not to develop a strict conformity or submission to prevailing ideas and attitudes; rather, because contemplative dialogue includes deep and compassionate listening, it lovingly encourages and nurtures the freedom of participants to authentically express themselves without fear of hostility or derision. Likewise, while contemplative dialogue can include the testing element of experiential learning, it is *not an effort to prove that someone is totally right while someone else is absolutely wrong*. It is instead a "conversation with a center, not sides,"[14] driven by the intention of members to explore things together, each agreeing to open oneself to possibilities not limited by personal habits, assumptions, or judgments.

In some initiatic traditions such dialogue may occur during the ritual experience, but in Speculative Masonry that is typically not the case. Even so, there is much to be gained in the practice of contemplative dialogue by candidates, ritualists, and audience members alike both before and after a Masonic initiation.

For example, prior to the ritual candidates and members of the lodge can come together in dialogue about the motives, intentions, and desired outcomes. Doing so helps candidates attain greater self-awareness and understanding of what they are seeking, why they are seeking it, and what they are willing to sacrifice in the quest. In exchange, lodge members get to reflect on their own initiatic experiences in ways that help the candidates determine whether they are on a suitable path.

Soon after the initiation, a new initiate's practice of reflection can be powerfully facilitated by members engaging the initiate in dialogue about the experience. As with dialogue before the event, new initiates benefit from sharing their own reflections and the meanings they find in them, as well as from listening to seasoned members. The benefits of contemplative dialogue are not limited to candidates, for even the most experienced Masons may come to see their initiatic work through new eyes and hear its words through new ears. Consider this testimony from an Oklahoma Mason:

> In my Masonic experience, one thing that has been very helpful to me is sitting down with a brother or group of brothers to have really good open discussions. That often happens after lodge in some quiet place where we won't be bothered. It also happens at our Scottish Rite reunions

> after a group meditation or during an education session. What's amazing is how guys just start sharing their thoughts about a symbol, and some of us have been students of Freemasonry for most of our lives, but the next thing you know we're all coming to a new insight together. It's a synergistic thing. That not only makes my own Masonic experience richer, but lots of things that have come out of those discussions are still with me when I do ritual work, sometimes right there in my mind while I'm speaking lines related to them. I know that makes me a better ritualist and instructor.

Study

For an earnest recommendation of study as the fourth cornerstone of initiatic contemplative practice, we again turn to Preston:

> Masonry is an art useful and extensive. In every art there is a mystery, which requires a progress of study and application to arrive at any degree of perfection. Without much instruction, and more exercise, no man can be skillful in any art; in like manner, without an assiduous application to the curious subjects treated in the different lectures of Masonry, no person can be sufficiently acquainted with its true value.[15]

Reading may well be the most common activity that comes to mind when speaking of study. For centuries reading has served as the linchpin of most disciplines in both public and private educational institutions. Reading is also a key element in the professional, philosophical, psychological, spiritual, or religious development of many people.

It is therefore not surprising to find an abundance of literature related to Masonry and many jurisdictions providing candidates and new initiates with specific texts for study. In some cases, reading those texts is mandatory. As there are many sources providing recommendations about *which* Masonic works to read, we now turn our attention to *how* contemplative reading is done and how it can enhance an initiatic experience. As with mindfulness, the best environment for contemplative reading is relatively free from distraction, enabling one to attend as fully as possible to the text at hand, as well as one's thoughts and feelings. One slows down in order to check any tendencies like making assumptions about the meanings of words, focusing on only one particular meaning, brushing past phrases that aren't immediately understood, or mentally leaping forward in anticipation of where the text may lead.

A slower, more careful consideration naturally leaves time and mental space for the processes of reflection. One pauses to review what has been read, not only to reflect on it in isolation, but to more completely grasp its place in the context of what came before. This kind of presence with a text becomes a kind of dialogue. There is a recurring inquisitiveness about meaning and direction, almost as if one is repeatedly asking the author for elaboration and a conversing with oneself about possibilities of meaning. One might even bring "others" into this solitary dialogue by consulting a dictionary, thesaurus, encyclopedia, or other texts to gain greater understanding.

These processes can reveal textual implications that the author may or may not have elucidated or even considered. Such an approach encourages critical thinking, increasing the likelihood that one will notice the strengths and weaknesses of logic and rhetoric in the text as well as in one's own interpretations. Furthermore, contemplative reading does not limit itself to strictly rational processes like analysis, comparing and contrasting, and forming associations. One also patiently holds a word, phrase, or sentence at the center of a relatively quiet and clear mental space, allowing for the possibility of intuition or inspiration, perhaps even revelation.

Affirming the value of contemplative study, a Mason from British Columbia writes:

> Before I was initiated, a friend and brother provided a few preparatory things to read. Among the terms that most captured my attention were "mystic tie" and "Masonic light." Already into meditation before becoming a Mason,

> I took first one and then the other into a series of meditations over several days, and also did a bit more reading. The practice was productive, giving me a richer backdrop for the initiatic experience. What I didn't yet know was how the work would pay off. Upon ceremonially being brought to light, there was a sudden coalescence of meaning in which I experienced Masonic light as the mysterious energy that is already the essence of our spiritual connection, or mystic tie, with Deity and each other. It dawned on me that we "sons of light" have committed ourselves, each in our own way, to seeking greater awareness of this truth and to labouring for its greater realization in this world. That epiphany still informs everything I do as a Mason, and most assuredly my presence in the initiation, passing, and raising of others.

This quote provides an example of how contemplative study has proven valuable to a candidate who now brings that value into the ritual work he performs for others. Studies such as this are sometimes prescribed for candidates and new initiates as the standing policy of a lodge or jurisdiction.

In any case, Masonic and related studies can be recommended and encouraged, and the fruits of such studies can be welcomed into fraternal communication so other Masons may take them into their own reflection and join together in dialogue about them.[16] Indeed, the Master Mason's lesson on the beehive teaches that Masons should "be endeavoring to add to the common stock of knowledge and understanding."[17]

Perfecting and Setting the Cornerstones

We note that each of these four cornerstones – mindfulness, reflection, dialogue, and study – is the product of careful labor. Part of that labor is their perfecting, which is to say that each should be refined to make it more beautiful and more effective, and thus more suitable for placement within the contemplative foundation of an individual or body of Masons.

A further aspect of this work is setting the cornerstones so that each is stable and properly oriented, complementing the others and contributing to their collective strength. In Operative Masonry, there is a point at which the perfecting and setting of cornerstones is complete. In Speculative Masonry the work is ever evolving because these cornerstones are practices that not only establish and maintain but also *improve* the wisdom, strength, and beauty of a Masonic edifice. We should consider that in Speculative Masonry, as with Operative Masonry, the execution of such work requires tools, techniques, training, and motive.

The Primary Tool

As these four cornerstones of initiatic contemplative practice depend on proper application of the mind, we can deduce that the primary working tool is consciousness itself. However, as is known by anyone who has attempted any sort of craftwork, it is not enough to possess the necessary tool; one must understand and be skilled in the techniques. Everyone uses their mind in ways that are both instinctive and learned, but many are not well versed or experienced in the techniques of contemplative consciousness.

The Primary Technique

As with the Masonic compass, consciousness may be closed down to a very narrow radius, producing a circle so tight as to be nearly indistinguishable from its focal point. On the other hand, consciousness can be opened to its utmost limit, providing a space large enough for the insertion of various figures or the tracing of numerous lines on different arcs and angles, some parallel, some intersecting. The technique of mental focus, like any other skill, requires training and practice.

The Primary Training

Numerous methods of meditation can be helpful in developing the ability to tune one's focus between the extremes. Even so, none is more fundamental or ubiquitous than silently sitting for the careful and sustained observation of one's own mind. With this practice, we experience how our attention may home in on the smallest detail of the mind's contents, expand to trace the path of ideas and emergence of images, or open to the immeasurable expanse of consciousness extending beyond our ability to comprehend. One experiments and gradually becomes adept finding and holding an optimal focus of attention.

The Primary Motive

As with any form of work, energy is required for the inner training of one's consciousness. The energy involved is not limited to the force applied in executing a task, such as the swing of a gavel, but must first manifest in the internal drive to pick up the gavel and swing it. In other words, the force that executes any kind of intentional work is stirred by the energy of one or more motives.

Masons have different reasons for why they sought initiation. These include desiring self-improvement, belonging to a great institution, respecting tradition, bonding with individuals for whom they have admiration and affection, seeking wisdom, devotion to truth, service to others, and so on. In reflecting on these motives, it is worth noting that all the functional terms – desiring, belonging, respecting, bonding, admiration, affection, seeking, devotion, service – are also used when trying to explain the nature of love. Thus, the primary force moving anyone into Speculative Masonry may be understood as a manifestation of love. Love is the primary motive and guiding force for initiatic contemplative practice.

To be open to this possibility, to deeply investigate it within oneself and embrace and nurture whatever truth may be found there, is to recognize and tap into the channels of power that transform a ceremony of membership into a genuine initiatic experience.

1 The author gratefully acknowledges those who responded to a public query about personal experiences of ritual initiation integrated with contemplative practice. By agreement, all such testimony in this essay remains anonymous. Some editing has been done.

2 Note that we are particularly referencing the Preston/Webb versions of Masonic ritual and monitorial instructions.

3 Mackey, Albert G., *Encyclopedia of Freemasonry*, New Edition, Revised and Enlarged (Chicago: The Masonic History Company, 1946), vol. 1, 241.

4 Harper, Douglas, *Online Etymology Dictionary* (2010-2018). Web:. 15 February 2018.

5 Preston, William, *Illustrations of Masonry*, Photographic Reproduction of the 1867 Edition (New Orleans: Cornerstone Book Publishers, 2016), 18. This language has been adapted to an opening charge used in many jurisdictions, as shown by Sickels, Daniel, *The General Ahiman Rezon and Freemason's Guide* (New York: Masonic Publishing and Manufacturing, 1871), 23.

6 Preston, *Illustrations of Masonry*, 7. For an example of this statement's presence in official monitorial instructions, see *Monitor of the Lodge, Monitorial Instructions in the Three Degrees of Symbolic Masonry, As Exemplified in the Grand Jurisdiction of Texas, A.F. & A.M.* (Waco: Waco Printing, 1982), 45.

7 The author originally wrote about these and other methods of Masonic contemplation in the manuscript *Contemplative Masonry: Basic Applications of Mindfulness, Meditation, and Imagery for the Craft* (2000), anonymously published on MasterMason.com. That text was then incorporated into *Contemplative Masonry: Basic Applications…*, Revised and Expanded Edition (Plano: Stone Guild, 2016). For more on the nature and variety of contemplative practices, see Plante, Thomas G., et al, *Contemplative Practices in Action: Spirituality, Meditation, and Health* (Santa Barbara: ABC-CLIO, 2010). Also see *CMind,* The Center for Contemplative Mind in Society (2000-2015). Web. 15 Feb. 2018.

8 For a comprehensive introduction to subtle energies as they are addressed in different geographical traditions, see Lockhart, Maurine, *The Subtle Energy Body: The Complete Guide* (Rochester: Inner Traditions, 2010).

9 Kolb, David A., *Experiential Learning: Experience as the Source of Learning and Development* (Englewood Cliffs: Prentice-Hall, 1984), 38.

10 Ibid, 21.

11 Sickels, *Ahiman Rezon*, 133-134.

12 Wirth, Steven, "The Path of Contemplative Dialogue: Engaging Collective Awareness," The Centre for Contemplative Dialogue (2012). Web: 15 February 2018, 7.

13 Sickels, 194.

14 Isaacs, William, *Dialogue and the Art of Thinking Together: A Pioneering Approach to Communicating in Business and Life* (New York: Random House, 1999), 17.

15 Preston, 19.

16 For more on the integration of contemplative techniques with educational experiences, see Komjathy, Louis, *Introducing Contemplative Studies* (Hoboken: John Wiley & Sons, 2018).

17 Sickels, 211.

Initiation in the Western Esoteric Tradition: A Personal Account

Herbie Brennan

"The Society of the Inner Light's prime purpose is to maintain and expand the bridge that exists between outer life in the world and spiritual forces upon the inner planes. It was founded in 1924 by Dion Fortune – Violet Mary Firth – at the instance of an inner plane Master. That is to say by a spiritual being who, having experienced and learned the lessons of life on Earth, has no further need physically to incarnate and has undertaken to help humanity progress by giving spiritual insights to those who are attuned to receive them. The general aim of this is the balanced earthing of spiritual principles under the general headings of Power, Love and Wisdom."

From the Society's current statement of its aims and work at http://www.innerlight.org.uk/index.html

On the evening of 5 July 1964, I was in London, facing a 7:30 pm deadline and utterly unable to find a taxi. Even when I stumbled across a whole rank of them, the first two declined to take me anywhere and the third looked blank when I asked for Steele's Road. "Chalk Farm," I told him tersely. He sucked his teeth. "That's a long way out, gov." I'd had enough of taxi drivers by this time. My experience was that an Irish accent encouraged them to find the longest way around while reciting their life stories. I settled myself firmly in the backseat and said, "Can you make it by 7:30?"

In fact he made it by 7:25 and I rang the bell of No. 38 with minutes to spare. A stern, unsmiling man opened the door. He seemed to know who I was because he gestured me to come in without asking my name, then led me to a small room somewhere in the bowels of the house. "You've brought your robe?" The robe was something I'd purchased mail order from an ecclesiastical supplies store in London.

In the catalogue it was identified as a single-breasted cassock, half lined, a neck-to-feet black garment that buttoned all the way down the front. I was disappointed to find it did not have a hood. I patted my briefcase. "In here."

"Please robe," said the unsmiling man. "Then I would suggest you meditate until someone comes to collect you." He closed the door silently behind him.

I put on the cassock – the buttons were fiddly and took forever – with the black socks and soft black slippers specified in the Society's instructions. Then I sat down on the straight-backed wooden chair, the only piece of furniture in the room, closed my eyes and worried. The reality of my situation fell on me like an avalanche. I was alone in a strange city, in a strange house, filled with strange people who engaged in weird rites and believed in magic. I realised suddenly how little I actually knew about the Society of the Inner Light. My nerves were stretched to breaking point by the time the door opened again.

A tiny woman in her seventies came in wearing a black robe and an Egyptian nemyss with a stylish golden cobra rising from the forehead. She had the sort of lines on her face that come from laughter. She had dark, twinkling eyes. "Hello," she said. "I'm Margaret Lumley Brown."

Apart from listings of the few books and articles she wrote and some surviving correspondence with Arthur Conan Doyle, the little that's known about Margaret Lumley Brown's early life tends to be anecdotal. But what anecdotes. Her eccentric father taught her to read using only books published in the 18th century and introduced her to Ovid – at the age of 8 – by way of a Latin grammar and a dictionary dated 1715. In the 1920s, she worked with Marie Stopes, campaigning for sex education and birth control. Then, out of nowhere, she began to develop fearsome and peculiar psychical abilities.

It started with a weird mental version of the moving glass, which I'd witnessed at a spiritualist séance. A letter of the alphabet would slide into her consciousness then, when it had clearly impinged, fade away to be replaced by another. In this way words, then whole sentences would be spelled out. The messages themselves were of no great importance, almost as if someone was chatting to her. Margaret mentally answered back, but after three nights she was losing sleep, increasingly confused and occasionally subject to threatening hallucinations. She was living on London's Edgware Road at the time and discovered there was a black cloud enveloping her house.

Her situation grew steadily worse. At one point it seemed as if a multitude of voices entered her head, all seeking her attention, all speaking at once. When she looked out of a window, misshapen figures crawled among the debris of former houses. There is sometimes a very narrow dividing line between psychism and madness and Margaret seemed close to crossing it. She found herself taken over, in the way that mediums are possessed by spirits of the dead. But the entity, a male, proved calming and protective. Poltergeist manifestations broke out. Flying discs of light appeared in her room, candle-like flames flickered at random, then went out. Black shapes manifested, like medieval woodcuts of demons with their faces grotesquely sunk into their bloated bodies. She was terrified and paralyzed.

At this point a new voice spoke to her, telling her not to be frightened because fear "only makes them worse." The creatures were, he said, devils and the haunting was associated with the room she was in. Margaret had a brief out-of-body experience in which she found herself floating near the ceiling, then returned to normal consciousness and fled.

Unfortunately she was in no position to leave the house altogether, so she endured days of illness while the phenomena continued. These included foul smells, apparitions, voices, glowing letters traced on a window blind and the spontaneous movement of objects like a rug and a dressing gown. Eventually the family called in an occultist and clairvoyant, who told them their home stood on the site of a much older building that had once housed an opium den, and this was where the current manifestations were coming from. What had caused the trouble, he said, was the interaction between the conditions existing in the house and Margaret's rare psychic qualities. Powerful and unusual spirits had been trying to communicate with her. He advised her to leave the building as soon as possible, otherwise the experiences might kill her. The occultist in question was Bishop Robert King of the Liberal Catholic Church.

I don't know if Margaret did leave the house at this point, but she clearly survived the trauma. More to the point, she got her psychism under control. And extraordinary psychism it was. Like William Blake, she had constant visions of nature spirits, elementals and even, to judge from her sketch pad, towering angelic figures. She developed a particular affinity for the fairy kingdom. A mutual friend once described how she would gently brush the little creatures off cushions so visitors could sit down. She made contact with what she believed to be the spirit of Oscar Wilde, who acted as her guide and mentor for a time. In the mid-1940s, she joined the Fraternity of the Inner Light. For a few years she maintained a low profile but following Dion Fortune's death in 1946 she moved abruptly into a central position within the organisation, taking over from the founder to channel those inner plane communications on which the spiritual life of the Society depended. Although virtually unknown outside the fraternity, she was recognised within it as the finest medium and psychic of the century. She eventually became known as a "cosmic mediator," a term that described someone capable of contacting the very highest of spiritual entities. Although I had no idea of her background or position at the time, this was the woman who had been patiently training me in magico-spiritual techniques for the past four years, my supervisor on the SIL training course.

"You're not wearing a watch, are you?" she asked me, then took my wrist and looked for herself. "You'll have to take that off – it'll be quite safe here. No other jewellery? They don't like jewellery on the Inner Planes. You can keep your wedding ring, but that's all. They'll spot watches and pendants like a shot. They're very eagle-eyed on the Inner Planes."

"Just the watch," I said and took it off.

Margaret looked me up and down like a sergeant-major inspecting troops, then did a strange thing. "It's your birthday, isn't it?" she said. I nodded. I was 24 that day, the youngest age at which the Society would accept an initiate. Margaret leaned forward and kissed me. She was so tiny she had to stand on tip-toe to do it. "Happy birthday," she said, smiling.

She produced a length of black cloth. "Are you ready to go? You're not nervous, are you? There's no need to be nervous – I know you're going to be fine. I have to blindfold you now, so you'll have to scrunch down: you're far too tall for me to reach." I scrunched down like a lamb, wondering how my wife would take it when I told her I'd fallen in love with a little old lady.

Had I been seeking admission to the original Golden Dawn, I would have been required to swear a ritual oath of secrecy under penalty of expulsion and voluntary submission to "a deadly and hostile current of will set in motion by the chiefs of the Order by which I should fall slain and paralyzed without visible weapon as if slain by the lightning flash." The Inner Light was less dramatic. Although members valued their privacy – and still do – you were required only to exercise discrimination in deciding with whom you would share details of the Society's activities, although any papers you might receive containing Inner Plane communications were to be kept under lock and key and returned to the Society if you ever resigned. I'm not sure whether discrimination would reasonably stretch to sharing my initiatory experiences in published form, but that is, in any case, an academic question since now, more than fifty years later, my memory contains only impressionistic glimpses of what happened.

Margaret led me from the waiting room to the door of the Lodge room. I recall the feel of her hand, small as that of a child, in mine. She knocked and was answered by a muffled response. I heard the sound of the door opening and felt the most extraordinary sensation as Margaret gently nudged me over the threshold. It was similar in many ways to that feeling you get when you walk from a cold street into a heated building, as if you have met with an invisible wall. There was an invisible wall across the threshold of the Lodge room, but not a wall of heat. It was comprised in equal parts of incense smoke and something I can only reasonably call energy. I have experienced the same phenomenon again since then, but never to quite the degree I experienced it then, perhaps because being blindfold sharpens the senses.

Being blindfold also forces you to visualise when you are involved in an initiatory ceremony. Dramatic pictures certainly swam into my mind as I was ritually challenged by the guardian of the threshold and gave the ritual response prompted by whispers from Margaret. It was all very Masonic, similar in some respects to what my father must have gone through when he joined the Craft. The guardian (presumably) stood aside and Margaret assisted me into the room. Underfoot felt like carpet, but my mental impression was of a vast outdoors.

After that, the experience becomes even more impressionistic. I felt Margaret let go of my elbow so that I stood vulnerable and alone. There might have been more ritual questions and responses, but I can scarcely remember. There was certainly a homily from the magus, who had, I noted with relief, a reassuringly Northern Irish accent. Then the blindfold came off and I was in a room that was both surprisingly small and surprisingly large – small by comparison with the vast open spaces of my visualisation, large by any other measure, since it readily contained more than twenty people, an altar, twin pillars and a magus throne. Margaret reappeared to lead me around the assembled company in a ritual procession of formal introduction. I was grinning smugly by this stage. I was one of them now. I joined in my first group pathworking through a vivid desert landscape…

Everyone who attended the rite, myself included, was required to submit a report of what they saw, heard and experienced. (I wrote mine before I left London.) All but one were simply held in Society archives. The exception, a description by the Society's Cosmic Mediator of Inner Plane activity during the ceremony, was circulated among the members of the Society. When I received my copy, I discovered Margaret had been psychically aware of an unusual intruder. One of Blavatsky's spirit guides, the Master M, had turned up to witness my initiation.

Initiations, Light and Dark

Mark Booth

This old Chinese story was chosen as one of his favourites by the great Argentinian writer, Jorge Luis Borges. It has mystic power.

It was the Hour of the Rat and the Emperor was dreaming. He dreamt that it was a beautiful night – as indeed it was – and that he had decided to go for a walk. He slipped out of the palace and began walking in the gardens beneath pleasantly scented trees.

Suddenly, he felt a weight on his feet. He looked down and was not as alarmed as he would have been if he had been awake to see a great green dragon prostrating itself at his feet, its head resting on his slippers. Was that tears on his slippers? Or was the dragon slavering all over them?

"Please help me, your Highness," said the dragon. "I have come to ask a boon. The stars have told me that your prime minister will behead me before midnight tomorrow."

The Emperor was flattered that this great dragon should come to him for help, and he promised to do all he could. He awoke at dawn and summoned the prime minister. He did not want to command the minister not to behead a dragon – by any standards that would be an odd request and awkward to explain. Besides, the Emperor had come to depend on his prime minister and was perhaps a little afraid of him. So instead he gave the minister a long list of administrative tasks, including some very tedious stock-taking that he knew would keep him busy indoors and take up the whole day, and he also invited the prime minister to join him for a game of chess in the evening.

The prime minister was already very tired out by his busy and very boring day when he arrived to play chess, and the Emperor played an unusually cautious game to spin it out. He smiled to himself when at about eleven o'clock, the minister nodded off. The minutes ticked away and midnight approached. Nearly there … What could possibly go wrong now?

Moments before midnight, two soldiers burst into the Emperor's room carrying the bloodied head of a giant green dragon, which they said had just fallen out of the sky and landed in the palace gardens.

The commotion awoke the prime minister. "That's funny," he said. "I've just been dreaming that I was beheading a dragon like that."

***

This story pleases us, as it pleased Borges, because of 'the shock of recognition'. Although it doesn't read like an account of something that actually happened, ie a historical event, the story reminds us that we too have experienced dreams which seem to give us access to a higher reality, a reality that, perhaps, even influences the world we experience while awake.

As I show in my book *The Sacred History*, people have always recorded dreams like these. And what we may call 'veridical dreams' have sometimes changed the course of history in dramatic and surprising ways.

In the Hebrew Scriptures, or Old Testament, Joseph was a dreamer and an interpreter of dreams, and the fortunes of his people depended on this. Healing dreams were often recorded at the shrine of the Greek healing god, Asclepius, sited at Epidaurus. There the sick would go and stay overnight for the 'healing sleep'. In one case, onlookers saw a snake lick the toe of a sleeping man. In the morning, when he awoke, he found he was cured and it turned out he'd had a dream of his toe being dressed in bandages by a godlike young man. In esoteric circles, the passage in chapter 3 of the Gospel of John, which recounts Nicodemus coming to Jesus *by night*, means hermeneutically that they were both initiates who met when asleep and out of their fleshly bodies. Similarly, by following a dream in which Jesus Christ appeared to him, Emperor Constantine decided to lead his army into a decisive battle that would unite the Roman Empire. A young girl called Genevieve would become the patron saint of Paris after a dream showing her that Attila the Hun would not press home his advantage and take the city by force. Because she was able to convince the people of Paris of the reality of her dream, they did not capitulate and the city was saved. Even the Holy Roman Emperor Charlemagne, founder of Europe, received instructions for his world-changing deeds in dreams.

Ansgar was a ninth-century mystic known as the Apostle of the North because of his mission to Northern Europe. He was guided through his life by a series of visions. As a young man, he entered a monastery, but the chill of the monastery soon made him cold to the marrow. When he heard news of the death of the Emperor Charlemagne, Ansgar felt fear and horror, which he tried to combat with prayers, fasts and spiritual exercises. On the Feast of Pentecost, he had an intimation that he would die very soon, and this pleased him. He fell sick, his sickness increased day by day, and he felt his body grow colder.

He was praying in front of the altar when the ground started to shake:

I heard a voice say "*Arise!*" and I felt my spirit suddenly ripped from my body. A figure with a shining face and bright apparel came to greet me, and began to lead me up. I looked down to see my body lying there on the stone floor, pale and dead to the world.

We walked in silence across a broad flat plain towards a glow on the horizon, which I understood to be the rising of the summer sun. We continued through a wide valley.

At once, the way ahead grew dark and full of shadows. The darkness thickened until I could see nothing but the shining of my guide's robes ahead of me, and then he disappeared, leaving me alone. I heard many people crying out in misery, and mixed with these lamentations, I heard crude laughter. Dark spirits crowded in around me, monkeys with flaming eyes.

"This one is ours!" I heard one say.

I thought I was lost. I struck out. Two came towards me with bodies hairy like thistles and holding ploughshares. These they stuck into me, on the head and feet, embedding the cold blades deep in my flesh and twisting them so that my insides were full of a freezing pain.

I cried out to God for help and looked around. I saw a light in the sky, a star shining in the black. It grew brighter, bigger, and came quickly towards me. I had cried out and been answered as the guardian angel always answers thoughts and reflections, and the demons vanished, and the cold went away.

"Is this Hell?" I asked.

"Not Hell as you understand it," replied the angel.

We turned right, towards the rising of the winter sun. We travelled north towards two mountains. There was a cavern between these two mountains, and when I drew near I could see a narrow bridge crossing over. Underneath bubbled and crackled a sea of fire, reeking of sulphur. Heads poked above the surface and some had nails sticking out of their heads or through their tongues or in their eyes. I saw souls in the form of weeping blackbirds trying to escape the flames but falling back into them again and again.

As I set foot on the bridge I saw it was a thousand paces long. It was narrow, in places so narrow it was sharp and there were, besides, thorns embedded in it that pierced my feet. I saw the forms of men in front of me on the bridge. Some fell with screams into the river below, while my angel led me forward by the hand.

I understood then that our deeds and thoughts are not scattered to the wind, and in the end they will be shown to us by good angels or by the enemy.

On the far side of the bridge there was a wall that seemed so high it was impossible to glimpse the top. It was completely smooth and without marks or openings. There were no doors or windows – or any means of climbing. Yet suddenly – and I don't know how – we were at the top, walking along the wall, and stretched out below us was a vast, sunny plain, with a great multitude of people dressed in white, carrying crosses, banners, candles and golden palm leaves.

My angel guide touched me on the shoulder, but I didn't want to stop looking. I could smell flowers, and the people were singing a beautiful song. I wanted to go down and join them.

They all faced east, I saw. Some bowed, others lifted their heads and stretched out their arms. Then I saw the twenty-four Elders also gazing eastwards and singing praises to God.

Everything was filled with a dazzling luminosity. I could not see the source of this light, but I believed Him to be there, surrounding, sustaining and protecting everything.

"You have to go back!"

I felt a sweet sense of delight run through me and in my heart. In that instant I could hardly tell if I was alive or dead and living in eternity.

I did not want to go back, I did not want to live, but suddenly I shrank back down inside this foul, disgusting body. I looked around and saw I was undergoing funeral rites. I sat up on the bier and my brothers fell back in amazement. They thought I had been dead for three days. They were glad to see me alive…

But tears streamed down his face. Ansgar continued to lead a solitary life, eating only bread and water. He prayed continually. His cell was by the banks of the river and often he would plunge into it saying prayers or singing psalms. Sometimes he went in up to his neck, and he would never take off his cold, wet clothes when he emerged. Sometimes in winter he had to break the ice to get in the river and would stand in the water surrounded by shards of it.

"We are amazed, brother, that you are able to endure that cold," the other brothers said to him sometimes.

"I have seen a greater cold," he would reply.

Such visionary dreams did not end with the Middle Ages. A beautiful, numinous painting, *The Dream of St Ursula* by Carpaccio, shows the saint sleeping in bed and an angel approaching the foot of it. We understand that the sleeping woman is dreaming of the angel. In the 16th century, the proto-Rosicrucian magus Paracelsus boasted that he could appear in other people's dreams at will. In the 20th century, Carl Gustav Jung kept detailed accounts of his dreams, so he was able to confirm that things he'd been shown while dreaming later checked out in waking life. I used to work with a healer called Joseph Corvo, and I know that on at least one occasion he appeared in a dream to a patient who was very sick, and in her dream he called her back into life.

In the esoteric and mystical view of the cosmos, human spirits have been dipped into matter and enclosed in material bodies, cutting them off from other spirits. But while we are asleep our spirit may emerge temporarily and partially from our body, and it is then that we dream. In dreams we may to some extent communicate with other spiritual beings, be they angels, spirits of the dead, or spirits of living humans – as happened in the case of Nicodemus or Joseph Corvo – perhaps even spirits of animals (as we shall shortly see).

Of course, dreams usually give us quite jumbled, even nonsensical impressions of the spiritual realms. But occasionally spiritual beings come to us with an important message, something they clearly intend us to understand and take notice of. These dreams are compelling.

While we may not understand these dreams completely, they often seem to be an expression of the care that the cosmos has for us, as this beautiful Native American Indian story shows:

An Iroquois warrior called Nekumonta married Shanewis. He was a great hunter and warrior and she was beautiful, and they were much in love. But shortly after they married the snows came and kept coming. It was an exceptionally severe winter, and soon food was in short supply and members of the tribe began to fall sick. Nekumonta watched as one by one, his father, mother, brothers and sisters and his wider family in the village all fell sick and died. Was the whole tribe going to be wiped out?

Then Shanewis began to feel ill. Nekumonta cried out to the heavens in pain. He prayed to the Great Spirit, asking for help. Where could he find the herbs to save his beautiful wife, whom he loved so much?

Covering her with many layers of furs and placing water within easy reach, he set off in the snow. He climbed over huge drifts and tried to find places where the snow was less deep, so that he could dig for herbs. He found nothing. That night he fell asleep exhausted and woke to find a rabbit looking at him.

He said "Tell me where to find the herbs planted by the Great Spirit that will heal my wife." But the rabbit just twitched its nose, turned and hopped off amongst the trees.

Nekumonta prayed again to the Great Spirit and pressed on into the depths of the forest. On the second day he found the cave of a bear. He asked the bear the same question, but it turned its back on him and resumed hibernating.

On the third day Nekumonta saw no animals. Perhaps, he thought to himself miserably, I don't know how to pray? He kept walking and digging until finally he collapsed at the foot of a great rock.

He had a dream. All the animals, the birds, the trees, the plants were gathering around him. They remembered that he had always treated them with respect. He had never killed them except for food and clothing. He had never killed a deer, for instance, without asking permission from the spirit of the deer, and he saw and loved the sacred life running through the trees and plants as well. Now all prayed with him and for him and helped carry his prayers up to the Great Spirit.

Then his dream changed. He saw his wife, still lying sick. She was murmuring. Now she was singing a beautiful song and the sound rippled outwards. Nekumonta realized that what he was hearing was the sound of a spring. He listened more intently and could hear the words. The spirit of the water was saying "Find me, and beautiful Shanewis shall live."

Nekumonta awoke. He stood up and looked around. No spring. He went back to where he had been lying and began to dig. It was hard because the ground was frozen, and he also had to pull out rocks and old roots. He was just about to give up when he saw a glint in the bottom of the hole, and a small spring of water started to bubble upwards.

It grew stronger and soon the hole was full. Nekumonta jumped up with joy and drank from the hole and immediately felt his strength renewed. He ran back to his village, carefully carrying some water. He found his wife lying still, her eyes closed. He poured a few drops through her lips. She opened her eyes. They were as beautiful as he remembered.

What if we could gain access to this kind of wisdom at will? This has always been the promise of esoteric initiation.

In my book *The Secret History of the World*, I gathered evidence to show that there have always been secret societies dedicated to helping initiates achieve higher consciousness. I have written more recently about how initiation rituals aim to coax the soul partially out of the body – or even have it ripped out the body, as happened to Ansgar. When the soul is partly out of the body, as sometimes happens in dreams or when the spirit leaves the body entirely after death, angels and other spiritual beings can communicate freely with it, spirit to spirit.

The difference between the experience of these higher realities in dreams and when it happens during initiation is that in the latter the candidate experiences such things in a state closer to waking consciousness, as opposed to dreaming consciousness.

Secret sanctuaries where members of the elite were initiated into great secrets were well-known in the ancient world. Everyone knew where they were, for instance the famous initiation school at Eleusis near Athens. But only a chosen few knew its deeper secrets – what really went on *inside*. Initiates were sworn to secrecy on pain of death, and what has come down to us is mostly a matter of coded accounts such as those contained in *The Golden Ass* of Apuleius or *The Aeneid* by Vergil.

Many of the great and good were initiated at Eleusis, including Plato, Aristotle, Pindar, Sophocles and Euripides. Some famous initiates even dropped hints. The Roman statesman Cicero, for instance, would say that the great contribution Athens made to the history of the world flowed from Eleusis. He also said initiation taught him to live well and approach death with hope.

By piecing the diverse bits of evidence together, it becomes possible to trace an outline.

What were called the Greater Mysteries happened at an important turning point in the year, when darkness took over the earth and vegetation began to die. In mystical traditions in all times and places the spiritual world grows nearer then.

Candidates would have undergone a long period of training and preparation. Those wishing to be initiated by the philosopher and mathematician Pythagoras endured several years of training, including a special diet based on seeds and honey, and physical training too.

As the day for initiation approached, they would be taken to what Vergil calls the Painted Room and left there in solitude for three days, to contemplate – and fear – what they were about to experience. The paintings showed the horrors of Hell, monsters and forms of torture.

As the geographer Strabo describes it, a candidate was led underground along passageways going a considerable distance, perhaps miles beneath the surface of the earth. The candidate probably knew he would be spending a while underground, and initiation ceremonies were often said to last three days. The wonder-worker Apollonius – a contemporary of Jesus Christ and more acclaimed in their lifetimes – spent seven days underground before emerging, certain of his mission to teach the world.

At a certain point in his journey the candidate would be stripped of his clothes, washed and anointed with oils, then given a simple white linen robe to wear before being led along more narrow, dark passages.

He would reach an underground river and be rowed across in a frayed old coracle by a ragged old man.

He would drink at two underground springs, the waters of Forgetfulness and then the waters of Memory. This echos what happens after death, according to Mystery teachings. We forget our earthly lives and remember our divine essence.

Then the candidate would be led even further into the labyrinth, perhaps by priests wearing animal masks; this is what Egyptian depictions of initiation ceremonies on temple walls seem to show.

They would reach the Dividing of the Ways. Again, this represents what happens to the spirit after death. Were any candidates taken straightaway along the path to heaven? Probably not. Instead, the candidate would now be marched firmly down the road to Hell. In some larger initiation centres the candidate might find himself walking through the city of the dead. Caves of stalactites might give the impression of dead forests.

In initiation ceremonies all around the world the candidate must pass a series of ordeals or tests, perhaps encounter monsters – but he or she will always have been prepared to face these perils with magic spells or – as in Vergil's account – talismanic objects. According to the ancient geographer Pausanias, the candidate would suddenly find himself propelled down a chute into a snake pit, told to lie down, and then as the snakes came towards him, propitiate them with honey cakes – just as in *The Aeneid*, when the Sibyl who accompanies Aeneas propitiates the snake-haired Cerberus with sops soaked in honey and drugs. In the account of this stage of the ceremony by Philostratus – biographer of Apollonius – it is here that the candidate is menaced by reptiles; Philostratus does not specify snakes and it may be that in some Mystery centres other reptiles appeared. There were rumours in the ancient world of fantastic reptilian monsters that were stragglers, survivals from the times before the great flood.

Animals would be sacrificed in close proximity to the candidate, perhaps a mass slaughter of cattle like the one that Vergil describes. Their shrieks and roars of agony would be deafening, and the air would stink of blood and guts. We know that in the Mithraic mysteries there is an image of Mithras slaying the Cosmic Bull, apparently depicting a rite known as the *tauroctony*. This may have involved a real sacrifice in the early days of the cult that later became a mere sombre enactment or depiction of the rite, comparable to what happened in Christianity. Similarly, during the *taurobolium* of the Magna Mater initiation, candidates stood under a grill on top of which a bull was sacrificed and they were baptized in a shower of blood. These two elements of initiation are often confused, but there is debate among scholars about possible overlap and/or connection between the two cults.

The candidate would perhaps have to take an oath, swearing that he had confessed all his sins and had no intention whatsoever of sinning again, that no part of him still nursed any secret illicit desires. He had sworn that he deserved to die if he was not telling the whole truth – and by now he would be having doubts. Of course, he hadn't confessed *everything*, and of course he would never be able to keep all selfish, lustful, cowardly or wicked thoughts *entirely* out of his head forever … and perhaps the gods or the priests knew he had been lying? Perhaps they therefore intended to kill him? The candidate might feel a blade pressing into his chest. Or he might hear strange inhuman voices and think he was about to be torn apart by demons?

Proclus, the Neoplatonic philosopher, and Plutarch, priest and historian, remembered the terrifying sight of troops of demons advancing upon them.

The candidate would then be made at this stage of the initiation to press on through tunnels made even murkier by the smoke of animal sacrifice until finally in the inner sanctum he would spend a period in complete and utter darkness. His imagination would be running riot by now, fearful to the point of hysteria and on the verge of madness. Plutarch describes how suddenly and without warning you would receive a heavy blow to the forehead, which would knock you over. This blow was intended in theory to open up the skull and set your spirit free. As a spirit among spirits, you should now be able to communicate freely with the spirits of the dead and the gods. A blow to the head still takes place in Freemasonic initiation ceremonies today.

After a while you would see a faint light somewhere up above you, and priests would arrive to lead you to your encounter with long-lost relatives and the gods.

During initiation you undergo the most intense, the most meaningful, the most extreme experiences of your life. Tragic drama originated with the masked performances of priests in the initiation centres of ancient Greece. If we watch a grand tragedy like King Lear, we may be moved to intense emotions, the greatest heights and depths of which human nature is capable of feeling – even to the extent that we feel our very nature has been in some way altered for the better. But if you were initiated in one of the Mystery schools, you would not be having these experiences by way of sympathizing with the characters on the stage. You would not feel pity for Lear as he reaches the lowest point in his life and looks upwards for the first time. You would *be* Lear.

When it comes to assembling a narrative of the latter parts of the initiation ceremonies – the meetings with the gods – we have fewer scraps of evidence to work with, but we do know that many of the most brilliant and intelligent figures in Athens believed they had really met the gods and had experienced while still alive what the human spirit also experiences after death. According to Plutarch the newly made initiate would emerge with a radiant expression. He said that 'when people die they experience what initiates have already experienced'. Aristides, the orator, said 'I thought I felt the god draw near and I touched him. My spirit was so light – in a way that someone who hasn't been initiated wouldn't understand'. Pindar, the poet, said 'Happy is he who has seen the Mysteries, because he knows what happens after death'. Similarly, Sophocles, the playwright, said 'Thrice happy are those who have seen the Mysteries before they die'. In *Alcestis*, Euripides alludes to Eleusis and to being buried and rising again on the third day.

When the newly initiated person emerged at last from the network of tunnels they were taken to a private room and invited to sit on the Throne of Memory. There the priests would quiz them about what they had experienced.

If the priests saw that the person sitting on the throne did not truly believe they had met the gods, would they kill them? After all, the populace believed that candidates really were visiting the realm of the dead. It would hardly raise many eyebrows if the odd traveller to that 'undiscovered bourne' failed to return.

Unfortunately initiation ceremonies were also open to abuse. In the dying years of the ancient world, as Rome became decadent, initiation centres and oracles became decadent too, a sort of mixture of séance and carny ghost train. Examination of the carvings on the walls of ancient Mystery centres shows depictions of plants known to have hallucinogenic properties, including poppies, henbane, and belladonna. Were these infused into the bathing waters and the springs of forgetfulness and memory from which the candidate was asked to drink? A priest who had been a follower of Apollonius used to frighten people who came to him for help with a giant snake wearing a mask with a man's face.

How much could be achieved with smoke, mirrors, bullroarers and other scary sounds? The candidates would be very suggestible, half-starved by fasting, disoriented by sensory deprivation, told what to expect by priests with magnetic personalities. There is an account by a 5th century bishop Theodoret of uncovering such impostures in Alexandria – hollow statues made of bronze and wood with the backs fitted against a wall, so that priests could secretly climb inside them and make them appear to talk. This evidence of decadence and cynical manipulation opens up dramatic possibilities.

What if you wanted to kill someone? What better cover than luring him down into the Underworld? What if you believed someone was being led down into the Underworld and held against their will, that their life was in danger – and that only a real hero could rescue them?

Some worldly-minded leaders tried to force entry or even take over the Mysteries for their own purposes. The Caesars wanted to snuff out prophecies of the Christ and promote themselves in his place. Adam Weishaupt attempted to hijack Freemasonry for cynical, political purposes. What if you became a candidate for initiation in good faith and later discovered you were being initiated into an evil organization? Some enemies of Freemasonry claim that at the highest level of initiation it is whispered in your ear that all along you have been prepared for service to Lucifer.

When the Caesars closed the initiation centres of the ancient world, the hierophants fled and, according to Rudolf Steiner, the initiation stream was driven underground. Steiner wrote that 'it was Imperial Rome that, without warrant [by Imperial edict], unveiled the secrets of the Mysteries. The time was approaching when the initiate-priests could no longer resist the commands of the Caesars. And the violation of the spiritual life by the Roman emperors is reflected in the events of the time'.

Traces of this initiatic stream can be found both inside and outside the Church and in the histories of organizations such as the Knights Templar, the Rosicrucians and the Freemasons. In the Middle Ages rumours raged around Europe about a strange and mysterious place in the wilds of Ireland. St Patrick's Purgatory was said to be somewhere you could step through a portal into other worlds.

Approaching Patrick's Purgatory in Lough Derg you would come to the shore of a lake, then you should sound a horn and wave a white cloth on a pole left there for the purpose to attract the ferryman. He would row you over the lake to the small rocky island by means of a boat made from a hollowed-out tree trunk. You were met on the shore of the island by the three canons who lived there, perhaps carrying pine torches if evening was approaching. On the face of it there was not much to see on the island, only a small oratory made of stone, two small wooden shacks, one for the canons and the other for the pilgrim. There were also three beehive cells, characteristic retreats for holy men and women in early Celtic Christianity. The prior may have lived in one of these cells. Behind the oratory was the Purgatory itself. It had an iron door about three cubits off the ground, and behind the door there was a rocky cave big enough for about twelve people to stand in, with a sort of alcove at the back where St Patrick was said to have slept. Next to this alcove was what looked like a mill stone, and the monks would tell you it was an entrance to a well…

These details of what it was like to visit St Patrick's Purgatory have come down to us in a letter written by a visiting pilgrim from Italy. Another more extraordinary account is based on what happened to another pilgrim, Owen, a knight from the court of Stephen, King of England.

Many visited the island in those days, but few dared descend into the cave, for some had never returned. Owen fasted and prayed for fifteen days and then on the fifteenth day was led into a little chapel, where the prior gave him the most Blessed Sacrament and told him to keep the Holy Name on his tongue, for that alone would avail him should he stand near the gates of Hell.

Then, at a word from the prior, the three canons pulled his clothes from off him, signifying that his past life was stripped away, and he was laid out as though dead, covered by a plain white sheet, while two of the canons commenced to chant the Office of the Dead.

Faint with his fasting, Owen passed into a trance…

The prior spoke, and two of the canons, raising him to his feet, led him slowly to the mouth of the cave. Then the prior threw holy water over him and took his leave.

Owen moved uncertainly into the now-opened cave. Immediately the door was closed and locked, and shadows came over him. For a little while he stood upright in a horror of the deep darkness, then a great weariness compelled him to lie down to rest. Sleep and forgetfulness overtook him.

He seemed, in his wandering mind, to stand upright once again and to feel his way through the gloom, but suddenly the ground seemed to give way underneath him and he fell wildly onto the stones. A cold sweat enveloped his body.

When he opened his eyes, they were filled with a soft light that revealed twelve men before him in the garb of a religious order. The garment of each man was marked a great cross.

The men were watching him kindly. One, who had the air of being their superior, and who wore a chain around his neck, greeted Owen, and assured him that it was God who had put into his heart his wish to visit the fields of Purgatory. Let him but keep the Holy Name on his tongue and refuse the temptations of evil spirits, and all would be well. But if he were to turn, even for a moment, to look back, he would suffer eternal loss.

As he spoke, clouds seemed to cover him and his companions. Light and darkness passed before Owen's eyes in strange comminglement. At last the clouds and shadows disappeared and he saw an endless throng of faithful souls kneeling in silent prayer and supplication. The wonderful company stretched as far as his eyes could see. Their bodies seemed to tremble in an unseen flame, as fields quiver in the summer heat even when there is no wind.

Then there fell on Owen's ears a low and piteous cry, the sweet impatience of a child in pain, and over their yearning brooded the shadow of an infinite happiness.

Owen remembered then that it had been written in time of old that men must be purged by the exceeding mercy of God before they could bear to enter his sublime presence. These were the wide fields of Purgatory, he decided, and these people, like swarms of starlings crying in the misty reeds, were souls being tested.

Owen was wrapped in darkness again, and all around him he heard piteous cries. This time they were more terrible because he could not see whence they came. There followed a harsh sound of moving winds and of flame, and a dry wind blew into his very soul. He found himself hurried forward into a widening lake. He felt as if his past life was slipping away like a dream, and he cried out to the Blessed Virgin and her Son.

He saw now that he was by the shore of the lake and crossing by a stone bridge, narrow and perilous. On either side of him lay a seething mist of fire, and in this fire were living men. Around him loomed strange shapes and beings. He'd heard that such beings lived at the bottom of the sea. Their noise was as the moan that is everlasting, and through and over and around them wound a belt of fire, like a great worm that cannot die.

Owen nearly slipped into the red flood but remembered to keep saying the Holy Name until he reached the further shore.

He found himself standing on the edge of a beautiful garden. The air was filled with an unsurpassed sweetness. Time itself seemed to be standing still. Neither was there any season, for the trees were loaded with mellow fruit and at the same time with fresh young leaves. How long he stood in this beatitude Owen did not know. Five hundred years might be passing.

Suddenly a very soft music sprang up in the distance, filling the quiet air with unebbing harmony. As the sound thrilled his heart, Owen saw a great company passing through a distant glade. Saints, popes and kings passed in glorious succession, carrying the emblems of their rank. Behind them came the great religious orders in their robes, and after them the great order of God's workers bearing the humble tools of their trade. In the midst of these Owen saw the white bodyguards of the king. These were the ones who had passed through the river of strife and plucked the reeds of martyrdom at the water's edge.

Owen fell back into a quiet and deathlike sleep. He lay there until he heard the voice of the prior calling him from the cave's mouth.

"My son, my son, hast thou perished?"

Owen tried to reply, but the weakness of his flesh would not allow his tongue to move. Three times he raised himself up and each time fell back exhausted.

Weak as he was, his mind was quite awake now and he heard the canons talking softly to one another outside as the prior jangled his heavy bunch of keys.

***

If we compare Ansgar's dream with Owen's account of St Patrick's Purgatory, it suggests that the latter is a formal initiation by twelve men of the brotherhood wearing large crosses on their robes. (It's provocative that the king from whose court Owen came was a patron of the Knights Templar.) In the case of the former, Ansgar's experience does not, on the surface, seem to have been directed by a brotherhood. But the message conveyed by the spiritual word in both cases is similarly dark and cold: watch out, purge yourself of evil-doing or you will go to Hell.

My book *The Secret History of Dante* collects evidence and arguments showing that Dante's mentor, the occult writer Brunetto Latini, was an initiate of a lay brotherhood affiliated to the Knights Templar and that he, in turn, initiated Dante. The *Commedia,* then, is an account of Dante's initiation.

Dante's poem is much longer, more vivid and elaborate than the Ansgar or Owen accounts, but the episodes and images from the *Commedia,* which have sunk deeply into the human imagination, carry the same message.

If one considers initiation as a cultural phenomenon, and because the information is so sparse, the temptation is always to focus on what initiations have in common down the ages. But if, as claimed by Helena Blavatsky, Rudolf Steiner and others, the aim of initiation is to guide and accelerate the evolution of individuals, with the broader aim of helping humanity to do the same, we should expect initiations to change through the ages. In fact, the initiatic and esoteric teachings that have emerged from the Mystery schools and secret societies give us clues as to how it has changed if we bear the following question in mind:

The history of the world is divided into epochs and eras, distinct phases when human society, ideas and consciousness were wholly different. This much is universally accepted. What if the other world, the spiritual world we interact with in dreams, visions and initiations, the world where we go after death, has *also changed and gone through similarly distinct phases?*

Beliefs about what happens after death have changed from age to age. What if this is because what happens after death has changed?

Do dreams change similarly? Who today has dreams like the ones Freud wrote about and analysed?

***

Out of the Mystery schools of ancient Greece came sculpture, drama and philosophy, mind-expanding initiatives that helped humanity to evolve many faculties including its powers of imagination. The notion of conscience came out of the Mystery schools, too, in the plays of the initiate Euripides, and conscience can be understood as *moral imagination*.

The great spiritual impulse mediated through secret societies in the Middle Ages was that humanity should train and discipline the animal part of its nature, should try to purge itself of unruly urges and passions. In the long perspectives on human history afforded by initiatic literature, the primary aim of human evolution in this era was to prepare the way for developing objective, conceptual thinking.

Human intelligence, developed within scholastic theology in the Middle Ages, would lead to amazing developments in science and technology. During the European Renaissance, at a time of discovery of 'new worlds', a revolutionary impulse was communicated to humanity in dreams, the visions of mystics, and by the Rosicrucian brotherhood. This impulse and focus of initiation is in this era less judgmental, less concerned with obedience and discipline, less hierarchical and patriarchal. It is more concerned with healing, and above all, with love. It asks us to apply our intelligence in a way that enables us to appreciate that, although we seem to be separated by earthly bodies, there is a living connection between us. And that although we may seem, at times, to be living in a world that is indifferent to us, there is a greater reality which reveals that we are all connected, and the world is a living being who cares for us.

This impulse inspires the story of Nekumonta who married Shanewis, and the underground spring of love and healing in their story becomes in the 20th century a river beginning to surface.

***

I had qualms about writing this in the time of Trump and Brexit. The populist movements in America, Britain and around the world are fired by a belief that in the new global economy secretive elites get rich at the expense of everyone else. In my view, populist beliefs about the unfairness of the system and widening gap between rich and poor are accurate and true. This unfairness is not sustainable, and if nothing is done about it there will be violent uprisings. But I am equally sure that the populist leaders proposing to lead us out of this mess don't have any solutions, and that people who *do* have the solutions have not been identified or made themselves known.

We can't turn the clocks back and uninvent the technology that made the global economy possible. What we need is not a reactionary approach but a new enlightened one with roots in a higher level of consciousness. And as I've tried to show in my books *The Secret History of the World* and *The Sacred History*, there have always been secret societies working to help make this happen.

Of course there are also secret groups dedicated to selfish ends, some straightforwardly criminal. The Mob is, in this sense, the dark shadow of the true secret societies.

There are also secret societies made up of occultists, 'brothers of the left-hand path', who see the spirit realm not as the limitless multiverse of Dante, but as a shadowy and limited penumbra around the material world, a realm infested with spirits and demons. For them, it is a sort of wild west, a place where they can compel spirits to help them fight for money, power, and sex without fear of running contrary to any higher purposes or risking punishment from higher powers.

If history shows that doing a deal with the devil tends to end badly, that does not seem to bother them!

So, I am by no means denying that secrecy is open to abuse or that self-seeking cabals of the sort that conspiracy theorists fear exist and seek unfair advantage. We have already alluded to the way the Bavarian Illuminati, led by Adam Weishaupt, attempted to hijack Freemasonry. In my work as a publisher, I have often had privileged access to both special forces and security services, and I can confirm that they are doing the very things you might worry they are doing.

However, I believe this is only half the story. Dwelling on evil conspiracies and dark agendas not only has a reinforcing, sclerotic effect on our worldview – in a way that modern psychologists, including cognitive behaviour therapists, have done much to highlight – but it also has more drastic and dangerous effects when considered from an esoteric standpoint. In a mind-before-matter universe inhabited by intelligent but unembodied beings, there is a danger that if we dwell on dark forces we may empower them and 'let them in'.

The forces of light, spiritual beings who may now approach us in dreams or visions or initiations today, are working to grant us the experiences that helped Nekumonta save Shanewis, so we'll not only know in an abstract, conceptual way that we are all connected, but we'll feel it and experience it as a living reality.

Living in material bodies deludes us into thinking we are separated from other people and the world, but the experience of existing outside the physical body causes this sense of separation to fall away. One of the effects of an initiation of light may be a conviction that we are, at root, connected not only to our family, tribe, nation or 'soul group', but to the whole of humanity – indeed to the whole living cosmos.

Initiations of light may take you to hell and back – and beyond, to heaven. Dark initiations, on the other hand, take you to hell as an end itself. Their secret plans are to squeeze all the spirituality out of the world, so it becomes a place of dead matter and delusion.

A culture of conspiracy theories encourages people to see secret meanings everywhere. It bestows a feeling of intellectual superiority, which does not have to be earned. Its secret meanings are concerned with the lower parts of human nature – greed, the lust for power, and military might.

But initiations of light encourage us to use our greatest intelligence, our most refined sensitivity, perceptual powers and imagination to discern higher meanings. These meanings do not depend on human intention and are not a matter of human willing mapped onto the cosmos. They inhere in the cosmos because they are what the great cosmic mind intends for us all.

Initiation into Aleister Crowley's Magick

Richard Kaczynski

"Will" is the fundamental principle behind Aleister Crowley's occultism. It resides at the core of his famous definition of magick as "the Science and Art of causing Change to occur in conformity with Will."[1] It is paramount in his dictum "Do what thou wilt shall be the whole of the Law."[2] And it is key to his conceptualization of initiation. To be clear, Crowley draws a distinction between simple whims or desires and "Will," which he views along the lines of one's *raison d'être*, purpose, or calling. Alas, social norms, pressure and expectations – in addition to the distraction of whims and desires – can so obfuscate one's true nature that uncovering and realizing it takes work: the Great Work.

Thus in his *Confessions*, Crowley writes, "This question 'who art thou?' is the first which is put to any candidate for initiation. Also, it is the last."[3] This is because initiation involves "going into oneself, and making one's peace, so to speak, with all the forces that one finds there."[4] In *Magick in Theory and Practice*, Crowley defines initiation by drawing analogies to other occult practices:

> What, by our definition, is initiation? The First Matter is a man, that is to say, a perishable parasite, bred of the earth's crust, crawling irritably upon it for a span, and at last returning to the dirt whence he sprang. The process of initiation consists in removing his impurities, and finding in his true self an immortal intelligence to whom matter is no more than the means of manifestation. The initiate is eternally individual; he is ineffable, incorruptible, immune from everything. He possesses infinite wisdom and infinite power in himself. This

> equation is identical with that of a talisman. The Magician takes an idea, purifies it, intensifies it by invoking into it the inspiration of his soul. It is no longer a scrawl scratched on a sheepskin, but a word of Truth, imperishable, mighty to prevail throughout the sphere of its purport. The evocation of a spirit is precisely similar in essence. The exorcist takes dead material substances of a nature sympathetic to the being whom he intends to invoke. He banishes all impurities therefrom, prevents all interference therewith, and proceeds to give life to the subtle substance thus prepared by instilling his soul.[5]

The common theme in all these definitions is the preeminence of the initiate's pure, unadulterated essence. It is therefore no surprise that the two initiatory organizations associated with Crowley – the A∴A∴ and Ordo Templi Orientis (O.T.O.) – both seek to lead the initiate to the discovery of their True Will. The A∴A∴ offers a rigorous curriculum for internal alchemy, whereas O.T.O. is geared toward applying the principles of Crowley's philosophy of *Thelema* (Greek, "will") to everyday life, while gradually revealing the mystery preserved in its Sovereign Sanctuary.

A∴A∴

The A∴A∴[6] was founded in response to the demise of London's Golden Dawn (GD) at the turn of the 20th century. It uses virtually the same grade system as its predecessor but boasts a significantly bolstered system of training and instruction. Since Crowley's role in the fall of the GD is often exaggerated, a little history and context is useful.

The GD was founded in 1887 by three members of the Societas Rosicruciana in Anglia (SRIA), a Christian mystery school whose membership was restricted to Christian Master Masons: William Wynn Westcott, Samuel Liddell MacGregor Mathers, and William Robert Woodman. As shown in Table 1, the GD copied the SRIA grade system, which was likewise modeled upon the German *Orden des Gold- und Rosenkreutz*. The GD was founded as a ceremonial

Table 1. Comparison of the A∴A∴ Grades with Preceding Rosicrucian Organizations

Gold- und Rosenkreutz (est. 1750s)		Societas Rosicruciana in Anglia (est. 1865)		*Royal Masonic Cyclopaedia* (1877)[9]		Golden Dawn (est. 1887)		A∴A∴ (est. 1906)	
								---	Student
						First or Outer Order		*Order of the G.D.*	
						⓪=0	Neophyte	0°=0□	Probationer
I	Junioris	I	Zelator	9,1	Junioris	①=10	Zelator	1°=10□	Neophyte
II	Theoricus	II	Theoricus	8,2	Theoreticus	②=9	Theoricus	2°=9□	Zelator
III	Practicus	III	Practicus	7,3	Practicus	③=8	Practicus	3°=8□	Practicus
IV	Philosophus	IV	Philosophus	6,4	Philosophus	④=7	Philosophus	4°=7□	Philosophus
						Portal	Dominus Liminis	The Link	Dominus Liminis
						Second or Inner Order		*Order of the R.C.*	
V	Adeptus Minor	V	Adeptus Minor	5,5	Minor	⑤=6	Adeptus Minor	5°=6□	Adeptus Minor
VI	Adeptus Major	VI	Adeptus Major	4,6	Major	⑥=5	Adeptus Major	6°=5□	Adeptus Major
VII	Adeptus Exemptus	VII	Adeptus Exemptus	3,7	Adeptus Exemptus	⑦=4	Adeptus Exemptus	7°=4□	Adeptus Exemptus
								The Link	Babe of the Abyss
						Third Order		*Order of the S.S.*	
VIII	Magister	VIII	Magister	2,8	Magister	⑧=3	Magister Templi	8°=3□	Magister Templi
IX	Magus	IX	Magus	1,9	Magus	⑨=2	Magus	9°=2□	Magus
						⑩=1	Ipsissimus	10°=1□	Ipsissimus

magic society which would be open to all, including women, non-Masons, and non-Christians. According to its creation myth,[7] a musty London bookseller came upon a cipher manuscript which, when decoded, contained the outlines of initiation rituals and instructions to contact the German adept Anna Sprengel for authorization to found a lodge. With correspondence and charters achieved, the GD founders fleshed out the rituals with excerpts from esoteric works they had edited or translated, such as the *Pymander of Hermes*, the *Chaldean Oracles*, and *Kabbalah Unveiled*.[8]

The GD thrived, attracting over a hundred members from a cross-section of London's artists, intelligentsia and other luminaries. Things changed when Woodman died in 1891. Westcott succeeded him as Supreme Magus of the SRIA, subsequently playing a diminished role in the GD. Several months later, in 1892, Mathers moved to Paris, leaving the London lodge without the presence of its founders. Although it thrived under its capable leadership, Mathers sought to reassert his authority by demanding that all members sign an oath of allegiance exclusively to him. In an apparent effort to undermine any claim by Westcott, Mathers disclosed that the story of the cipher manuscript was a fabrication, and that Westcott had "either himself forged or procured to be forged" the Sprengel correspondence.[10] Mathers's revelation plunged the London body into a constitutional crisis, its members fearing that they had been initiating people under false pretenses. Rather than solidifying his position, Mathers undercut his own authority.

Into this tumultuous nadir of the London body stepped young Aleister Crowley, taking his first initiation in November 1898 at the age of 23. A serious and dedicated student of the mysteries, he moved steadily through the grades of the Outer Order up to Dominus Liminis. Yet owing to his colorful personality, promiscuity, and rumors of homosexuality – and no doubt because he had befriended Mathers – the London leadership denied him admission to the Second Order, with senior initiate William Butler Yeats explaining, "[W]e did not think a mystical society was intended to be a reformatory."[11]

Denied entry to the first of the GD's Rosicrucian grades, Crowley traveled to Paris and received his Adeptus Minor initiation from

Mathers himself. When Crowley returned to London and requested the instructional papers corresponding to his new rank, the London leadership took umbrage to this affront to their authority and refused him. In response, Crowley – acting as Mathers' envoy and plenipotentiary – went to the Second Order's headquarters and seized the rooms, insisting that every member appear before him and swear allegiance to Mathers, or be immediately expelled. Before long, a constable was summoned and the London leadership reasserted control of the room. After this incident, Crowley occupied himself with other things while the London lodge of the GD completed its disintegration.[12]

Crowley would go on to marry and take his honeymoon in Cairo. On this trip, in 1904, he penned *The Book of the Law*, the received text that formed the cornerstone of his philosophy of Thelema. In 1906, Crowley and his GD colleague George Cecil Jones renewed contact with each other and decided to revive the Order. Crowley had complained of the so-called secrets given to him at his Neophyte initiation:

> And now I was entrusted with some of these devastating though priceless secrets. They consisted of the Hebrew alphabet, the names of the planets with their attribution to the days of the week, and the ten Sephiroth of the Cabbala. I had known it all for months; and, obviously, any schoolboy in the lower fourth could memorize the whole lecture in twenty-four hours.[13]

Crowley is engaging in some *reductio ad absurdum* for effect, as the Hebrew alphabet forms the key to the GD's greatest accomplishment, which was to unify astrology, Tarot, Kabbalah, Enochian magic, and Rosicrucianism into a single elegant system: a Grand Unified Theory of occultism. It was clunky in places – the incorporation of Enochian is really a forced fit – but this system served as the foundation of Crowley's understanding of magick for the rest of his life and is the key to understanding many of his writings. Nevertheless, the core of Crowley's critique stands: namely that, for a teaching order, the GD taught very little in its preliminary grades. The Outer Order concerned itself primarily with memorizing symbolism and correspondences, and the only practical magic taught was the pentagram ritual. Crowley's new order, the A∴A∴, would address those shortcomings by creating a more expansive curriculum. In addition to magic and practical work, it notably introduced progressive exercises in yoga, meditation, and memorization – virtually unheard-of at that time.

The work of each grade in the A∴A∴ is scattered amongst several documents by Crowley:

"Liber XIII vel Graduum Montis Abiegni: A Syllabus of the Steps upon the Path," *The Equinox*, March 1910, I(3): 3-8.

"Liber A vel Armorum sub figurâ CCCXII," *The Equinox*, September 1910, I(4): 15-19.

"Liber Collegii Sancti sub figurâ CLXXXV: Being the Tasks of the Grades, and Their Oaths, Proper to Liber XIII, the Publications of the A∴A∴ in Class D from A to G," in Israel Regardie (ed.), *Gems from the Equinox* (St. Paul: Llewellyn, 1974; rpt. San Francisco: Samuel Weiser, 2007), 1107-1134.

"A∴A∴ Curriculum," *The Equinox* III(1): 18-38.

"One Star in Sight," Appendix II in *Magick in Theory and Practice*, 229-244.

The system and key tasks of each grade can be summarized as follows:

Student status is preparatory and involves acquiring "a general intellectual knowledge of all systems of attainment, as declared in the prescribed books."[14] Listed in the "A∴A∴ Curriculum," these books represent a veritable liberal arts education, covering sacred Hindu and Buddhist texts, Kabbalah, Gnosticism, Hermeticism, Rosicrucianism, alchemy, folklore, philosophy, science, and a long list of suggestive fiction. Naturally, the list includes a healthy selection of Crowley's works.

The one-year Probationer period begins with selecting a magical motto, filling out the Oath of a Probationer, and acquiring the appropriate robe. The tasks of this grade include memorization, keeping a magical record or journal, and beginning some regular practice to be recorded in the journal. This practice is not prescribed, although the "A∴A∴ Curriculum" includes instructions on solar adorations ("Liber Resh") and Crowley's version of a pentagram ritual (the "Star Ruby").[15]

During the eight-month Neophyte period, "The main work is to obtain admission to, and control of, the astral plane."[16] Aspirants also design and construct the first of the elemental weapons of ritual magic, the pentacle. They study a method of divination, such as geomancy or Tarot, and are examined in the Four Powers of the Sphinx (to know, to will, to dare, and to keep silent), assumption of god-forms, memorization, and the rituals of the pentagram and hexagram.

The work of a Zelator includes exercises in meditation, yogic posture (*asana*) and breath control (*prāṇāyāma*), and forging the second elemental weapon: the sword.

In addition to further meditation and memorization tasks, the Practicus studies the Kabbalah, practices control of speech, and forges the elemental cup.

The Philosophus passes examinations in evocation, rising on the planes, and constructing/consecrating talismans. Aspirants of this grade also engage in meditative practices dealing with devotion (*bhakti yoga*), control of action, and *mahāsatipaṭṭhāna*, for which Crowley's mentor, Allan Bennett, offers the following instructions:

> practise concentrating the mind in observing all the actions that you perform, all the sensations that arise in your body, all the thoughts that arise in your mind, and always analyse each concentration object thus (as in the case cited above, of the bodily action of walking). "What is it that walks?" and by accurate analysis you reflect that there is no person or soul within the body that walks, but that there is a particular collection of chemical elements, united and held together by the result of certain categories of forces, as cohesion, chemical attraction, and the like.[17]

As Crowley himself succinctly put it, "It is essentially an observation-practice, which later assumes an analytic aspect in regard to the question, 'What is it that is really observed?'"[18]

The Philosophus also cuts the wood for their third elemental weapon, the wand.

The Dominus Liminis "meditates upon the diverse knowledge and power that he has acquired, and harmonises it perfectly."[19] Members of this grade also master the yogic techniques of *pratyahara* (sensory transcendence) and *dhyāna* (concentration, or control of thought). Finally, they light the fifth and final elemental weapon, the lamp of spirit.

The Minor Adept acquires the Knowledge and Conversation of their Holy Guardian Angel, while the Major Adept "obtains a general mastery of practical Magick."[20] The Exempt Adept "must prepare and publish a thesis setting forth His knowledge of the Universe, and his proposals for its welfare and progress," thus becoming the leader of a school of thought.[21] Attaining the grade of Master of the Temple involves "the perfect annihilation of that personality which limits and oppresses his true self"[22] and mastery of the yogic trance of *samadhi* (ecstatic transcendence of the self), after which they tend to their garden of disciples. The Magus distills everything learned up to this point into a single word, whose utterance "transforms the planet on which he lives."[23] Finally, the Ipsissimus is beyond comprehension, but Crowley tells us that those who attain to this grade have "identified Being and not-Being and Becoming, action and non-action and tendency to action, with all other such triplicities, not distinguishing between them in respect of any conditions, or between any one thing and any other thing as to whether it is with or without conditions."[24]

To summarize the A∴A∴ system, members of the Order of the GD design, produce and consecrate the magical weapon corresponding to the element attributed to their grade. The Second Order concerns itself with mastery of magic, culminating in the Exempt Adept publishing a thesis on their understanding of the magical universe. After this, the focus of subsequent grades is less about the aspirant and more about facilitating the spiritual evolution of mankind: The aspirant obliterates their ego in the Ordeal of the Abyss, emerging into the first grades of the Third Order as a Master of the Temple.

This curriculum also includes the Eight Limbs of Patanjali's *Rāja yoga*. *Yama* and *niyama* (conduct and discipline) are established at the outset. Zelators practice both *asana* and *prāṇāyāma*, asserting mastery over the physical body. This covers the first half of the Eight Limbs. Aspirants are thus free to turn their attention to meditative states without physical distractions. Thus the Practicus works on principles of philosophical meditation (*jñāna yoga*), while the Philosophus practices *mahāsatipaṭṭhāna*. The Dominus Liminis returns to the fifth and sixth of the Eight Limbs: *pratyahara* (control of the senses) and *dhārṇā* (concentration). In the latter, the aspirant practices visualizing or otherwise concentrating on a single thought, counting the number of breaks occurring in the attention span, with the goal of reducing the number of breaks with sufficient practice. This is a precursor to the seventh limb, *dhārṇā*, which represents an effortless perfection of *dhārṇā*. From here, the adept advances to the Eighth Limb, the state of *samadhi*, where the distinction between observer and object dissolves into blissful oneness.

Ordo Templi Orientis

Like the A.·.A.·., O.T.O. was born out of the crucible of predecessor organizations. Its seed was planted at the turn of the twentieth century in an effort to introduce *hauts grades* Freemasonry, and similar esoterically-minded rites, into the German-speaking world. The goal was to form an Academia Masonica, an umbrella organization which held charters to administer all these varied rites. The key players included Austrian industrialist Carl Kellner, German Theosophist Franz Hartmann, and expat music publisher Henry Klein, but its prime mover was the colorful reporter, singer, and Prussian Secret Police spy Theodor Reuss. He contacted GD co-founder William Wynn Westcott to negotiate German charters for lodges of other organizations in which Westcott was an officer. These included the Swedenborgian Rite and the Societas Rosicruciana. While Westcott, as secretary of the Swedenborgian Rite, was authorized to charter a single lodge, Reuss and company's subsequent request to form a grand lodge required approval by the rite's head, Masonic scholar and critic of the Ancient and Accepted Rite John Yarker. He not only approved the Swedenborgian grand lodge, but also offered charters in other rites over which he had authority: the Rite of Memphis, the Rite of Mizraim, and the Cerneau Scottish Rite. Before long, the group's newsletter, the *Oriflamme*, touted the formation of a grand lodge of Freemasonry offering initiation into all of these rites.

Several controversies subsequently dogged Reuss. When a small group of unaffiliated lodges asked Reuss to heal their membership (to which he agreed), they were dismayed to learn that his grand lodge was unrecognized by the *Grosslogenbund*, or union of German grand lodges that recognized each other. Not long after, Reuss drew criticism for advocating the admission of women into Freemasonry. At one point, a member claimed – and soon recanted – that an instruction on the then-relatively-unknown concept of chakras was homoerotic;[25] disgruntled ex-members sought to create a scandal through a letter-writing campaign to both Masonic and anti-Masonic journals. Thus, when Reuss's press job required relocating to London, his enemies claimed that they had driven him out of town. In reality, Reuss and colleagues continued their work, eventually encountering Aleister Crowley in London and bringing him into the fold.

After some persuasion,[26] Crowley gladly took up the cause, having had his own disappointments and frustrations with Masonry. Crowley had received the 33° in Mexico City in 1900 from Don Jesus Medina-Sidonia.[27] The experience failed to impress him, but it piqued his curiosity in Freemasonry, which he viewed as "a system of communicating truth – religious, philosophical, magical and mystical."[28] While living in Paris in 1904, enmeshed in the community of writers and artists who frequented Le Chat Blanc in Rue d'Odessa, Crowley took his three Craft initiations at Anglo Saxon Lodge #343, an English-language lodge serving British and American expats living in France. His later request to attend lodge in UGLE was an unhappy experience with the treacherous waters of Masonic recognition: his initiations were not recognized in England,

and his request was denied. Crowley came to regard recognition and regularity as fickle, arbitrary and inconsistent.

A glowing review of Yarker's *Arcane Schools* (1909) in *The Equinox* gained Crowley Yarker's friendship:[29] Yarker recognized the word given to Crowley in Mexico City, issued him a new 33° charter, and authorized him to restart the fallow London bodies of the Antient and Primitive Rite. Thus, when Yarker's associate Reuss confronted Crowley in 1912 about publishing the innermost secrets of the Order – a charge he strenuously denied – Crowley conceded the importance of this secret and became Reuss's enthusiastic ally. Appointed Supreme and Holy King for Great Britain, he mixed the worlds of Yarker and Reuss with Thelema and produced therefrom the modern O.T.O.[30]

The elements for this reconstruction were largely in place when Crowley entered the picture. Reuss already held the patents in various esoteric rites. Just as the Antient and Primitive Rite was a form of the 97 degrees of Memphis and the 90 degrees of Mizraim reduced into a system of 33 degrees,[31] Yarker had subsequently written that the entire system could be further reduced to twelve degrees "without in the least impairing the design of the Rite."[32] The *Oriflamme* had published Reuss's reduced system of nine degrees [see Table 2] and referred to Hartmann as possessing the IX°. Kellner had led an occult circle or inner triangle within the Academia Masonica, revealing mysteries that were hinted at in Masonry but never openly taught: this undoubtedly involved the yoga that Kellner had written about, and about which Reuss later openly proclaimed in the *Oriflamme*, "Our Order possesses the KEY which unlocks all Masonic and Hermetic secrets; it is the doctrine of *sexual magic*, and this doctrine explains without exception all the riddles of Nature, all Masonic symbolism and all religious systems."[33] Reuss had already advocated admitting women as members, and in general promoted gender equality and sexual liberation.

Table 2. Theodor Reuss's Organization of the Order of Oriental Templars[34]

Degree	Title		Governing Body
I°	Candidate	1	Pronaos/Atrium
II°	Minerval	2	Synod
III°	St. John's (Craft) Freemason	3	St. John's Freemasonic Lodge
IV°	Scottish (St. Andrew's) Mason	4	Scottish Chapter
V°	Rose Croix Mason	5	Rose Croix Chapter
VI°	Rosicrucian Templar	6	Mystic Temple
VII°	Mystic Templar	7	Grand Council
VIII°	Oriental Templar	8	Secret Areopagus
IX°	Perfect Illuminate	9	Sovereign Sanctuary
X°	Supreme King (Outer Head of the Order)		

Although Crowley says he took Yarker's book of ceremonies into the Sahara and "fished out the very sparse plums and put the whole of Masonry and super-Masonry in the rituals of O.T.O.,"[35] the initial drafts of his rituals borrowed heavily from the Rite of Emulation.[36] Thus, some recognizable vocabulary, phraseology and other elements carry over, including the relationship of "super-Masonry" to the three Craft degrees. As Crowley explains, "The Minerval degree is a Prologue to the First; the degrees subsequent to the Third but pendants to it."[37] Similarly, in *Magick Without Tears*, he writes that, "All subsequent Degrees of the O.T.O. are accordingly elaborations of the II°, since in a single ceremony it is hardly possible to sketch, even in the briefest outline, the Teaching of Initiates with regard to Life. The Rituals V°–IX° are then instructions to the Candidate how he should conduct himself; and they confer upon him, gradually, the Magical Secrets which make him Master of Life."[38] This is very much how the degree of Master Mason is seen as the pinnacle of Masonry, with all pendant rites but elaborations upon it.

Despite these superficial similarities, Crowley severely edited the rituals, removing what he considered unnecessary speeches and proceedings, and reducing the number of officers. This cutting was abetted by Crowley's conviction that he had recovered the Lost Word: "So there you are, with 9/10ths of the rituals reduced to nonsense."[39] He retained the quintessence of what remained in a shorter form to make it "reasonably possible for men to learn them by heart under modern conditions."[40] But his alterations also ran deeper. Gone are the landmarks of Freemasonry. The characters, obligations and lessons of each degree he retooled to be uniquely Thelemic: "The 0°–III° rituals are not outwardly Masonic. No Solomon, nor Hiram, etc."[41] Similarly, the O.T.O. manifesto explicitly states,

> The O.T.O., although an Academia Masonica, is not a Masonic Body so far as the "secrets" are concerned in the sense in which that expression is usually understood; and therefore in no way conflicts with, or infringes the just privileges of, the United Grand Lodge of England, or any Grand Lodge in America or elsewhere which is recognized by it.[42]

He rounded out these skeletal rituals by introducing elements not present in Masonry, but which enhanced his reimagined symbolism and emphasized the esoteric and occult elements. In some cases – such as the introductory Minerval degree (which takes its name from the Illuminati Order) or the concluding Man of Earth initiation as a Perfect Initiate – there is no comparable ritual in Masonry, so the ceremonies reflect Crowley's pure ingenium. This wasn't revisionism but separating the wheat from the chaff in order to get back to the essence of the rituals. Consequently, Crowley would write that O.T.O.'s I°–III° ceremonies "claim to restore the lost meaning of the Three Craft Degrees."[43]

Table 3 shows Crowley's O.T.O. degree system. He summed up his conceptualization of the initiations as follows:

> I begin by showing the object of the pure soul, "One, individual and eternal," in determining to formulate itself consciously, or, as I may say, to understand itself.
>
> It chooses to enter into relations with the solar system.

Table 3. Aleister Crowley's O.T.O. Degree System[45]

The Third, or Man of Earth, Triad	0°	Minerval
	I°	Man and Brother, Woman and Sister
	II°	Magician
	III°	Master Magician
	IV°	Perfect Magician and Companion of the Holy Royal Arch of Enoch Perfect Initiate, or Prince of Jerusalem
Outside all Triads		Knight of the East and West
The Second, or Lover, Triad	V°	Sovereign Prince Rose-Croix, and Knight of the Pelican and Eagle
		Knight of the Red Eagle, and Member of the Senate of Knight Hermetic Philosophers
	VI°	Illustrious Knight (Templar) of the Order of Kadosch, and Companion of the Holy Graal
		Grand Inquisitor Commander, and Member of the Grand Tribunal Prince of the Royal Secret
	VII°	Theoreticus, and Very Illustrious Sovereign Grand Inspector General
		Magus of Light, and Bishop of Ecclesia Gnostica Catholica
		Grandmaster of Light, and Inspector of Rites and Degrees
The First, or Hermit, Triad	VIII°	Perfect Pontiff of the Illuminati Epopt of the Illuminati
	IX°	Initiate of the Sanctuary of the Gnosis
	X°	Rex Summus Sanctissimus
	XI°	Initiate of the Eleventh Degree (This degree is technical, and has no relation to the general plan of the Order)
	XII°	Frater Superior, and Outer Head of the Order

> It incarnates. I explain the significance of birth and the conditions established by the process. I next show how it may best carry out its object in the eucharist of life. It partakes, so to speak, of its own godhead in every action, but especially through the typical sacrament of marriage, understood as the voluntary union of itself with each element of its environment. I then proceed to the climax of its career in death and show how this sacrament both consecrates (or, rather, sets its seal upon) the previous procedure and gives a meaning thereto, just as the auditing of the account enables the merchant to see his year's transactions in perspective.
>
> In the next ceremony I show how the individual, released by death from the obsession of personality, resumes relations with the truth of the universe. Reality bursts upon him in a blaze of adorable light; he is able to appreciate its splendour as he could not previously do, since his incarnation has enabled him to establish particular relations between the elements of eternity.
>
> Finally, the cycle is closed by the reabsorption of all individuality into infinity. It ends in absolute annihilation which, as has been shown elsewhere in this book, may in reality be regarded either as an exact equivalent for all other terms soever, or (by postulating the category of time) as forming the starting point for new adventure of the same kind.[44]

In *Magick Without Tears*, Crowley offers a much more succinct summary, writing, "the object of the ceremonies being the Initiation of the Candidate, it is he whose Path in Eternity is displayed in dramatic form."[46] This sequence unfolds over the Man of Earth degrees as shown in Table 4:

Table 4. The Path in Eternity Symbolized by O.T.O. Initiations[47]

Degree	Stage	The Path
0°	Minerval	The Ego is attracted to the Solar System.
I°	Initiation	The Child experiences Birth.
II°	Consecration	The Man experiences Life.
III°	Devotion	He experiences Death.
IV°	Perfection, or Exaltation	He experiences the World beyond Death.
PI°	Perfect Initiate	This entire cycle of Point-Events is withdrawn into Annihilation.

As Yarker did with him, Reuss was generous in passing authority in his collection of rites along to those he considered sincere. In 1906, he gave authority in the Rite of Mizraim to Rudolf Steiner so that he could start Mystica Aeterna, Steiner's unique vision of what an initiatory order should be. Reuss was on friendly terms with Matthew McBlain Thomson years before the latter's 1922 conviction on ten counts of mail fraud in connection with his American Masonic Federation: Reuss had appointed him "Grand Representative General" in 1912, and, when Yarker died a year later, the death notice in *The Equinox* quoted extensively from Thomson's obituary of Yarker. In 1921, Reuss also issued honorary membership to H. Spencer Lewis of AMORC. None of these helped to advance O.T.O., and in the case of Thomson the amity was ill-considered; thus Reuss – despite occasionally resisting Thelema – must have thrilled to see Crowley breathe life into O.T.O. and promptly establish envoys in South Africa, Australia, Canada, and the United States. When Reuss died in 1923, Crowley succeeded him as Outer Head of the Order.

Conclusion

In forging his systems of initiation, Crowley took as his starting point two organizations that had a major influence on him: the Golden Dawn and Freemasonry. He eschewed that which he considered unnecessary, streamlining and distilling them to their quintessence. Then he re-envisioned them, bolstering what he considered to be deficiencies, adding content where necessary, and placing Thelema at its core.

At first glance, there appear to be structural similarities between the A.∴A.∴ and O.T.O. systems of initiation: both are divided into three "Orders" or "Grades." The Minerval degree, foreign to Masonry, may be inspired by the Probationer degree. The degrees of the Man of Earth triad, like those of the Order of the GD, can be taken as elemental. And just as the ⑤=6 degree of the original GD was an introduction to Rosicrucianism, the O.T.O.'s V° is similarly inspired by the Rose + Croix. However, as Crowley writes regarding O.T.O., "There is thus no connection with the A.∴A.∴ system and the Tree of Life. Of course, there are certain analogies."[48]

The goals of both orders are, furthermore, decidedly different. As Crowley writes, "The O.T.O. is a training of the Masonic type; there is no 'astral' work in it at all, nor any Yoga. There is a certain amount of Qabalah, and that of great doctrinal value. But the really vital matter is the gradual progress towards disclosure of the Secret of the Ninth Degree."[49] The A.∴A.∴ focuses on personal, internal alchemy, is largely solitary, and has a prescribed curriculum of study and supervision. By contrast, O.T.O. instructs members in principles of how to interact with each other and provides a social setting (the lodge) for support, encouragement, and a place to practice and hone these lessons, ultimately transferring them to their conduct outside the lodge. These different approaches to initiation nevertheless share the same goal: to help the initiate understand their true nature – their Will – and how it relates to the world in which they live.

1 The Master Therion [Aleister Crowley], *Magick in Theory and Practice* (Paris: Lecram, 1929-1930), xii.

2 Aleister Crowley, *The Book of the Law*.

3 Aleister Crowley, *The Confessions of Aleister Crowley*, ed. John Symonds and Kenneth Grant (London: Jonathan Cape, 1969), 31.

4 Aleister Crowley, "The Three Schools of Magick (3)," in *Magick Without Tears*, ed. Israel Regardie (St. Paul: Llewellyn, 1973), 89.

5 Crowley, *Magick*, 185.
6 The initials are commonly decoded as Argentium Astrum (Silver Star), although "The Name of the Order […is] not disclosed to the profane" (Crowley, *Magick*, 230).
7 For more on the prevalence of creation myths in Western esotericism, see Richard Kaczynski, "Inventing Tradition: The Construction of History, Lineage and Authority in Secret Societies." Paper presented at the annual meetings of the Association for the Study of Esotericism, June 2014, Hamilton, NY.
8 W. Wynn Westcott, *The Pymander of Hermes*, Collectanea Hermetica v. 2 (London: Theosophical Publishing Society, 1894); Sapere Aude [W. Wynn Westcott], *The Chaldæan Oracles of Zoroaster*, Collectanea Hermetica v. 6 (London: Theosophical Publishing Society, 1895); S. L. MacGregor Mathers, *Kabbala Denudata: The Kabbalah Unveiled, Containing 1. The Book of Concealed Mystery, 2. The Greater Holy Assembly, 3. The Lesser Holy Assembly* (London: Kegan Paul, Trench, Trübner & Co., 1887).
9 Kenneth Mackenzie, *The Royal Masonic Cyclopedia* (1877: rpt. Wellingborough, Northamptonshire: Aquarian Press, 1987), 617. It should be noted that Mackenzie is often mooted as the author of the GD cipher manuscript.
10 Letter of S. L. MacGregor Mathers to Florence Farr, February 16, 1900, GBR 1991 GD 2/4/3/1, Library and Museum of Freemasonry, London.
11 W. B. Yeats to Lady Gregory, 25 April 1900, in Allan Wade, *The Letters of W. B. Yeats* (New York: MacMillan, 1955).
12 For an account of the GD's history, see Ellic Howe, *The Magicians of the Golden Dawn: A Documentary History of a Magical Order, 1887-1923* (London: Routledge and K. Paul, 1972); Robert A. Gilbert, *The Golden Dawn: Twilight of the Magicians* (Wellingborough: Aquarian Press, 1983).
13 Crowley, *Confessions*, 177.
14 Crowley, "One Star in Sight," 231.
15 [Aleister Crowley], "Liber Resh vel Helios sub figurâ CC," *The Equinox*, September 1911, I(6): 29-32; "The Star Ruby" in Frater Perdurabo [Aleister Crowley], *The Book of Lies: Which is also Falsely Called Breaks. The Wanderings or Falsifications of the One Thought of Frater Perdurabo, which Thought is in Itself Untrue* (London: Wieland & Co., 1913), 34-35.
16 Crowley, "Letter F," in *Magick Without Tears*, 16.
17 Ananda Metteya [Allan Bennet], "The Training of the Mind," *The Equinox*, March 1911, I(5): 56-57.
18 Aleister Crowley, "Science and Buddhism," in *Sword of Song* (Society for the Propagation of Religious Truth: Benares, 1904), 149-192.
19 Crowley, "Liber XIII," 7.
20 Crowley, "One Star in Sight," 232.
21 Ibid., 236.
22 Ibid., 235.
23 Ibid., 234-235.
24 Ibid., 234.
25 Kellner, in 1896, published one of the first Western papers on yoga: the same year that Swami Vivekananda's seminal text on *Raja Yoga* introduced Patanjali's yoga

sutras to the west. See Carl Kellner, *Yoga: Eine Skizze über den psycho-physiologischen Teil der alten indischen Yogalehre* (München: Kastner & Lossen, 1896); Swami Vivekananda, *Yoga Philosophy: Lectures Delivered in New York, Winter of 1895-6 ... on Râja Yoga or Conquering the Internal Nature, also Patanjali's Yoga Aphorisms, with Commentaries* (London: Longmans, Green, and Co., 1896).

26 For details on this encounter, see Richard Kaczynski, *Perdurabo: The Life of Aleister Crowley* (Berkeley: North Atlantic Books, 2010), 251-252; Richard Kaczynski, "Wstp," in Aleister Crowley, *Liber CCCXXXIII: Księga Kłamstw* (Gdansk: Lashtal Press, 2018), v-xiv.

27 Crowley, *Confessions*, 202. According to Masonic researcher John Hamill, Don Jesus Medina led "a miniscule irregular body" (quoted in Martin P. Starr, "Aleister Crowley: Freemason!" Ars Quatuor Coronatorum, vol. 108 (1995), 150-161). This article offers a comprehensive treatment of Crowley's encounters with Freemasonry.

28 Crowley, *Confessions*, 700.

29 John Yarker, *The Arcane Schools: A Review of Their Origin and Antiquity; with a General History of Freemasonry and Its Relation to the Theosophic, Scientific, and Philosophic Mysteries* (Belfast: W. Tait, 1909); Aleister Crowley, "The Arcane Schools" [review], *The Equinox*, September 1910, I(4): 240.

30 For a detailed account of O.T.O. and its backstory, see Richard Kaczynski, *Forgotten Templars: The Untold Origins of Ordo Templi Orientis* (s.l.: the author, 2012).

31 Introduced in 1865 by Harry J. Seymour. See Kaczynski, *Forgotten Templars*, 149-150.

32 See the entry ghost-written by John Yarker in Jeremiah How, *The Freemason's Manual; or, Illustrations of Masonry, containing in addition to the rites sanctioned by the United Grand Lodge and Grand Chapter of England and Wales, the Mark and Mark Master, a full account of all the degrees included in the ancient and accepted rite, etc.* (London: J. Hogg, 1881), 373.

33 *Oriflamme*, September 1912, 7(1): 21.

34 "Organisation des Orientalischen Templer-Ordens," *Oriflamme*, September 1912, 7(1): 32.

35 Letter of Aleister Crowley to W.B. Crow, 16 July 1944, Yorke Collection.

36 Martin P. Starr, *The Unknown God: W.T. Smith and the Thelemites* (Bolingbrook, Ill: Teitan Press, 2003); Richard Kaczynski, "The O.T.O. 0° Initiation: History, Development and Parallels," paper presented at the annual meetings of the National Ordo Templi Orientis Conference, August 2007, Salem; Richard Kaczynski, "The O.T.O. I° Initiation: History, Development and Parallels," paper presented at the annual meetings of the National Ordo Templi Orientis Conference, August 2009, Seattle; Richard Kaczynski, "The O.T.O. II° Initiation: History, Development and Parallels," paper presented at the annual meetings of the National Ordo Templi Orientis Conference, August 2013, Sacramento; Richard Kaczynski, "The O.T.O. III° Initiation: History, Development and Parallels," paper presented at the biennial meetings of the National Ordo Templi Orientis Conference, August 2015, Austin; Richard Kaczynski, "The O.T.O. IV° & PI Initiations: History and Development," paper presented at the biennial meetings of the National Ordo Templi Orientis

Conference, August 2017, Orlando.

37 [Aleister Crowley], "Liber CXCIV: An Intimation with Reference to the Constitution of the Order," *The Equinox*, March 1919, III(1): 241.

38 Aleister Crowley, "System of the O.T.O." in *Magick Without Tears*, 123-124.

39 Letter of Aleister Crowley to W.B. Crow, 1 May 1946, Yorke Collection.

40 Letter of Aleister Crowley to J.W. Parsons, 27 March 1946, Yorke Collection.

41 Letter of Aleister Crowley to Hugh George de Willmott Newman, late September, 1944, Yorke Collection.

42 L. Bathurst IX°, "Liber LII: Manifesto of the O.T.O.," *The Equinox*, March 1919, III(1): 202-203.

43 A Past Grand Master [Aleister Crowley], "The Crisis in Freemasonry," *English Review*, August 1922, 35(2): 127-134.

44 Crowley, *Confessions*, 701-702.

45 Taken from the United States Grand Lodge of O.T.O., "Initiation," http://oto-usa.org/oto/initiation/ [accessed January 28, 2018].

46 Crowley, "System of the O.T.O.," 123.

47 Based on Crowley, "System of the O.T.O.," 123.

48 Crowley, "Letter G," *Magick Without Tears*, 19.

49 Crowley, "System of the O.T.O.," 124.

Initiation by Spirits in Western Magic

Donald Tyson

I have been studying and working magic in its various forms for over forty years, and with each year that passes I become more and more convinced that without direct communication with a higher spiritual teacher, or teachers, through whom a living system of ritual magic is communicated, the practice of true high magic is impossible. The transmission of this living magic from spirit teacher to human disciple usually takes the form of an initiation ordeal during which the old self symbolically dies so that the new magical self may be born.

What is spirit initiation? The transformation of human consciousness that enables an understanding and use of magic, brought about by the successful completion of a ritualized ordeal during which there is a visionary union with a higher spiritual teacher.

Before I delve deeper into the practical aspects of initiation by spirits, it will be useful to examine the conventional ways initiation is understood, so that we may distinguish conventional forms of initiation from spirit initiation.

Mundane Initiation

Initiation is usually understood to be the ceremony by which a person is admitted to some sort of club, fraternity, or society. It can be ritualized and complex, or very simple. Hunter S. Thompson wrote in his book *Hell's Angels* that initiation into the Angels consisted of allowing a new set of Levi's to be soiled by the excrement of the club members. "A bucket of dung and urine will be collected during the meeting, then poured on the newcomer's head in a solemn baptismal. Or he will take off his clothes and stand naked while the bucket of slop is poured over them and the others stomp it in."[1]

We see here one form of the ordeal that so often accompanies the initiation rite, even in mundane forms of initiation. College fraternities may subject new members to various forms of humiliation or pain. Street gangs sometimes beat new initiates with their fists until they can't stand up. This is regarded as barbarous and sadistic, but it is also something more. It is an echo of the sacred ordeals that initiates were compelled to pass through before becoming members of the ancient mystery schools of Greece, Rome and Egypt.

It often happens that the highest and most sacred things become debased over the course of history, and their sacred origins all but forgotten. Greek theater was originally put on for the entertainment of the gods, not of the human onlookers. In ancient times, dance was sacred, song was sacred, poetry was sacred, wine was sacred. The casting of dice was a form of divine sortilege and only later degenerated into a form of gambling. So it is with initiation, which began as a most sacred rite and degenerated over the centuries into a foolish bit of buffoonery required to gain entry into a club.

The most complex form of mundane initiation is that used by the Freemasons. Although Freemasonry is a purely secular organization, its leaders pretend to a long mystical tradition. Their symbolism is imbued with latent occult meaning, although few Masons understand its practical application in magic.

The candidate for entry into Freemasonry must swear that if he should betray any of the secrets of the fraternity, he will be subjected to violent penalties, or (which is more probable) that he shall be branded as a liar, a person void of all moral worth, unfit for the society of honorable men. He is entrusted with some secret bits of Masonic lore, such as the secret handshake of an Entered Apprentice Mason.

In ancient Greece, a candidate for one of the mystery schools took his or her vow quite seriously because those who betrayed the secrets actually were torn limb from limb by the furious members of that school. Even strangers who happened to look upon the ceremonies of the mystery schools, when discovered, were swiftly put to death. For this reason, we know relatively little about the mystery schools of ancient Greece. Their secrets never were completely betrayed. We have only hints.

In our own time, we have such fraternities as the Skull and Bones of Yale University, founded in 1832, to which many American leaders have belonged, including former president George W. Bush. The secrets have been kept, and the teachings and true purpose of this society remain a mystery.

In my view, these modern secret societies are hollow and ultimately meaningless because they have no higher spiritual purpose. Men inducted into Skull and Bones may gain some practical networking advantage with fellow members of the club, but their secret teachings are void of value. They are merely playacting, in the degenerate sense of the term. By contrast, initiation into modern occult lodges, like that of the ancient mystery schools, is performed before the spirits who preside over those organizations, with their aid and approval, and for this reason occult initiation may be potent with the highest spiritual and magical meaning.

The Arbatel of Magic

I say that initiation into an occult lodge "may" be potent with spiritual and magical meaning because it depends entirely on the lodge. If the lodge is presided over at the highest level, not by men and women but by spirit teachers who are present during initiation ceremonies, and who give the esoteric teachings of the lodge to its members, then those teachings may have great value for the initiates. But if the lodge is moribund and has been abandoned by spirit teachers, the teachings it has to offer will never resonate at the highest level with its members, even though in earlier times those same teachings may have held great significance for those who received them from the spirits.

There is a mystery here that is not well understood. The teachings of magic must be matched to the mind and soul of the student who receives them, and the student must be transformed on both a physical and mental level before he can truly comprehend the teachings or be able to work those teachings to advantage in his own life. Very few are the magicians who have grasped this reality of magic.

One of them was the author of the grimoire known as the *Arbatel of Magic*, or sometimes as the *Isagoge*. This is an incomplete work that was first published in Latin in 1575. The original Latin title is *Arbatel de Magia Veterum* (*The Arbatel of Ancient Magic*). The complete work projected by the anonymous author was to have been in nine books, but it was never finished. *Isagoge* (Greek, meaning "Introduction") is the name of the first book, which is the only book that was completed.

The great truth that an initiate must receive magic from spirit teachers, not from men alone, is revealed by the anonymous author of the *Arbatel*. It is a truth everywhere observable in Western magic, but it was the genius of the author that he recognized from many diverse examples their single uniting principle.

After describing the Olympic hierarchy of spirits, he wrote in Aphorism 18 of his *Isagoge*:

> There are other names of the *Olympick* spirits delivered by others; but they onely are effectual, which are delivered to any one, by the Spirit the revealer, visible or invisible: and they are delivered to every one as they are predestinated: therefore they are called Constellations; and they seldome have any efficacie above 40 yeers. Therefore it is most safe for the young practisers of Art, that they work by the offices of the Spirits alone, without their names; and if they are pre-ordained to attain the Art of Magick, the other parts of the Art will offer themselves unto them of their own accord. Pray therefore for a constant faith, and God will bring to pass all things in due season.[2]

The seven Olympic spirits are planetary spirits. Their natures derive from the seven crystalline planetary spheres of ancient astrology. The names of the Olympic spirits empower those spirits for the magician who speaks and writes the names and enables the spirits to cause change in the world. But the true names of these spirits are unique for each magician who seeks to use them and must be revealed by the magician's tutelary spirit – the being described in the *Arbatel* as "the Spirit, the revealer, visible or invisible."

It is the function of this teaching spirit to reveal the key to magic to the practitioner of the art. This revelation occurs during a ritual of initiation in which the consciousness of the practitioner is transformed and elevated. The practitioner casts away his former identity and embraces a new identity. Sometimes this metamorphosis is symbolized by the adoption of a secret name or motto, a distant but living echo of the ancient mysteries.

Elsewhere in the *Isagoge*, in Aphorism 9, our author gives the hierarchy of wisdom received by various beings:

> That is the chiefest wisdom, which is from God; and next, that which is in spiritual creatures; afterwards, in corporal creatures; fourthly, in Nature, and natural things. The Spirits that are apostate, and reserved to the last judgement, do follow these, after a long interval. Sixthly, the ministers of punishments in hell, and the obedient unto God. Seventhly, the Pigmies do not possess the lowest place, and they who inhabit in elements, and elementary things.[3]

We see from this that the highest teachings come from God directly, and God is a spiritual creature – the supreme spirit. The next best teachers are the spirits of God, or angels, and those spirits of a celestial nature who have not fallen. After them, the best teachers are enlightened sages and prophets. Next follow the lessons to be learned by the study of the natural world, what we today call science. Then, after a long gap, come the fallen angels who remain rebellious toward God, and after them the demons who administer the punishments of hell and, in this sense, are obedient to God. Finally, but not in the lowest place, come the spirits of the elements, such as the salamanders of fire, the sylphs of air, the undines of water, and the pygmies or gnomes of earth, that were distinguished by Paracelsus.[4] That they are not in the lowest place suggests that we still have useful things to learn from them.

In the *Arbatel*, Aphorism 11, it is stated: "This Art [of discerning and commanding spirits] is not delivered, but divinely. Unto whom God will, he revealeth his secrets; but to whom he will not bestow any thing out of his treasuries, that person shall attain to nothing without the will of God." In Aphorism 12 is stated: "There is no other manner of restoring these Arts, than by the doctrine of the holy Spirits of God; because true *faith cometh by hearing.*"

In the prayer to God that appears in Aphorism 14, the aspirant asks God to supply him with a spirit who shall act as teacher:

> *Because I earnestly desire perfectly to know the Arts of this life and such things as are necessary for us, which are so overwhelmed in darkness, and polluted with infinite humane opinions, that I of my own power can attain to no knowledge in them, unless thou teach it me: Grant me therefore one of thy spirits, who may teach me those things which thou wouldest have me to know and learn, to thy praise and glory, and the profit of our neighbour. Give me also an apt and teachable heart, that I may easily understand those things which thou shalt teach me, and may hide them in my understanding, that I may bring them forth as out of thy inexhaustible treasures, to all necessary uses. And give me grace, that I may use such thy gifts humbly, with fear and trembling, through our Lord Jesus Christ, with thy holy Spirit.* Amen.

In Aphorism 17-5, the important point is made that no one can seize magic by force of will alone – magic must be given from on high by a spirit: "A man that is a true Magician, is brought forth a Magician from his mother's womb: others, who do give themselves to this office, are unhappy. This is that which *John* the Baptist speaketh of: *No man can do any thing of himself, except it be given him from above.*"[5] This is another way of saying that true initiation into magic can only come from God, or from the spirits of God.

Many of the greatest sages, prophets and teachers received their occult initiation and instruction directly from God, or at least, so it is claimed by those who later wrote about them. It will be objected by some readers that the men I am going to consider here were prophets and holy men, not magicians. In my opinion they were, indeed, magicians, even if the holy texts that refer to them do not present them as such, and even if they themselves did not think of themselves as magicians.

Moses

When Moses went up upon the slope (not the peak) of Mount Horeb[6] and encountered the burning bush, he learned that it was the initial revelation of the spirit of the mountain, Yahweh, his teacher in the arts of magic. Yahweh gave him detailed instructions as to what he must do to liberate the Hebrews from slavery in Egypt. Moses was empowered by the spirit of the mountain to do three acts of magic in order to impress the Pharaoh of Egypt – he was shown how to turn his wooden walking staff into a writhing serpent, and back to a staff; he was enabled to make his hand white with leprosy, then instantly return it to good health; and he was shown how to turn a pitcher of water he drew out of the River Nile into what appeared to be red blood as the water was poured onto the dry ground.

When Moses came before Pharaoh, he performed the serpent trick and the water-into-blood trick, but not the leprosy trick. As it transpired, the priests of Egypt, who were also magicians, were able to duplicate both tricks,[7] and Pharaoh was not impressed. Thereafter, Moses continued to communicate with the mountain god via prayer and meditation, and by returning to the mountain. Throughout the plagues that subsequently visited Egypt, the spirit of the mountain continued to counsel and instruct Moses, who relied on the learning and eloquence of his brother, Aaron, to debate points of legality with the Egyptians.

The final initiation of Moses into the wisdom of the occult arts came upon the peak of Mount Sinai, in the third month after the liberation of the Hebrews from Egypt, where he received the Ten Commandments and the other laws which he set over the Hebrews. Yahweh no doubt imparted to Moses secret teachings that Moses never revealed, except perhaps to his brother Aaron, but about this little is written.

Moses represents the entire Hebrew nation, so in a sense his initiation is *their* initiation. Yahweh vowed to make the nation of the Hebrews a nation of priests. This occurred when they were given the covenant: "And Moses took the blood, and sprinkled it on the people, and said, Behold the blood of the covenant which the Lord hath made with you concerning all these words."[8]

To receive his final initiation, Moses undertook an ordeal of fasting and exposure to the elements that lasted for forty days and nights. This ordeal transformed him and made his face to shine brightly in imitation of the face of Yahweh, which was too blindingly brilliant to even look upon. During this period, he was taught how to construct the tabernacle, the altar, and all the instruments of religion used thereafter by the Hebrews. This is usually looked upon as the reception of a system of religion, but it can also be viewed as the reception of a system of magic, since religion was used for magical purposes in ancient times.

What we have in the story of Moses is a magician who receives a complete system of magic from his spirit teacher, Yahweh, who from an occult perspective may be regarded as the tutelary spirit of Moses.

Solomon

Let us consider another great figure in Jewish lore, King Solomon, son of King David, whom scholars believe reigned at Jerusalem during the tenth century BC. He is said in the Old Testament books to be the wisest of all men, who received his gift of wisdom from Yahweh during sleep. The story goes that when Solomon was a young boy, he had a dream in which Yahweh appeared to him and asked what gifts he would wish to receive in return for the magnificent burnt offering of a thousand beasts that Solomon had just made. Young Solomon asked for an understanding heart and discerning judgment, so that he might judge his people wisely. The spirit Yahweh was pleased with his modest request and assured him that he should receive not only the gifts of understanding and good judgment, but also riches and honor, as well as a long life.[9]

What is not mentioned in the books of the Old Testament is that Solomon became a master of the art of magic and was able to command the demons of hell to do his bidding. Who taught Solomon this art? It is reasonable to assume it must have been either God or the angels of God. Indeed, in the first century pseudepigraphical work known as the *Testament of Solomon*, he received from the archangel Michael a magic ring impressed with a seal in the shape of a pentagram that could be used to control demons by impressing the seal on the ring into the demon's flesh.

Using this ring, Solomon gained control of Beelzebub, who is said to have been the highest angel in heaven before being cast down to the earth. Solomon commanded Beelzebub and his demons to build the first Temple at Jerusalem, the dimensions of which were communicated to Moses. This would have been difficult for human stonemasons because one of the conditions of God was that all the stones used in the Temple were to be natural, unshaped by hammer and chisel. Natural stones preserve their original occult potential. For the same reason, Moses was told that the early altars built to Yahweh should be of natural stones only.

There is little mention in the Bible of Solomon's magical abilities. However, it is said in I Kings 11:9-13 that God became angry with him because, despite God's explicit command to Solomon that he not go after foreign gods, Solomon turned to foreign gods. What does this mean? Does it only imply that Solomon worshipped foreign gods? Or, as seems more likely, does it suggest Solomon went to foreign priests seeking to enlarge his knowledge of magic? Or perhaps even that Solomon communicated with foreign gods to learn secrets of magic directly from them?

Solomon's fame as a magician was so widespread, numerous texts on magic were ascribed to him, the most famous being the *Key of Solomon*, which is widely used by modern Western magicians as a source text. This grimoire purports to be the legacy left by Solomon to his son, Roboam. It is asserted in the introduction that it was written in cipher on the bark of trees, with the occult sigils that are its primary component inscribed on plates of copper, and that it was preserved in the Temple at Jerusalem.

Treasure up, O my son Roboam! the wisdom of my words, seeing that I, Solomon, have received it from the Lord.

Then answered Roboam, and said: How have I deserved to follow the example of my father Solomon in such things, who hath been found worthy to receive the knowledge of all living things through [the teaching of] an angel of God?

And Solomon said: Hear, O my son, and receive my sayings, and learn the wonders of God. For, on a certain night, when I laid me down to sleep, I called upon that most holy name of God, IAH, and prayed for the ineffable wisdom, and when I was beginning to close mine eyes, the angel of the Lord, even Homadiel, appeared unto me, spake many things courteously unto me, and said: Listen O Solomon! thy prayer before the most high is not in vain, and since thou hast asked neither for long life, nor for much riches, nor for the souls of thine enemies, but hast asked for thyself wisdom to perform justice. Thus saith the Lord: According to thy word have I given unto thee a wise and understanding heart, so that before thee was none like unto thee, nor ever shall arise.

And when I comprehended the speech which was made unto me, I understood that in me was the knowledge of all creatures, both things which are in the heavens and things which are beneath the heavens; and I saw that all the writings and wisdom of this present age were vain and futile, and that no man was perfect. And I composed a certain work wherein I rehearsed the secret of secrets, in which I have preserved them hidden, and I have also therein concealed all secrets whatsoever of magical arts of any masters; any secret or experiments, namely, of these sciences which is in any way worth being accomplished. Also I have written them in this Key, so that like as a key openeth a treasure-house, so this

> [Key] alone may open the knowledge and understanding of magical arts and sciences.[10]

After the death of Roboam, it is asserted that the book was laid in the sepulchre of King Solomon, where it remained until found by "certain Babylonian Philosophers." By this is meant the Magi of Babylon, a priestly cast renowned for their skill in the arts of magic throughout the ancient world. None of them could decipher the meaning of the text, not even the oldest and wisest of them all, Iohé Grevis, until he humbled himself by falling on his face on the ground, weeping and striking his breast, and praying to "God, the Creator of all" that the secret of the *Key* be revealed to him. An angel of God appeared to him, and after making him promise never to reveal the text to the unworthy, suddenly the obscure text became plain to his understanding.

One of the points to be observed from this fable is that the text of Solomon's book, which presumably was intelligible to his son, was obscure to the Magi of Babylon until one of them humbled himself (ordeal) and was initiated by an angel of God. Why was the text plain to Roboam and obscure at first to Iohé Grevis? This harks back to the instruction in the *Isagoge* that living magic cannot endure much beyond forty years, and that after that period, illumination must be sought from the spirits. Roboam received the magic directly from Solomon – a son, directly from his father. Because of this occult connection, the wisdom which was given to Solomon by the angel of God was able to be passed on by Solomon to Roboam.

It is a common practice in both the East and West for magicians to take disciples and pass on their magic to them. Quite often their disciples are their own sons. This practice stems from ancient shamanism, where it was the practice of a shaman to teach his son magic, provided his son was suited by nature to receive the teaching. In the East, it is said that the guru passes on occult wisdom to his disciple, when the disciple is ready to receive it, by means of a mantra, which acts as a key to both occult knowledge and a wellspring of occult power. The mantra can only be passed from *guru* to *chila*. To anyone else, it would be meaningless and useless.

The divine inspiration that allows a magician to grasp the art of magic extends itself for one generation, from father to son, or from master to pupil, but after that it must be refreshed by direct communication with the spirits, who provide a new and different key to the occult mysteries.

Jesus

Jesus was the disciple of John the Baptist, who you will remember is mentioned in Aphorism 17-5 of the *Isagoge*: "This is that which *John* the Baptist speaketh of: *No man can do any thing of himself, except it be given him from above*." Everything I am trying to convey in this essay is summed up in this statement by John. No true mastery of magic is possible without the initiation of spirit teachers.

It must be emphasized here that in writing about Jesus, I am writing about the way in which an enlightened man acquired the art of magic from spiritual beings. I treat Jesus as a man, and I treat God as a spirit. No blasphemy or irreligion is intended, but I can find no clear demarcation between magic and miracles.

The baptism by John was Jesus's initiation rite of entrance or beginning, just as it is the initiation rite of all Christians.

> And Jesus, when he was baptized, went up straightway out of the water: and, lo, the heavens were opened unto him, and he saw the spirit of God descending like a dove, and lighting upon him. And lo a voice from heaven, saying, This is my beloved Son, in whom I am well pleased.[11]

It seems likely that as a young man Jesus was the member of a secret sect of scholars and sages prior to venturing forth to teach and preach. Some occult authors have claimed he acquired his higher wisdom from the Essenes, but as I have tried to suggest, if he studied with the Essenes he gained only the dead bones of wisdom from their esoteric books. It was not until the spirit of God descended upon him that he was illuminated and became fully capable of understanding the ways of magic. It was God, or the angels of God, who taught him his own unique form of magic, which he could never have acquired from books. But before his knowledge could be perfected, it was necessary that he pass through an occult ordeal in which his worth was proven.

After initial contact was made with his spirit teacher, Jesus underwent the ordeal in the wilderness, in which he left the towns and villages of humanity and went forth alone into the waste places of the earth, where dwell the demons and evil spirits. He did not go forth of his own initiative but was led there by his spirit teacher: "Then was Jesus led up of the Spirit into the wilderness to be tempted of the devil."[12]

We see in this a pattern that repeats itself. The magician John Dee did not leave the security and comfort of his family house at Mortlake to undertake a long and dangerous journey to Bohemia because he wanted to – he did it because the Enochian spirits compelled him to do it. Similarly, when S. L. MacGregor Mathers moved from London to Paris, it was not because he wanted to do so, but because the Secret Chiefs told him to do so.

The devil tempted Jesus in the wilderness in various ways, but Jesus cast him away by invoking the power of the name of God. The author of the Gospel of Matthew writes: "Then the devil leaveth him; and behold, angels came and ministered unto him."[13] The parallel here with the forty days and nights that Moses endured on Mount Sinai before being given the great revelation by God is completely intentional. Immediately after the successful completion of his ordeal, Jesus began to collect his disciples.

After the ordeal on the cross, when Jesus ascended to yet a higher and more refined level of being, his disciples were confused and dispirited. They did not know what to do. Jesus had cured the sick, raised the dead, cast out demons, and performed other miracles, but his disciples could do none of these things. Why would anyone follow them or pay attention to their teachings? All this changed on the Pentecost, when the spirit of God, which had descended upon Jesus following his baptism by John, descended upon the heads of his disciples and caused them to begin to speak in strange languages.[14] They found themselves able to work the wonders Jesus had worked, merely by invoking his name. But only the twelve who had received the gift of the Holy Spirit were able to do this – anyone else who tried to use his name alone to cast out demons, without a soul inflamed by spiritual wisdom, failed miserably.

During the period when they followed Jesus, he taught them the dead bones of esoteric lore. They learned both the outer teachings he gave to the public who came to hear him preach, and the secret teachings he reserved only for his closest followers. But this teaching was not energized and empowered until the Holy Spirit descended on their heads and made them able to use it, as their master had used it. Again, we see that without the spirit teacher that transformed each disciple, the teachings of Jesus would have remained barren.

It is not enough merely to establish contact with spirits. Countless trance mediums have managed to do this, and they are unchanged by it, having no magical abilities of any kind. Spirit communication is only of value if those spirits become our teachers and work with us to transform us, not only on the intellectual and emotional levels, but on the physical level of our nervous systems. Spirit communication is the first step in becoming a true magician, but of itself it is not the fulfillment. It opens the door, but you must pass through that door with the guidance and help of your spirit teachers.

Mohammed

As we come to the prophet of Islam, the overall pattern we've been examining begins to sound familiar. In the year 610, when Mohammed was approaching his fortieth birthday, he had a vision of the archangel Gabriel, who commanded him to "Read!" Mohammed told the angel he didn't know how to read, whereupon the angel hugged him fiercely to his breast. Again he told Mohammed to read, and again Mohammed was forced to declare his ignorance. Again the angel hugged him. The same thing happened a third time, but after hugging him the angel told him to recite the following verse, which later was to appear in the Koran:

Proclaim! (or Read!)
In the name
Of thy Lord and Cherisher,
Who created –

Created man, out of
A (mere) clot
Of congealed blood:
Proclaim! And thy Lord
Is Most Bountiful, –
He Who taught
(The use of) the Pen, –
Taught man that
Which he knew not.[15]

It is important to know that in Arabic, the word for "read" is the same word for "recite aloud." The angel was ordering Mohammed to recite or proclaim that God himself taught mankind by his sacred texts "that which he knew not."

Mohammed had already started to take himself apart from other men so that he could meditate. He would go alone to a cave some three miles outside his native city of Mecca and in that place he began to have spiritually meaningful dreams. There followed a second vision of Gabriel while he was climbing a mountain, in which Mohammed saw the angel between the sky and the earth. Whichever direction he looked, he saw the angel.

The earliest biographer of Mohammed, Ibn Ishãq, puts a different spin on the climb Mohammed made up the mountain. He says Mohammed was so shaken and horrified by his initial encounter with Gabriel, he decided to commit suicide by throwing himself off a high place, rather than risk becoming a man possessed by spirits. However, Gabriel came to him three times on the mountainside and prevented him from killing himself.

Thus began his spiritual instruction by Gabriel. It was only after achieving this union with the angel that Mohammed was enabled to become a prophet. He was not happy about it in the beginning, but sometimes the spirits do not give any choice about acquiring higher wisdom. Some are called and cannot decline the call. Mohammed only began preaching his message after the transforming encounter with his tutelary angel, and after passing through the ordeal of belief that caused him to attempt suicide.

How do we know that Mohammed was a magician? He is reported to have performed numerous magical works, which are referred to as miracles. Religions like to refer to their magic as miracles. These differ only in name from similar wonder works performed by recognized magicians of the ancient world, such as Apollonius of Tyana and Simon Magus. I will give a few examples. When requested to give proof of his magical power, Mohammed is said to have split the moon into two halves. At the Battle of Tabuk he caused water to pour forth from the dry ground and slaked the thirst of thousands of his soldiers – there was so much water they were even able to wash in it. During the Battle of Badr he took up a handful of dust and threw it in the direction of the enemy, and many of the enemy soldiers were instantly blinded. During the Battle of Khaybar, he spat into the blind eye of Ali, his son-in-law, and Ali's eye was instantly healed.

Structure of Spirit Initiation

We don't know all the details in the lives of these great religious figures, particularly their early lives, but what we do know should be enough to offer a general pattern. They are of a meditative inclination of mind and are visited by a spirit who sometimes identifies itself as a god, sometimes as an angel, and becomes their teacher of esoteric secrets. After passing through a crisis or ordeal, they emerge transformed and empowered, able to use the secrets they have acquired to the fullest degree. They go on to create a school where their disciples receive the same teachings they received from their tutelary spirit.

It will be useful to lay out the basic pattern of occult initiation by spirits. It consists of the following six stages:

Preparation
Training
Ordeal
Initiation
Revelatio
Union

Bear in mind that not all accounts of spirit initiation contain all six steps. The steps are usually there, but in the retelling of the events sometimes steps are minimized or glossed over.

The first stage, *preparation*, is when the person seeking occult knowledge and power begins to dwell on spiritual and esoteric matters. He spends a lot of time on his own, apart from society, and has little interest in the pastimes of his family and friends. He becomes thoughtful, silent, brooding. He may neglect his appearance because the impression he makes on others no longer seems important to him. He seeks out mystics and questions them intensely and reads any books he can find on magic and spiritual attainment.

At this initial stage he will begin to exercise himself in magic by walking through magic rituals recorded in the grimoires, wearing ritual robes, acquiring and making ritual instruments and furniture, memorizing occult information such as the names of the zodiac signs and the order of the planets.

Stage two, *training*, occurs under the guidance of spirit teachers. The student may not be aware of their presence, but they shape his interests so that he begins to devote all his time and energy to one form of occult practice. As he practises, he begins to evolve his own unique exercises at the direction of his tutelary spirit, or spirits. These exercises are designed to transform him into a magician. Such a transformation is neither quick nor easy. To develop the will, the imagination, and the nervous system, so that they are capable of prolonged spirit communication, is no easier and no quicker than body building. It requires years, although good progress can be seen within a few months of intense training.

The third stage, *the ordeal*, is essential to the passage from ordinary self to magical self. You will find it in all shamanic practices around the world, and it has descended to the Western occult lodges, although usually in a symbolic form. Indigenous Americans knew it as the vision quest. The ordeal is both mental and physical.

Alexandra David-Néel (1868-1969), a French woman who traveled through Tibet during the early decades of the 20th century, described in her 1929 book *Magic and Mystery in Tibet* a ritual called *chöd*, a shamanic ritual of the old Tibetan *bon* religion that was absorbed into Tibetan Buddhism when Tibet became Buddhist in the latter half of the 7th century.

The young monk takes himself to a place where the corpse of a person newly dead has been dismembered and left on the ground for the vultures and other scavengers. He calls demons to him, and they begin to dismember his living flesh and cut him into small pieces, which they consume, until there is nothing left of him. At that point the monk commands the demons to return and restore his body, which they do. He then dismisses them, having demonstrated command over the lower spirits, and over his own fears.

The ritual does not always work out well for the monk. David-Néel encountered a young monk whom this ritual had rendered raving mad. An older monk explained to her that the young monk had undertaken the *chöd* ritual, but had failed to master his fear, and therefore had not been able to achieve dominance over the demonic spirits. The experience drove him completely insane. He was constantly seeing demons and hearing their taunting voices screaming at him. She was told that sometimes such afflicted monks found their way back to sanity, and sometimes they did not.

> "Rimpoche," I said, "I warn you seriously. I have some medical knowledge; your disciple may gravely injure his health and be driven to madness by the terror he experiences. He really appeared to feel himself being eaten alive."
>
> "No doubt he is," answered the lama, with the same calm, "but he does not understand that he is himself the eater. Maybe that he will learn it later on…"
>
> I was about to reply, arguing that the poor novice might, before that time came, give other candidates for secret lore the opportunity of performing *chöd* before his own corpse. Perhaps the lama guessed what I was about to say, for without allowing me time to utter a word, he added, slightly raising his voice:
>
> "You seem to imply that you have had some kind of training in the 'Short Path.' Did your spiritual teacher not

> inform you of the risks and did you not agree that you were ready to run these three: illness, madness and death?"[16]

The *chöd* ritual of *bon*-infused Tibetan Buddhism is very similar in spirit to the corpse-sitting ritual (*śāva sādhanā*) that is used in the short path of Hindu tantric magic. The practitioner procures the corpse of a young man without defect in body and carries it to a place of cremation, a deserted house, or other place where spirits are thought to congregate. After washing the corpse, the practitioner draws a magic circle of protection around it and inscribes a magic mandala design on its back. He then sits upon the back of the corpse (details vary – some practitioners sit upon the chest, or stomach). By meditation and the use of mantra he calls into the corpse the god Shiva, who blesses him with the ability to create mantras and unites with him to produce in him an egoless consciousness.

I mention the *chöd* ritual of Tibet because it illustrates that when the magical initiation is genuine, the ordeal is not merely symbolic, but very real and dangerous. The primary danger, apart from any physical punishments the ordeal may involve, is the loss of reason. When you invite spirits into your mind to freely communicate with you, and they come, it is not always easy to send them away again, or to silence their voices. The key to doing so is the realization that such spirits are not real, but only shadows of your own fears. Once you realize that you are generating these spirit voices and visions, you realize you have the power to control them because they stem from your own mental process.

It is easy to make the error of thinking that because some spirits are mere shadows, all spirits must be shadows. This is not true. Those who fall into this trap are prevented from advancement by their own materialism. The magician understands that spirits are both real and illusion at the same time. He must be able to hold two points of view that are contradictory in his mind simultaneously, without dismissing either of them.

The fourth stage, *initiation*, is often bound up with the ordeal. The working through of the ordeal is a part of the initiation process, and when the ordeal has been successfully completed, the initiation can fulfill itself.

The fifth stage, *revelation*, comes at the end of the initiation ritual. During the initiation, the student comes into communication with the highest spiritual being of whom he has been made aware during his preparation and training. This supreme spirit, who may be an angel or a god, but is always a being of great power and wisdom, radiant with light, will reveal to the student certain esoteric secrets that have special meaning and application in the student's life. The student will usually be told to keep this revelation secret, except to his own disciple or disciples.

The final stage of spirit initiation, *union*, is a sense of peace and oneness with the highest spiritual source, coupled with the inner awareness that the world is evolving according to plan, that nothing is out of place or defective, but everything is unfolding like the petals of a flower in harmony and order. This awareness is extremely powerful and may be likened to the *samadhi* of Eastern mystics, which is sometimes called the attainment of universal consciousness. The euphoria it brings lasts for days or weeks, but slowly declines as the mind returns to its normal, everyday state.

The initiation ritual, whatever form it may take – and the forms are varied – functions as a kind of marriage ceremony with the higher tutelary spirit who will give the gift of true magic to the magician. During the training period he may be assisted by other lesser spirit teachers who may become his familiar spirits. They can prepare the student for the ordeal and initiation but cannot convey the highest revelations that follow successful initiation. These come only from the spirit who is sometimes referred to as the Higher Self, and characterized by Christians as the light of God, or Christ, that shines within each individual human being.

Establishing contact with a spirit teacher should be the primary goal of anyone who seeks to understand and practice magic. It may happen that contact is thrust upon a human being by a spirit, when the spirit teacher knows the potential of its student better than the student himself, but more often it must be diligently courted by a long regimen of prayer, meditation and study.

Once communication has been established, the spirit teacher will guide and shape the consciousness of the student, rendering his mind suitable for the performance of magic. This is accomplished over an extended period but culminates with a ritual ordeal that embodies all that has gone before it, and symbolically represents death and rebirth. Passage through this ritual ordeal awakens the self-awareness of the student to his own magical potential and initiates his new life as a magician.

Sometimes this is symbolized by the adoption of a second magical name that remains secret, or the replacement of the birth-name of the individual by the magical name. Sometimes, in occult fraternities that presume to teach systems of magic, this adoption of a second magical name, or change of the birth name, takes place before the magician has actually undergone the ordeal and received the revelation. In these cases, it may be regarded as a foreshadowing by the student of what he wishes to accomplish – the transformation of the old and familiar into something new and significant.

Faust

Spirit initiation is not always by angels into the light of holy spirit. There is a dark side of magic, and a dark form of magical initiation that accompanies it. Contrasting with the magician who practices high magic, or thaumaturgy, is the black magician who works goetic magic and derives his abilities from a pact with Satan. He attains nothing on his own merits. His unearned power is simply given to him, or the devil merely appoints a serving demon to fulfill the black magician's wishes in exchange for the pledge of the magician's soul.

The thaumaturge may employ the services of lower spirits in works of a grossly physical nature, but he always does so from a position of authority and command. His authority stems from the highest spirit of light that instructed and initiated him in the art of magic. The goetic magician has no authority over the lower spirits who do his bidding, but relies on the authority of the spirit with whom he has made a pact. Such was the case with the most famous European black magician, Johann Faust, who in folklore was given a demon to serve his wishes.

According to folklore, Faust tried to summon the devil to visual appearance by a ritual of evocation. Instead, the demon Mephistopheles appeared and offered to serve him. The story is told in a 1587 English pamphlet titled *Historia & Tale of Doctor Johannes Faustus, The sorcerer, wherein is described specifically and veraciously: His entire life and death, How he did oblige himself for a certain time unto the Devil, And what happened to him, And how he at last got his well-deserved reward.*

The pamphlet relates that Faust was an educated man who received a doctorate in theology from the University of Wittenberg. He had an insatiable thirst for knowledge, which led him to the study of forbidden books of black magic. We see here the initial two stages of spirit initiation, but alas, initiation in the black arts does not entail the ordeal that leads to personal transformation and higher spiritual knowledge.

Faust attempted to summon the devil at a crossroad deep in the Spesser Wald forest near Wittenberg. After many frightening and amazing apparitions, a spirit came to him and agreed to visit his living chamber the following morning. Faust was disappointed to learn that the spirit was not Satan, the lord of hell. The spirit, who later in the pamphlet is identified as Mephostophiles, explained:

> Now thou shalt know, Fauste, said the spirit, that among us there is a government and sovereignty, just as on earth, for we have our rulers and governors and servants – of whom I am one – and we call our kingdom Legion. For although the banished devil Lucifer brought about his own fall through vanity and insolence, he raised up a Legion, nevertheless, and a government of devils, and we call him the Oriental Prince, for he had his sovereignty in Ascension. It is thus a sovereignty *in Meridie, Septentrione* and *Occidente* as well. Therefore, inasmuch as Lucifer the fallen angel now hath his sovereignty and principality beneath the Heavens, we must, on account of this transformation, betake ourselves unto mankind and serve them. But with all his power and arts man could

> not make Lucifer subservient, except that a spirit be sent,
> as I am sent.[17]

The idea that a person can voluntarily pledge their immortal soul into the keeping of Satan may seem odd to modern readers, but it was a common view in the 16th century. In his occult diaries, the magician John Dee several times mentions that he has put his "soul in pawn" to Edward Kelley. What did Dee mean by these strange words? He meant that he had voluntarily offered his own soul in place of the soul of Edward Kelley, his crystal gazer, should Kelley ever find himself damned because of his service to John Dee. It was a way of reassuring Kelley that after death he would not go to hell because of his obedience to Dee's instructions. Instead, the devil would take Dee's soul, and leave Kelley's untouched. Of course, Dee did not believe his work to be devilish, or that his own soul would ever be threatened.

The figure of Faust the magician is based on a real person, although there is some doubt about his specific identity. It seems likely to me that he was Johann Georg Faust (1466-1541). He was an alchemist, astrologer and magician who, like so many scholars at the time, wandered around Europe seeking wealthy patrons. The actual Faust died of an alchemical explosion in which his body was horribly mutilated.

It is interesting to note that Faust became the archetype of the black magician through the play *The Tragical History of Doctor Faustus* by Christopher Marlowe, first published in 1604, and John Dee became the archetype of the white magician through William Shakespeare's play *The Tempest*, which was first published in 1623. John Dee and Johann Faust were contemporaries. Indeed, it is not beyond the bounds of possibility that they actually met each other during one of Dee's travels through Europe.

Faust angrily told the spirit he had summoned that he would not damn his soul. The spirit replied in a mocking way that Faust was already damned due to the sins he had committed in his past life, so what did selling his soul matter? Enraged, Faust banished the spirit, but the spirit came to him later in the day and set down his terms of service in three points: (1) that he should serve Faust for a set number of years, after which Faust should belong to him, (2) that Faust would give himself over to the spirit with a contract written and signed with his own blood, and (3) that Faust must renounce the Christian faith.

The author of the pamphlet declares that this black pact was found in Faust's house after his death and gives its wording. In part it reads:

> Now therefore have I summoned the spirit who calleth himself Mephostophiles, a servant of the Hellish Prince in Orient, charged with informing and instructing me, and agreeing against a promissory instrument hereby transferred unto him to be subservient and obedient to me in all things.
>
> I do promise him in return that, when I be fully sated of that which I desire of him, twenty-four years also being past, ended and expired, he may at such a time and in whatever manner or wise pleaseth him order, ordain, reign, rule and possess all that may be mine: body, property, flesh, blood, etc., herewith duly bound over in eternity and surrendered by covenant in mine own hand by authority and power of these presents, as well as of my mind, brain, intent, blood and will.
>
> I do now defy all living beings, all the Heavenly Host and all mankind, and this must be.
>
> In confirmation and contract whereof I have drawn out mine own blood for certification in lieu of a seal.
>
> Doctor Faustus, Adept.[18]

Thereafter, for the term of 24 years, his familiar spirit supplied Faust with all the wine, food, and fine clothing he desired, along with an allowance of 24 gold crowns per week. When Faust expressed a desire to marry, he was sternly told by the devil himself that this could not be, but Mephostophiles offered to supply him with whichever women he might desire, by entrancing them and bringing them to Faust's bed. To satisfy his lust for knowledge the spirit gave him "a great book containing all manner of sorcery and *nigromantia*."

When his 24 years were up, Mephostophiles came for Faust in a great storm wind during the hour after midnight and dashed out Faust's brains on the walls of his bedroom, then threw his still-twitching corpse onto a dung heap. So says the pamphlet, upon which the legend of Faust the black magician is based.

We see in the progress of Faust a seeking after forbidden knowledge, which attracts a spirit teacher. For Faust it was the spirit Mephostophiles. The seeker is compelled to sign a contract pledging his or her soul to the spirit. For Faust it was necessary that he write out the contract in full. Bear in mind that Faust knew how to read and write, being an educated man, but most common people of the 16th century were not educated. It is my own belief that a pledge of fidelity or solidarity with the spirit teacher was all that was needed to seal the pact, and the pledge did not even necessarily need to be spoken aloud. After the pledge of service, gifts are given to the black magician by the spirit, but there is no spiritual attainment involved. The mind of the black magician is not transformed by higher consciousness, nor is there any ordeal to fulfill, for the ordeal of the black magician comes after death, not during life, and that ordeal has no transformative saving grace.

Abramelin

I move on to the grimoires here to show that the general pattern of spirit initiation occurs there as well, and more importantly, that the presence of spirit teachers is absolutely essential for obtaining a living system of magic that will prove effective and rewarding. Someone can go through the motions of ceremonial magic by imitating the rituals and using the seals that are found in the grimoires, but one is not a true magician until his spirit teacher opens his mind to his own unique forms and instruments.

One of the most famous grimoires, at least for those of us who actually study the occult arts, is the *Book of the Sacred Magic of Abramelin the Mage*. This is a German grimoire that was translated from a French manuscript in the *Bibliothèque de l'Arsenal* into English by the magician of the Hermetic Order of the Golden Dawn, Samuel Mathers, and published in 1898.[19] It had a profound influence on the philosophy and magic of the members of the Golden Dawn, including Aleister Crowley, who made the magical process of *Abramelin* the centerpiece for his own magical evolution.

The Golden Dawn was a secret order that taught practical magic in the Western tradition. Started by three high-ranking Freemasons, its grade initiations incorporated elements of Masonic ritual, but the symbolism of the Golden Dawn was much more esoteric. One of the three founders, Samuel Mathers, was not only a Freemason but a seer and a mystic who spent much of his time studying occult manuscripts in the British Museum. It was through Mathers and his equally mediumistic wife, Moïna, that the Golden Dawn system of magic was received from spirits calling themselves the Secret Chiefs.

It must be mentioned that the manuscript Mathers used as his source for his translation of *Abramelin* was imperfect and incomplete. The *Abramelin* has more recently been translated into English by Stephen Guth from a 2001 German translation.[20] The most important difference between Mathers' translation and the modern translation occurs in the section of the text devoted to magic squares. In the Mathers version, most of the magic squares, which consist of ranks and files of letters, are incomplete. This led many magicians, Crowley among them, to assume that they were intended to be incomplete. In the Guth translation all the squares are complete, as they are in the original German version of the text.

In the Mathers version, which most English-speaking magicians have used for the past hundred years and more, the text is divided into three books. The first book is a kind of memoir written by Abraham the Jew to his son, Lamech, and relates the ten-year quest of Abraham to find what he described as "the True Mysteries of the Lord."[21]

In Egypt, Abraham discovered the sage Abramelin, who taught him the method of gaining communication with his Holy Guardian Angel. This is the heart of the *Abramelin* text, and without it the rest of the text has little value. The Holy Guardian Angel is the highest personal expression of divine power and wisdom that an individual human being can attain. It is equivalent to the tutelary daemon so well known to the ancient Greeks.

The Greeks believed that each human being has a spirit who watches over him and attempts to guide his path through life. Some individuals are blessed with the ability to perceive the warnings and encouragements of their personal daemons. The philosopher Socrates was renowned for not only his wisdom, but for his daemon, which warned him of impending dangers by means of certain signs that the philosopher understood.

It is my belief that all the spirits who initiate us as magicians and who teach us true, living systems of magic are our Holy Guardian Angels, or aspects of our Holy Guardian Angels. The quest of any person for spirits who will teach the secrets of magic is always, at root, a quest for the conversation of the Holy Guardian Angel.

Concerning his quest for the "true Mysteries" Abramelin wrote:

> I arrived in Egypt at the house of an Ancient Sage who was called ABRAMELIM, who put me into the true Path as I will declare it unto thee hereafter, and he gave me better instruction and doctrine than all the others; but this particular grace was granted me by the Almighty Father of all Mercy, that is to say, ALMIGHTY GOD, who little by little illuminated mine understanding and opened mine eyes to see and admire, to contemplate, and search out His Divine Wisdom, in such a manner that it became possible unto me to further and further understand and comprehend the Sacred Mystery by which I entered into the knowledge of the Holy Angels, enjoying their sight and their sacred conversation, from whom at length I received afterwards the foundation of the Veritable Magic, and how to command and dominate the Evil Spirits. So that by way of conclusion unto this chapter I cannot say that I have otherwise received the True Instruction save from ABRAMELIM, and the True and Incorruptible Magic save from the Holy Angels of God.[22]

I want you to note the last part of this quotation. Abraham asserted that he received "true instruction" from the sage Abramelin, and the "true and incorruptible magic" from the holy angels. Abramelin's instruction did not teach magic, but merely enabled Abraham to reach the angels, who then taught him the system of magic he sought.

The second book of Mathers' *Abramelin* teaches in great detail the ritual process that the sage Abramelin passed on to Abraham. It is a daunting process of prayer and meditation that requires six months, or lunar cycles, of constant, focused, mental and spiritual attention (the Jews used a lunar calendar, the months of which were marked by the cycles of the moon).

Abraham wrote, "The Holy Guardian Angels at the end of the Six Moons or Months will manifest unto thee that which is sufficient for the possession of this Sacred Magic."[23] Notice that the Guardian Angel is spoken of in the plural. You may receive instruction from a single angel, or as is more common, a number of angels, but these are (as I believe) offshoots or expressions of your one unique Holy Guardian Angel, who is your living spiritual conduit to the Divine Source.

In the new translation of the work by Stephen Guth from the German text, the term of prayer is even longer. Instead of six moons or months, it lasts for eighteen months. This, merely to gain communication with the Holy Guardian Angel. Those who have not delved deeply into the ways of Western magic may think this term of preparation is unnecessarily prolonged, but in my own practice, and in the practices of other magicians that I have observed, I have found that at least a year is required to fully open communication with the angels.

If I may make an anecdotal comment, it took me slightly more than a full year of daily ritual practice, often as much as six or eight hours a day of meditation, prayer, prana yoga, ritual work, and regulated diet, to attain the conversation I now enjoy with my spirit guardians, who have at my request worked two major miracles for me, both of which completely transformed my life. Without the intervention of these spirits in my life, I would probably not be alive.

It took my wife, Jenny, precisely one year to complete her intensely rigorous training in spiritual alchemy, which was entirely regulated and overseen by spirit teachers and culminated in a frighteningly potent three-day initiation ordeal, as is set forth in detail in her book *Spiritual Alchemy*.[24] The attainment of true magic is not quick, and it is not easy.

The culmination of the six (or eighteen) month period of prayer and austerity is the achievement of the conversation of the Holy Guardian Angel. Curiously enough, Abraham describes the use of a young child as the magician's seer. The child acts as an intermediary between the magician and the angel. It is the child who, with his natural psychic ability, sees and hears the initial communications of the angel. The child relates the words and actions of the angel to the magician, who keeps his eyes cast downward during the operation.

This use of a young child may seem very strange to modern readers, but it was the practice of magicians in Egypt, Babylon and Greece to use a child as a seer. Children are more naturally psychic than adults, and it is easier for a child to see visions and relate them to the magician than for the magician to see visions directly.

Mathers makes the reasonable point that if the magician is a seer himself, the use of a child in the *Abramelin* operation is unnecessary.

> But for my part I cannot understand the imperative necessity of the employment of a Child in the Angelic evocation, if the Operator be pure in mind, and has developed the clairvoyant faculty which is latent in every human being, and which is based on the utilisation of the thought-vision. This thought-vision is exercised almost unconsciously by everyone in thinking of either a place, person, or thing, which they know well; immediately, coincident with the thought, the image springs before the mental sight; and it is but the conscious and voluntary development of this which is the basis of what is commonly called clairvoyance.[25]

As it happens, Mathers was a highly skilled clairvoyant. To a lesser degree, so was Aleister Crowley, who made the *Abramelin* operation the center of his magical development. The point of using a seer is that the conversation of the Holy Guardian Angel can be achieved without the direct seeing or hearing of the magician. This was essential to the many magicians who did not have the second sight, and who could not see spirits at will. John Dee was a prime example. He had very poor abilities as a crystal scryer, but thanks to Edward Kelley, who was employed as his scryer, he was able to communicate with the Enochian angels.

If a seer is used in the *Abramelin* operation, there is no need that it be a child. Any mediumistic person can be used to act as a communication link between the magician and the Holy Guardian Angel, when it comes to actual sight or articulate speech. Once contact is made with the Guardian Angel, the magician will be able to feel and sense its presence, even if he is not psychic enough to see the angel standing before him or hear the angel's actual words.

The six-month process of preparation for the coming of the Holy Guardian Angel is simplicity itself. It consists of purification of the body and the oratory, where the altar is placed before an open window, and the confession of sins and speaking of prayers to God. During the first two months, the magician enters his oratory precisely one-quarter of an hour before sunrise, opens the window before which stands his holy altar, and kneels in front of the altar facing the window. He then confesses his sins, prays to God that his sins be forgiven, and asks God to favor him and grant him his Holy Guardian Angel to be a guide throughout his life.

The author of this second book, who is not Abraham but perhaps is Abramelin, makes the crucially important point that the prayers must be composed by the magician. He provides no prayers but tells readers to compose their own prayers.

> But it is absolutely necessary that your prayer should issue from the midst of your heart, because simply setting down prayers in writing, the hearing of them will in no way explain unto you how really to pray. This is the reason that I have not wished to give unto you any special form of prayers and orations, so that ye yourselves may learn from and of yourselves how to pray, and how to invoke the Holy Name of God, our Lord; and for that

> reason I have not been willing that ye should rely upon me in order to pray.[26]

In a footnote Mathers emphasized the importance of this, saying, "This is the great point to be studied in all Magical Operations soever, and unless the whole heart and soul and faith go with the ceremony, there can be no reliable result produced."[27]

Over the next two months the magician continues with the purifications of his body and household and kneels before his altar not only at sunrise, but at sunset. During the final two months he kneels to pray at sunrise, at noon before having his midday meal, and at sunset. It's important that the stomach be empty during these periods of prayer. Finally, the magician, purified and barefoot to signify his humility toward God, enters the oratory with his child seer just before sunrise, opens the window, and knees before the altar. He recites a special orison akin to the one that is written out in the book, but the author clearly states that the orison is given only as an example:

> This is the Prayer which I myself made use of in my Consecration; the which I give not here to confine you (to a certain form), nor to oblige you to employ the same, nor to tell it you over as I would to a parrot whom I should wish to teach to talk; but only and solely to give unto you an idea of the manner in which we should pray.[28]

The wording of the orison is also significant. The author asks God that he "may become worthy of the Conversation of thy Holy Angels" and that he may be granted the power God gave to his prophets over "all the Evil Spirits."[29]

You may be asking yourself why it is necessary that the magician obtain power over evil spirits, when it is the holy angels of God who are given such emphasis and importance in the text. The reason is practical. The holy angels are too exalted to perform mundane works of magic. Lower spirits are much better suited to lesser tasks, because there is more of the elementary world in their natures. Lower spirits can be safely commanded by the authority of the higher angels, and the authority of God, but only if the magician has truly achieved communion with his Holy Guardian Angel.

Stephen Guth, who translated the text from its original German, chose to render what Mathers calls "evil spirits" into the less emphatic "unredeemed spirits" – "trapped or lost spirits, rather than directly destructive or manifestly evil entities."[30]

The culmination of the whole operation covers a period of seven days. The first of these days, on which the orison is spoken, is known as the consecration. The next three days involve the convocation of the holy spirits, and the final three days serve for the convocation of the evil spirits. "Evil" is perhaps too harsh a word for most of them. They are not so much evil as they are natural and pagan. The spirits of the fields and streams known to the ancient Greeks would be a good example. They are, for the most part, spirits ignorant of the blessings of the God of the Jews and Christians.

On the first day of the convocation of the good spirits, the magician robes himself in a robe of mourning, puts ashes on his forehead, and enters the oratory just before sunrise, with his child seer. Communication with the holy angels is made via a small square silver plate that has been placed on the altar top. The child brings this to the magician, who studies it for any special and particular sign that must be made in order for the magician to see the Holy Guardian Angel.

This sign I take to be the angel's personal seal. It will be unique for each person who does the operation. The use of the silver plate is fascinating because it seems unnecessary – the child is able to see the angel make the seal and mimics its shape to the magician. I suspect it may be that the cool air of morning, falling upon the polished silver, causes beads of moisture to form, which may be interpreted by the magician as writing from the angel. I suspect this is why the window is so carefully specified to be open during the operation. The magician is to copy whatever written instructions from the holy angels appear on the silver plate before having his child seer replace it on the altar.

The second day of the convocation of holy spirits is spent in fervent prayer, at morning, noon, and evening, that God may grant the magician a vision of the holy angels. On the morning of the third day the magician discovers if all his work over the past six months has been fulfilled. If he has done the work well, the Holy Guardian Angel appears to him in all its glory. The child seer is no longer needed as an intermediary. The angel converses with him "in words so full of affection and of goodness, and with such sweetness, that no human tongue could express the same."[31]

But the Guardian Angel does more than this: "After this he will show unto you the True Wisdom and Holy Magic, and also wherein you have erred in your Operation, and how thenceforward you should proceed in order to overcome the Evil Spirits, and finally arrive at your desired ends."[32]

This is a key point that should not be missed. Only after the Holy Guardian Angel has appeared is the magician shown the "true wisdom and holy magic." The operation of Abramelin is not a system of magic in itself, it is a method to obtain the conversation of the Guardian Angel, who then teaches the magician a system of magic uniquely tailored to the magician's mind and personality. Part of that magic includes the way in which evil or unredeemed spirits are to be mastered and commanded.

There is nothing vague about this communication. The magician is to remain in his oratory all day long, "receiving from the Holy Angel distinct and ample information regarding the Evil Spirits and the manner of bringing them into submission, carefully writing down and taking notes of all these matters."[33] It is emphasized that the Holy Guardian Angel is his teacher, not any other source.

The last three days of the operation involve the conjuration and binding of the evil spirits. The conjuration to be used is described in general terms, but its exact wording is not given. The magician must perform the conjuration "with feeling and freely by heart; and not by writing, because in using that composed by others, the Spirits thence judge that we ourselves are ignorant, and render themselves straightway more intractable and stubborn."[34]

By these conjurations all the lower spirits are summoned and bound in service to the magician by their oaths. The author stresses the importance of heeding the instruction of the Holy Guardian Angel in this operation. "But while invoking God your Lord for strength and surety, and your Holy Angel for counsel and assistance, never forget what the latter will have taught you, for it is a necessary point."[35]

These references to the *Abramelin* operation should be sufficient to show how much importance it placed on the direct communication and teaching of the Holy Guardian Angel, and how little value is given to what the author calls "Seals, and Conjurations, and Superstitious Figures, and Pentacles, and other Abominations, written by Diabolical Enchanters."[36]

The seven days at the end of the six-month operation constitute a kind of spirit initiation of the practitioner into the holy secrets of magic. The final three days, during which the evil spirits are bound, is an ordeal. The evil spirits must be faced without fear but with a steady heart and mind, and an assurance that the power of God and the angels is assisting the conjuration. Once this final ordeal is successfully passed, the practitioner can well and truly call himself a magician.

S. L. MacGregor Mathers

The man who translated the French manuscript of the *Book of Abramelin* into English received his living system of magic from three beings whom he identified as the Secret Chiefs of his occult school, the Hermetic Order of the Golden Dawn. It was during communications and actual meetings with these Secret Chiefs that Mathers obtained the teachings that have gone on to become, in their various evolutions and off-shoots, the most widely used formal system of magical training in the Western world.

Golden Dawn magic is not only practiced today by most English-speaking magicians, even those who do not realize that they are using the Golden Dawn system, but it is at the root of the ritual magic of modern Satanism and modern witchcraft as well. Both Gerald Gardner, the father of modern witchcraft, and Anton LaVey, the founder of the Church of Satan, derived their magic from the Golden Dawn system. Even today it remains the most intelligent and coherent system for teaching Western ritual magic that has yet been devised.

Samuel Liddell "MacGregor" Mathers (1854-1918) was a strange, otherworldly man who appeared to those around him to be perpetually lost in thought, both present and absent at the same moment. He had one of those faces that seems ageless, and this merely added to his personal mystique among his fellow occultists. The poet William Butler Yeats, who became a member of the Golden Dawn in 1890 and continued his association for thirty years, wrote of Mathers in his 1926 *Autobiographies*, "In body and in voice at least he was perfect; so might Faust have looked in his changed ageless youth. In the credulity of our youth we secretly wondered if he had not met with, perhaps even been taught by, some old man who had found the elixir."[37]

Mathers and his two Masonic friends, William Robert Woodman and William Wynn Westcott, who made up the three human chiefs of the Golden Dawn, founded the first Golden Dawn temple in London in 1888. One of the three, Woodman, died in 1891 before the formation of the more esoteric Second Order and was never directly involved in the composition of the Golden Dawn teachings. Westcott referred to himself as "Praemonstrator of the Kabbalah to the Isis-Urania Temple of the G. D."[38] He contributed important source materials on the Kabbalah to the Golden Dawn system, but this was existing lore. There was nothing original in his teachings.

All the rest came through Mathers and his psychic wife Moïna, a remarkable woman who was the sister of the noted French philosopher Henri Bergson. Moïna was responsible for the art of the Golden Dawn, including its colorful Vault of the Adepts and the imagery of its Tarot. She had been trained as an artist and met Mathers while painting in the British Museum. After the death of her husband she became the head of the Order.

When Mathers first made contact with the Secret Chiefs is not known, but he wrote in his Manifesto of 1896 that before the creation of the Vault of the Adepts the Secret Chiefs had selected him to be the conduit of esoteric secrets from them to the members of the Golden Dawn. At his request they graciously allowed his wife to aid him in this work. Part of the requirement was probably that both must abstain from sexual union to maintain their purity and conserve their vital energies.[39] But this was not a burden since their marriage was sexless in any case, as his wife confided in an 1895 letter to Annie Horniman: "I have always chosen, as well as S.M.R.D. [Mathers] to have nothing whatever to do with any sexual connection – we have both kept perfectly clean I know, as regards the human, the elemental, and any other thing whatsoever."[40]

Mathers began his efforts to obtain the communications of the Secret Chiefs by using the familiar devices of Spiritualism, which was then in vogue, such as table rapping. He was, however, highly mediumistic himself and soon began to receive teachings either psychically or during actual physical meetings with mysterious figures he took to be the Secret Chiefs, as he wrote in an 1896 document he titled his Manifesto:

> Almost the whole of the Second Order Knowledge has been obtained by me from them in various ways; by clairvoyance, by Astral projection on their part and on mine – by the table, by the ring and disc, at times by a direct Voice audible to my external ear, and that of Vestigia [Moïna Mathers], at times copied from books brought before me, I know not how, and which disappeared from my vision when the transcription was finished, at times by appointment *Astrally* at a certain place, till then unknown to me; and appointments made in the same manner and kept in the same manner as in the case of those rare occasions when I have met them by appointment in the physical body.[41]

Who were these Secret Chiefs that met with Mathers? He believed them to be high-ranking Rosicrucians who had mastered the secrets of alchemy and the elixir of eternal life, but he was not prepared to jump to any conclusions about them:

> Concerning the Secret Chiefs of the Order, to whom I

> make reference and from whom I have received the wisdom of the Second Order which I have communicated to you, I can tell you *nothing*.
>
> I do not even know their earthly names.
>
> I know them only by certain secret mottoes.
>
> I have but very rarely seen them in the physical body; and on such rare occasions the *rendezvous* was made astrally by them at the time and place which had been astrally appointed beforehand.
>
> For my part I believe them to be human and living upon this earth; but possessing terrible superhuman powers.
>
> When such a *rendezvous* has been in a much frequented place, there has been nothing in their personal appearance and dress to mark them out as differing in any way from ordinary people except the appearance and sensation of transcendent health and physical vigour (whether they seemed persons in youth or age) which was their inevitable accompaniment; in other words, the physical appearance which the possession of the Elixir of Life has traditionally supposed to confer.
>
> On the other hand, when the *rendezvous* has been in a place free from easy access by the Other World they have usually been in symbolic robes and insignia.[42]

The Golden Dawn itself is a Rosicrucian Order, as its symbol of the rose and cross demonstrates. Mathers was not certain if the beings from whom he received his teachings were living men or spirits, but if they were living men they were so exalted in power and wisdom that the distinction between flesh and spirit scarcely had any meaning.

The three Secret Chiefs are named in Golden Dawn teachings. They are asserted to be Hugo Alverda, Franciscus de Bry and Elman Zata, three great figures in Rosicrucian lore, but Mathers does not name them when referring to them. Their names are mentioned in the Adeptus Minor Ritual, where they are called "the three Highest Chiefs of the order."[43]

If the Secret Chiefs had any corporeal existence, it was so exalted and refined that it can only be likened to the corporeal nature of the angels who are reported to have visited human beings in the Old Testament.[44] These angels should not be regarded as corporeal beings in the usual sense, though they may have dressed themselves in flesh in order to communicate better with earthly men and women.

These tutelary encounters with the Secret Chiefs were more than an ordeal for Mathers.

> … the sensation was that of being in contact with so terrible a force that I can only compare it to the *continued* effect of that usually experienced momentarily by a person *close* to whom a flash of lightning passes during a violent storm; coupled with a difficulty in respiration similar to the half-strangling effect produced by ether; and if such was the result produced in one, as tested as I have been in practical Occult Work, I cannot conceive a much less advanced Initiate being able to support such a strain even for five minutes, without Death ensuing.[45]

For the purposes of this essay, the important point to gather is that the higher teachings of the Golden Dawn did not come from the minds of men, but from spiritual beings who chose Mathers to be their instrument. Mathers suspected that these beings were exalted Rosicrucian sages who had transcended death and the limitations of the body. Others might see them as angels, but whatever their true nature, they were not common men.

This pattern exists throughout the entire field of Western occultism, but it is surprisingly obscure to most magicians, who assume that they can acquire magic effectively from other human beings and from existing grimoires and schools. This is an error, as I have done my best to indicate. True initiation in magic is spirit initiation, and the highest and most potent teachings in practical magic always come, not from human beings, but directly from spirits.

Aleister Crowley

This was certainly the case in the life of the most famous member of the Golden Dawn, Aleister Crowley (1875-1947). As a young man Crowley studied the Golden Dawn system with intense enthusiasm and idolized Mathers. Then he had a falling out with his idol, changed his mind, and decided that Mathers was a black magician with feet of clay. He went forth on his own to work the *Abramelin* procedure in Scotland, using Mathers' translation, while living at an 18th century manor he called Boleskine House. Although he did not complete the operation, he was able to obtain union with his Holy Guardian Angel, a being calling itself Aiwass.

While Crowley and his wife were visiting Cairo, Egypt, in 1904, Aiwass dictated psychically to Crowley the document titled *Liber AL vel Legis*, also known as the *Book of the Law*. This book has three chapters and was received by Crowley during three hour-long sessions beginning at noon on three consecutive days, 8-10 April. In his *Confessions*, Crowley remarked concerning the reception of this book, "My entire previous life was but a preparation for this event, and my entire subsequent life has been not merely determined by it, but wrapped up in it."[46]

At the time of its dictation Crowley did not understand its importance, but in later decades he came to realize that the dictation of his Guardian Angel was the most important expression of his life as a magician. The *Book of the Law* is the very heart of Crowley's magical philosophy of Thelema. Crowley's modern-day followers, who style themselves Thelemites, regard *The Book of the Law* as prophetic. It is in a very real sense their Bible and describes in horrific terms the coming of the Aeon of Horus, which will be marked by the period of strife and chaos that was foretold in the Revelation of John the Divine.

Thelema (Greek for will) may be summed up in two sayings that form part of the *Book of the Law*. They became Crowley's personal mantras. He used them to greet strangers and disciples alike. "Do what thou wilt shall be the whole of the Law,"[47] Crowley would say to those he met, and if they knew his teachings they were expected to answer, "Love is the law, love under will."[48]

These teachings are not from any human teacher, they are spirit inspired. Without the conversation of his Holy Guardian Angel, Crowley would never have received them, and the cult of Thelema would never have existed. There is a wonderful poetry and cohesive strength in the *Book of the Law* that becomes apparent only after repeated readings. Of all Crowley's writings it is undoubtedly the most important, foretelling, as it does, the vicissitudes and misfortunes of the very times in which we presently live. The *Book of the Law* predicted the decline of Christianity that we now see happening.

Crowley considered himself to be in psychic contact, not only with Aiwass but with the Secret Chiefs, whom he believed had abandoned Mathers because of his black magic and shifted their allegiance to Crowley. He was not the only one to claim a psychic link with the Secret Chiefs of the Golden Dawn. After the death of Mathers in 1918, several Golden Dawn members and former members claimed to receive teachings from the Secret Chiefs, or those of other spiritual beings even more exalted, among them Annie Horniman, Florence Farr, and A. E. Waite.

By virtue of these spirit connections, all declared themselves to be the true leader of the Order. All of them failed. It seems that the tutelary spirit of one person cannot become the tutelary spirit of another, regardless of what it may name itself, and regardless of who the person in communication with it believes it to be.

Although the *Book of the Law* was dictated by Aiwass, Crowley's personal Guardian Angel, the actual authors of the three chapters of the book are three Egyptian gods. Aiwass merely conveyed their words to Crowley. The first chapter is spoken by the goddess Nuit, the second chapter by the god Hadit, and the third chapter by Ra-Hoor-Khuit.

In the first chapter, Crowley is referred to by Nuit: "the chosen priest & apostle of infinite space is the prince priest the Beast."[49] Nuit refers to herself as "Infinite Space and the Infinite Stars."[50] She is, of course, the goddess of the unbounded starry night sky. Elsewhere Nuit calls Crowley "My scribe Ankh-af-na-Khonsu the priest of the princes."[51] It is clear that Crowley has been chosen by Nuit to reveal her secret teachings to a chosen few who have the wit to heed them. She says, "Let my servants be few & secret; they shall rule the many and the known."[52]

It is a common feature of initiation by spirits that the initiate is enjoined to keep the secret teachings hidden; yet at the same time, paradoxically, it often happens that the one chosen to receive the secret teachings is also enjoined to record them for the benefit of a select few, who may be his sons, his disciples, or the members of his school.

This was the case for John Dee, who received the Enochian magic from the angels with the understanding that he not reveal it, yet he was required to record and preserve it with care for the use of someone who would come after him. Who this might be has never been revealed. In Crowley's case, the one who was to follow and actually make full use of the teachings of the gods was to be his son, who would be the Antichrist of Revelation. Nuit tells Crowley that he "shall not behold all these mysteries" but that they must wait their revelation by his son. "The child of thy bowels, he shall behold them."[53]

The parallel between John Dee and Aleister Crowley on this point is exact. Both are receivers of the magic of heaven, but both are denied its ultimate fulfillment by the very spirits who teach them the magic. They are like Moses, who leads his people to the Promised Land, but is himself denied entry.

Crowley presumed that the child promised him by Nuit must be his natural-born son, despite her admonishment that he should "Expect him not from East nor from the West, for from no expected house cometh that child." When Crowley began to doubt whether he would ever have a natural son, he began to believe that the child must be a magical child – perhaps his disciple Frater Achad, or perhaps a moon-child engendered through a magic working on a mortal woman. But like the person who was to unfold the mysteries of Enochian magic after its reception by John Dee, the child of Crowley's bowels has never been revealed, although many pretenders have claimed the honor.

In the second chapter of the *Book of the Law*, the god Hadit declares himself to be the bridegroom of Nuit,[54] and later calls himself "the Snake that giveth Knowledge and Delight."[55] The imagery of the serpent is intended in part to represent the penis, but also to suggest the giver of gnosis to mankind in the Garden of Eden. In a more geometrical sense, Hadit identifies himself as the infinitely tiny dot at the center of the circle. He is the center which is everywhere, and his lover Nuit is the circumference which is nowhere.[56] Hadit calls Crowley his "prophet" in several places and says, "I am the Master: thou art the Holy Chosen One."[57]

One of the prophecies given to Crowley, his prophet, is this:

> There is a veil: that veil is black. It is the veil of the modest woman; it is the veil of sorrow, & the pall of death: this is none of me. Tear down that lying spectre of the centuries: veil not your vices in virtuous words: these vices are my service; ye do well, & I will reward you here and hereafter.[58]

It may be suspected that Islam is intended by the "veil that is black." The laws of Islam are in direct conflict with the laws of Thelema. Thelemites are told to "Tear down that lying spectre of the centuries" – can this be Mohammed? I can see no other obvious interpretation. This prophecy seems to speak of a war between the West, as transformed by Thelema, and traditional Islam in the East.

The third chapter is given over to the god Ra-Hoor-Khut, a name elsewhere spelled Ra-hoor-Khuit and Ra-Hoor-Khu. This is Ra-heru-khuti, or Horus of Behutet. Different cities in Egypt had different forms of the major gods, with slightly differing shades of meaning. The Horus of one city was not exactly the same as the Horus of another city. In this third chapter Crowley is called by the god "warrior" and "o blesséd Beast."

There is another prophecy in the third chapter which refers to Crowley's Abbey of Thelema in Cefalù, on the island of Sicily. First Horus orders that Crowley "Choose ye an Island! Fortify it!"[59] It seems self-evident to me that the island is Sicily, and the fortification is the house Crowley chose to call his "Abbey of Thelema," a reference to the 1534 novel *Gargantua and Pantagruel* by the French satirical writer Francois Rabelais. The fortifications are magical, not physical. Elsewhere Horus says: "But your holy place shall be untouched throughout the centuries: though with fire and sword it be burnt down & shuttered, yet an invisible house there standeth and shall stand until the fall of the Great Equinox, when Hrumachis shall arise and the double-wanded one assume my throne and place."[60]

Horus refers to the end of his astrological age, when after approximately two millennia the sign of Aquarius shall be replaced by the sign of Capricorn. At the end of the Aeon of Horus "another prophet shall arise, and bring fresh fever from the skies."[61] It was generally believed by Western magicians that the transition from one astrological age to another would necessarily carry with it a period of great strife and turmoil, as the old age gave way grudgingly to the new age.

Crowley's "holy place" is, of course, his Abbey of Thelema, which despite being abandoned for decades is still standing on the hillside where it overlooks the city of Cefalù. The roof has fallen in, but the walls are intact and still bear traces of Crowley's paintings of demons and gods. It has not been torn down, and nothing new has been erected on its foundations. It is dreaded and shunned by the people of Cefalù as an unlucky place to visit, and they usually keep their distance, especially at night.

The primary gift that Horus gives to Crowley is a warrior spirit. "I am Ra-Hoor-Khuit and I am powerful to protect my servant. Success is thy proof: argue not: convert not: talk not overmuch."[62] Crowley is being told that he does not need to preach – his living example is enough to gather his followers, who will receive the secret teachings of the *Book of the Law*, not from Crowley who can only guide them, but from the gods themselves, if they are worthy to receive it. Again, teaching takes place from spirit to disciple directly, with the sage who received the original system of magic acting as a guide and as an example of what to strive after. Crowley did not have the power to give enlightenment, he could only point the way to its attainment.

Horus tells Crowley not to even try to unravel the mysteries of the *Book of the Law*, because he will fail, "but one cometh after him, whence I say not, who shall discover the key to it all … It shall be his child & that strangely. Let him not seek after this, for thereby alone can he fall from it."[63] The obscurity of this wording suggests to me that the child who will obtain the full knowledge of the secrets of the book cannot be Crowley's child in the normal sense, even though elsewhere Horus prophesizes that Crowley shall have a child on his Scarlet Woman, who at the time was his wife, Rose. Horus says, "Then will I lift her up to pinnacles of power: then will I breed from her a child mightier than all the kings of the earth…"[64]

Crowley did have children on his various Scarlet Women, two girls and a boy, but none of them appeared to fulfil the prophecy of the one who should come after him to unravel the secrets of the *Book of the Law*. Though many have claimed this honor, none have clearly demonstrated their fitness to receive it.

Conclusion

In this essay I have tried to show that there is another form of initiation for magicians that is different from the initiation into a mundane social organization, and different from the initiation into an occult lodge or school. This third kind of initiation is performed by spirits who assume the role of teachers of the mysteries. These mysteries are conveyed in their fullness only after an ordeal during which the courage and worth of the magician is severely tested. At times, the full understanding of the mysteries is reserved for a chosen one who will follow after the magician who receives them.

In my opinion, only systems of magic which are conveyed directly from the spirits are of real value. By that I mean, systems concocted by individuals from grimoires alone are never effective, because after a relatively brief period (the *Arbatel* sets it at 40 years), the magic conveyed by spirit teachers loses its potency and remains only as a dry and lifeless example of a magical system, just as a butterfly, after it dies, remains only as the lifeless carcass of a butterfly.

It is intimated by writers on magic that the efficacy of a true system of magic can, in certain cases, be passed on from the individual who received it directly from the spirits to a student or disciple, particularly if there is a tie of blood between teacher and student. Even in these cases, the system taught to the disciple is only the framework of a living system of magic. It remains for the spirits to enter into direct communication with the disciple and teach the living symbols and words of power that energize the system.

Without this initiation of a disciple by the spirits themselves, and the conveyance to the disciple directly of a living system of magic, the achievement of notable success in the art of magic is not possible. Those who believe otherwise delude themselves.

1 Thompson, Hunter S. *Hell's Angels: A Strange and Terrible Saga.* New York: Ballantine Books, Trade Edition, 1996, chapter 6.
2 Turner, Robert (translator). *Arbatel of Magick: Tome One, Isagoge.* New Jersey: Heptangle Books, 1979, p. 29.
3 Ibid., p. 11.
4 Paracelsus, *On Nymphs, Sylphs, Pygmies, and Salamanders*, date uncertain.
5 John 3:27.
6 Exodus 3.
7 Exodus 7:11, 22.
8 Exodus 24:8.
9 I Kings, 3:5-14.
10 Mathers, S. Liddell MacGregor (translator). *The Key of Solomon the King.* York Beach, ME: Samuel Weiser, 1974, p. 2.
11 Matthew 3:16-7.
12 Matthew 4:1.
13 Matthew 4:11.
14 Acts 2:1-4.
15 *Koran* 96:1-5.
16 David-Néel, *Magic and Mystery In Tibet.* (French: 1929; English translation: 1932). New York: Dover Publications, Inc., 1971, pp. 162-3.
17 *Historia & Tale of Doctor Johannes Faustus*, chapter 3.
18 Ibid., chapter 6.
19 Mathers, S. L. MacGregor (translator). *The Book of the Sacred Magic of Abramelin the Mage.* London: John M. Watkins, 1898. Second edition reprinted by Dover Publications Inc., 1975.
20 Guth, Stephen (translator) and Georg Dehn (editor). *The Book of Abramelin, A New Translation.* Lake Worth, FL: Ibis Press, 2006.
21 Mathers, *Abramelin*, p. 5.
22 Ibid., pp. 6-7.
23 Guth, *Abramelin*, p. xvii.

24 Tyson, Jenny. *Spiritual Alchemy: Scrying, Spirit Communication, and Alchemical Wisdom*. Llewellyn Publications, 2016.
25 Mathers, *Abramelin*, p. xxvii.
26 Ibid., p. 65.
27 Ibid., p. 65, footnote.
28 Ibid., p. 80.
29 Ibid., pp. 79, 80.
30 Guth, *Abramelin*, p. xx.
31 Mathers, *Abramelin*, p. 84.
32 Ibid.
33 Ibid., p. 85.
34 Ibid., p. 88.
35 Ibid., p. 92.
36 Ibid., p. 90.
37 Howe, Ellic, *The Magicians of the Golden Dawn* [1972]. York Beach, ME: Samuel Weiser, Inc., 1978, p. 43.
38 Ibid., p. 47.
39 Ibid., p. 128. Mathers wrote that the Secret Chiefs required him to "keep his body in such a condition of physical health and especially of vital energy, that the ordinary chances of corporeal illness and exhaustion should not be permitted to become any bar to his constant efforts and exertions."
40 Ibid., p. 118.
41 Ibid., pp. 130-1. From Mathers' Manifesto.
42 Ibid., pp. 129-30. From Mathers' Manifesto.
43 Regardie, Israel. *The Golden Dawn.* Sixth Edition. St. Paul, MN: Llewellyn Publications, 1989, p. 237.
44 Judges 13:16-23.
45 Howe, *The Magicians of the Golden Dawn*, p. 130. From Mathers' Manifesto.
46 Crowley, Aleister. *The Confessions of Aleister Crowley*. London & NY: Arkana, 1989, p. 393.
47 Crowley, Aleister. *The Book of the Law*. South Stukely, Quebec: 93 Publishing, 1975, pp. 18-9.
48 Ibid., p. 25.
49 Ibid., p. 10.
50 Ibid., p. 12.
51 Ibid., p. 17.
52 Ibid., p. 10.
53 Ibid., p. 24.
54 Ibid., p. 33.
55 Ibid., p. 38.
56 Ibid., p. 33.
57 Ibid., p. 50.
58 Ibid., p. 45.
59 Ibid., p. 57.
60 Ibid., pp. 64-5.

61 Ibid., p. 65.
62 Ibid., p. 68.
63 Ibid., p. 72.
64 Ibid., p. 70.

About the Contributors

Susanna Åkerman, b. 1959, BA at Stockholm University 1982, PhD. in Philosophy at Washington University in St. Louis 1988, Research fellow in the History of Ideas at Uppsala and Stockholm Universities 1991-1996. Since 2001 secretary and program coordinator at Swedenborg Forum, Stockholm. Member of The Lord's New Church which is *Nova Hierosolyma*. Author of several books and articles on Queen Christina of Sweden, Paracelsus, and Swedenborg.

J. H. Brennan is a New York Times best-selling author whose work has appeared in more than fifty countries. Brennan has published more than 111 books with international sales estimated at 10 million copies. Herbie has a powerful reputation for challenging conventional assumptions with penetrating intelligence and a clear, easy style. This is reflected in his interests, which range from transpersonal psychology, spirituality, reincarnation and psychical research to comparative religion and quantum physics. He holds a Master's Degree in Western Esotericism from Exeter University.

Mark Booth (aka Jonathan Black) was educated at Ipswich School and Oriel College, Oxford, where he studied Philosophy and Theology. He has worked in publishing for over twenty years. He is perhaps most well-known for his internationally bestselling books *The Secret History of the World* (2007) and *The Sacred History: How Angels, Mystics and Higher Intelligence Made Our World* (2013).

Chuck Dunning is a teacher and facilitator of contemplative practice and the author of *Contemplative Masonry: Basic Applications of*

Mindfulness, Meditation, and Imagery for the Craft. He is the founding Superintendent of the Academy of Reflection, a chartered organization for Scottish Rite Masons interested in contemplative practice. Chuck holds a Master's Degree in Counselor Education and a Bachelor's Degree in Psychology, both from the University of North Texas.

Jedediah French is a member of Templum Rosae Lodge, No. 863 in Oakland, California. He is also a member of the Sacramento York Rite Bodies and a 32° in the Sacramento AASR. His articles have been published in *Philalethes: The Journal of Masonic Research and Letters*, *The Plumbline*, and *The Square*. He holds a Master's Degree in Religious Studies from the University of California and regularly gives talks in lodges on Masonic education. Find more of his work at his blog: *Sir Knight Jedediah French: ESOTERIC FREEMASONRY AND THE WESTERN MYSTERY TRADITION.*

Joscelyn Godwin was born in England, educated as a musicologist and composer at Cambridge and Cornell Universities, and taught from 1971-2016 at Colgate University in Hamilton, New York. He has written, edited, and translated many books on "speculative music" and on the Western esoteric traditions, most recently *Symbols in the Wilderness: Early Masonic Survivals in Upstate New York* (with Christian Goodwillie), *Macrocosm, Microcosm and Medicine: the Worlds of Robert Fludd,* and a translation of *Introduction to Magic, Volume II: The Path of Initiatic Wisdom* by Julius Evola and the UR Group.

Richard Kaczynski is an American writer and lecturer in the fields of social psychology, metaphysical beliefs and new religious movements. He is known for his biography *Perdurabo: The Life of Aleister Crowley*, described by the *Times Literary Supplement* as "the major biography to date," and by the Norwegian daily *Aftenposten* as being regarded as the best biography of Crowley.

Greg Kaminsky is the host and producer of the Occult of Personality,

a highly regarded and long-running podcast that explores the occult and esoteric with authors and experts in the field. His desire to create the Occult of Personality podcast in 2006 began with a life-long compulsion to learn more about ancient civilizations, world religions, symbolism, and the underlying hidden wisdom which they contain, but only convey to those with eyes to see and ears to hear. With well over 150 episodes completed and tens of thousands of listeners every month, the podcast continues to grow in popularity and prestige. You can find Occult of Personality podcast at:
http://occultofpersonality.net/.

Adam Kendall is an editor for the Scottish Rite Research Society and a member of their governing board. He is the former collections manager and curator of exhibits for the Henry W. Coil Library and Museum of Freemasonry at the Grand Lodge of California. From 2013 to 2015, he served as president of the Masonic Library and Museum Association. An enthusiastic advocate for the preservation of Masonic and fraternal history and culture, Kendall has published several essays in notable Masonic and academic publications and has presented at many international symposia. He is a past master of San Francisco's Phoenix Lodge No. 144, the Northern California Research Lodge, and is a full member of Quatuor Coronati No. 2076 in London, England. He is currently pursuing a graduate degree in American history at California State University, Los Angeles, and is a member of the Phi Alpha Theta honor society.

Jeffrey S. Kupperman has studied Hermetics, Kabbalah, and the Western Mystery Tradition for more than 25 years and is a hierarch of the *Ekklesia Neoplatonismos Theourgia*. He is the author of *Living Theurgy: A Course in Iamblichus' Philosophy, Theology, and Theurgy* (Avalonia, 2014), and the founder and publisher of the *Journal of the Western Mystery Tradition* (http://jwmt.org). He is currently working on his next projects, an illuminated *Theurgist's Book of Hours* and *High Magic in the Age of Steam*. Jeffrey lives in central Wisconsin, where he teaches martial arts, spends his time researching, writing, painting non-traditional Byzantine icons, and raising his daughters.

Not necessarily in that order. You may follow his blogs at *A Thirteen Petalled Rose, A Cup of Blessing* (http://cupofblessing.blogspot.com) and *The Writer's Tome* (http://jeffreyskupperman.com).

Angel Millar is the author of *The Crescent and the Compass: Islam, Freemasonry, Esotericism and Revolution in the Modern Age* (2015), *Freemasonry: Foundation of the Western Esoteric Tradition* (2015), and *Freemasonry: A History* (2005). His writing has also been published in *Quest* magazine, *The Journal of Indo-European Studies*, and at Disinfo.com, and EurasiaReview.com, among others. *New Dawn* magazine has called his work, "highly significant ... of extra ordinary importance in this time of cultural and even spiritual conflict."

Timothy Scott is the author of *Symbolism of the Ark* (Fons Vitae) and numerous articles on religion and symbolism. He lived and taught Religious Studies in Düsseldorf, Germany, and Oxford, UK. He has worked as a copy-editor and proof-reader helping in the preparation of the works of Ananda Coomaraswamy. Timothy is a contributor to the journals *Sacred Web*, Vancouver, and *Sophia*, Washington DC. His research focuses on the universal language of traditional symbolism with a particular focus on biblical symbolism and the mystical traditions of Judaism, Christianity and Islam. Between 2007 and 2009 Timothy was editor-in-chief of *Eye of the Heart: A Journal of Traditional Wisdom* for the Philosophy and Religious Studies Program at La Trobe, Bendigo. From 2010 till 2016 he taught a range of Humanities at Girton Grammar School, Bendigo. He currently resides in Geelong where he is pursuing his writing and teaching.

Richard Smoley is the author of nine books on spirituality, religion, and philosophy, including *Inner Christianity: A Guide to the Esoteric Tradition*; *Forbidden Faith: The Secret History of Gnosticism*; and *Supernatural: Writings on an Unknown History*. He is former editor of *Gnosis: A Journal of the Western Inner Traditions* and is currently editor *of Quest: Journal of the Theosophical Society in America*. His website is www.innerchristianity.com.

Donald Tyson was born in Halifax, Nova Scotia. His first nonfiction book, *The New Magus* (expanded as *New Millennium Magic*), revolutionized the way practitioners of Western magic look at this ancient art. He originated rune dice, a unique way of divining with runes, and the symbol set known as Power Glyphs, which simplifies the creation of spirit sigils and charms. He has annotated and edited such classic texts as the *Three Books of Occult Philosophy* by Cornelius Agrippa, the *Fourth Book of Occult Philosophy*, and the *Demonology of King James I*. In *Sexual Alchemy and Liber Lilith* Tyson explored sexual magic. For the past few years he has devoted himself to the writing of fiction. His horror stories have appeared in numerous anthologies. *The Lovecraft Coven*, a novel about H. P. Lovecraft (Hippocampus Press) and a collection of ten short stories about Abdul Alhazred, author of the *Necronomicon*, titled *Tales of Alhazred* (Dark Renaissance Books), are both currently available.

